Urban Ghana and Privacy in the Digital Age

This book explores privacy practices and the role of digital technologies in the lives of urban Ghanaians, considering how they use language, materiality, and culture to maintain sharp boundaries between the private and public. Focusing on the harbour town of Tema, it offers rich ethnographic portraits that cover topics such as nightlife, domestic architecture, religion, and social media. The volume demonstrates how transformations across Africa such as Pentecostal reformation, neoliberal reforms, and rapid digitisation all raise the need for privacy among middle-class urbanites who use brand new (and very traditional) strategies to uphold an image of their economic or religious state. Overall, the book highlights how digital technologies intertwine with local cultures and histories, and how digital anthropology enhances our understanding of the offline as much as the online. It makes a valuable contribution to discourse about the right for privacy and surveillance in the digital age, and will be of interest to scholars from anthropology and African studies.

Elad Ben Elul is an anthropologist who lectures at Tel Aviv University and specializes in digital cultures and modern African studies.

Materializing Culture
Series Editors: Daniel Miller and Paul Gilroy

This provocative series focuses on the social relations involved in material practices. The study of material culture has stimulated a new body of research which brings together areas as diverse as the artwork of record sleeves, shopping, bitter conflicts over ancient monuments, digital fonts, craft skills, and the political economy of consumption. This series demonstrates the innovative and critical edge that a material culture perspective may bring to bear upon a wide range of academic concerns.

The Japanese House
Material Culture in the Modern Home
Inge Daniels

Material Culture and Authenticity
Fake Branded Fashion in Europe
Magdalena Craciun

Ethics and Nationalist Populism at the British Seaside
Negotiating Character
Ana Carolina Balthazar

Urban Ghana and Privacy in the Digital Age
An Ethnographic Exploration
Elad Ben Elul

For more information about this series, please visit: www.routledge.com/Materializing-Culture/book-series/BLANTMC

Urban Ghana and Privacy in the Digital Age
An Ethnographic Exploration

Elad Ben Elul

LONDON AND NEW YORK

First published 2022
by Routledge
4 Park Square, Milton Park, Abingdon, Oxon OX14 4RN

and by Routledge
605 Third Avenue, New York, NY 10158

Routledge is an imprint of the Taylor & Francis Group, an informa business

© 2022 Elad Ben Elul

The right of Elad Ben Elul to be identified as author of this work has been asserted in accordance with sections 77 and 78 of the Copyright, Designs and Patents Act 1988.

All rights reserved. No part of this book may be reprinted or reproduced or utilised in any form or by any electronic, mechanical, or other means, now known or hereafter invented, including photocopying and recording, or in any information storage or retrieval system, without permission in writing from the publishers.

Trademark notice: Product or corporate names may be trademarks or registered trademarks, and are used only for identification and explanation without intent to infringe.

British Library Cataloguing-in-Publication Data
A catalogue record for this book is available from the British Library

Library of Congress Cataloging-in-Publication Data
Names: Elul, Elad Ben, author.
Title: Urban Ghana and privacy in the digital age : an ethnographic exploration / Elad Ben Elul.
Description: Abingdon, Oxon ; New York, NY : Routledge, 2022. | Includes bibliographical references and index.
Identifiers: LCCN 2021051964 (print) | LCCN 2021051965 (ebook) | ISBN 9781032017334 (hardback) | ISBN 9781032034690 (paperback) | ISBN 9781003187424 (ebook) | ISBN 9781000570083 (adobe pdf) | ISBN 9781000570106 (epub)
Subjects: LCSH: Internet—Social aspects—Ghana. | Technology—Social aspects—Ghana. | Data privacy—Social aspects—Ghana. | Internet—Religious aspects—Christianity. | Technology—Religious aspects—Christianity. | Pentecostalism—Ghana. | Ghana—Religious life and customs. | Ghana—Social life and customs.
Classification: LCC HN832.Z9 I564 2022 (print) | LCC HN832.Z9 (ebook) |
DDC 302.23/109667—dc23/eng/20220202
LC record available at https://lccn.loc.gov/2021051964
LC ebook record available at https://lccn.loc.gov/2021051965

ISBN: 978-1-032-01733-4 (hbk)
ISBN: 978-1-032-03469-0 (pbk)
ISBN: 978-1-003-18742-4 (ebk)

DOI: 10.4324/9781003187424

Typeset in Times New Roman
by codeMantra

Contents

	List of figures	vii
1	Introduction: studying privacy, digital anthropology, and Pentecostalism	1
2	Method and reflection	23
3	Setting the field: people, place, language, and technology	38
4	Treasures of darkness: nightlife & surveillance	59
5	Hidden and incomplete: Middle-Class houses	86
6	In a relationship with God: the discretness of Social Media	121
7	Conclusions: towards an ethnography of privacy	158
	Index	171

Figures

1.1	"Listen to God", church plasma screen	1
3.1	View of a pedestrian road, architectural plans of Tema, 1961, TDC	41
3.2	The streets of Tema	42
4.1	Hidden alleys in Tema	60
4.2	Sitting away from the light	69
4.3	Community surveillance at night meme	73
4.4	Nigerian man disapproving a public display of affection meme	74
5.1	Sketch of a typical house in Tema	88
5.2	Unfinished house	90
5.3	Envisioning the 'dream house'	93
5.4	Gates: status symbols or security measure?	98
5.5	Design blocks: see without being seen	100
5.6	The modern compound	100
5.7	"View of a veranda in a multi-story block of flats", Architectural plans, 1961, TDC	102
5.8	"Typical" Ghanaian living room	104
5.9	The living-roomisation of streets	107
6.1	Vodafone Ghana advert links family and technology	122
6.2	Monitoring profile pictures, Instagram post	126
6.3	Motherhood and privacy, Instagram post	127
6.4	Facebook and Christianity	130
6.5	Visual communications, WhatsApp meme	136
6.6	Two secret lives collide, Instagram post	147
6.7	Importing "call and response" prayers to Facebook's Pentecostal realm	149
6.8	Overcoming jealousy and evil intentions	151
6.9	keep your good news, Facebook post, 2016	151
7.1	The physical is a metaphor for the virtual, Instagram post	160

1 Introduction

Studying privacy, digital anthropology, and Pentecostalism

1.1 Introduction

It's a typical Sunday morning in Tema. The children are not at school, office and factory workers are resting, and most of the shop and restaurant owners will open their businesses later in the day after they've attended church. The people begin to gather in the various churches as early as 7 AM, so the streets are peaceful, and the weather is mild. They all come wearing their 'Sunday Best,' looking colourful and stylish. Inside the church, nuclear families fill the long benches while others sit on plastic chairs, the choir prepares the stage, and then the pastor begins his service.

Technology has an immense presence in the room: microphones for the pastors; loudspeakers for the band; tablets and smartphones for the churchgoers, who are snapping pictures and shooting videos; generators in case the electricity shuts off; colourful lights and (at least) a couple of large plasma screens hung up high. The screens display biblical quotes and messages, lyrics for songs and hymns (to encourage sing-alongs), the contact information of pastors, and slides stating the various segments of the service (e.g., 'prayers' or 'donations'). A specific display caught my attention: it showed a picture of white earphones with the title 'Listen to God' (recreated in Figure 1.1).

Figure 1.1 'Listen to God,' church plasma screen. Author recreation.

DOI: 10.4324/9781003187424-1

2 *Introduction*

This visual and textual encounter between digitisation, technology, and modernity on the one hand and faith, divine intimacy, and God on the other calls for a closer look. Bonding with the divine while connecting to the digital is a fascinating tale of cultural transformation. As Meyer phrased it describing Pentecostal media in Ghana's public sphere: 'media are far more than just instruments. They are substantial ingredients through which the power of God is made tangible' (Meyer, 2012: 99). However, this particular image refers to what people do when they are entirely alone: do they use their privacy for spiritual or sinful activities?

Both pastors and worshippers know well that the rapidly increasing ownership of portable devices such as mobile phones, laptops, and tablets means people in Ghana can challenge social boundaries and explore new ideas like never before. Ghana's urban middle class is currently negotiating between two dramatic forces of contemporary globalisation: Christianity and digitisation. In other words, they are enthusiastic consumers of two global markets: internet usage, smartphones, and social media on the one hand and international Pentecostal/Charismatic Evangelism on the other. Their dynamic urban landscape, therefore, is full of tensions and transformations that privacy plays a crucial role in the church, with its rigid boundaries between good and evil, the family with its hierarchal and demanding traditional structures, and the latest digital technologies with their multiple functions of personalisation and interaction.

This ethnographic book argues that privacy in Ghana is not perceived as a civil or natural 'right' obtained by an autonomous individual as it does in many Western liberal contexts but as a shield from the precariousness of modernity and as a tool for aspiring middle-class urbanites to liberate themselves from constraining communal forces. It asks how privacy is experienced and perceived in this particular urban and theological landscape? How does digitisation influence these experiences? Also, what can this tell us about privacy at large?

I will answer these questions by describing the daily lives of middle-class Ghanaians who live in Tema, a young city built in 1961 (four years after Ghana's independence from the British empire) on the outskirts of Accra. I interviewed over 30 informants, lived with several families, and conducted participant observation over the course of three years. This participant observation combined six months of traditional fieldwork with digital ethnography (Postill and Pink, 2012; Pink et al., 2015) and digital content analysis. I anonymised the participants in this study to protect their privacy and changed their names to pseudonyms that remain connected to their ethnic origins and Christian names.

Taking a place-based ethnographic approach means I was able to explore privacy as a daily and grounded practice by observing middle-class Ghanaians in various locations and situations. Ethnography proved to be highly suitable for the study of privacy due to its attentive, nuanced, and contextual virtues, both offline and online. I examined practices of privacy in three key sites (or 'urban spaces') that demonstrate ongoing tensions between publicity and privacy and between visibility and invisibility:

Introduction 3

1   **Nightlife and darkness (Chapter 4)**: Once the sun sets on Tema, a plethora of bars, clubs, street markets, and other night services come to life. The dark conditions, enhanced by irregular and unstable electricity, become an opportunity to step away from public surveillance and attend intimate, secret, and forbidden activities. Ghana's sunsets are like a flickering light switch, moving from full daylight to complete darkness very quickly. The binary of darkness and light, day and night, becomes a symbol of morality, security, and spirituality. It also divides and arranges urban life as a temporal interplay between privacy and publicity.
2   **Private houses (Chapter 5):** As I step into the yards, gates, exteriors, and interiors of middle-class houses, I map the material and metaphorical boundaries between inside and outside, private and public, and kin and stranger. These boundaries are not dichotomous but set a certain spectrum that includes semi-private areas and distinguishes between visitors and family members in a strict set of social conduct. I take a material culture approach to discuss trends and conventions of domestic living, such as placing chairs outside the house to welcome guests or installing high walls and large gates around it to maintain privacy and security. I also address the introduction of digital technologies into the house and how they challenge familiar notions of the house as a relatively enclosed unit.
3   **Social media platforms (Chapter 6):** After the exploration of physical 'offline' urban spaces (while referring to the presence of digital objects within them), a nuanced and contextual reading of online social media practices among middle-class Ghanaians is made possible. In these sites, I argue, people employ a familiar system of boundaries and codes to regulate their visibility. However, with their constant updates and improvements, these platforms and applications also introduce Ghanaian users to new and exciting opportunities for privacy and invisibility. Each social media application reveals unique practices of sharing and withdrawing as people balance between participating in, and escaping from, public spheres dominated by the family and the church. This chapter engages with current debates in digital anthropology to demonstrate practices of privacy in a new and rapidly evolving environment by directly addressing its visual and textual contents alongside its place-based cultural context.

In this introductory chapter, I situate this study within three main theoretical frameworks: studies in sociology, media, and anthropology about privacy, the emerging discipline of digital anthropology, and the theoretical role of Pentecostalism and Christianity in the field. In Chapter 2, I will focus on the methodological and reflexive aspects of this study, and how they contribute to the understanding of the topic at hand. Addressing the subjective angles of my presence in the field was an integral part of an open-ended ethnographic endeavour. In Chapter 3, I will provide some historical background about the city of Tema and its complicated relationship with rural life. This chapter also includes information about this study's key demographics: Ghana's rising middle-class. I discuss this group's technological,

4 *Introduction*

architectural, and theological infrastructures, as well as their enthusiastic consumption of mobile phones. The three key sites of this ethnography are described and analysed in the following three chapters (Chapters 4, 5, and 6), leading to an overall concluding chapter (Chapter 7) that will tie them together towards a better understanding of privacy through ethnography.

I base the structure of this book on the well-established claim in digital anthropology that technological transformations always take place (literally) in particular socio-cultural, geographical, and historical contexts (Miller and Slater, 2001; Miller and Horst, 2012; Miller et al., 2016). Therefore, the book opens with the more 'traditional' spaces of the city and then describes how they are reflected, challenged, and continued in the digital space. The links, parallels, continuities, and oppositions between all these urban spaces are constantly present as, for instance, a middle-class lawyer uploads a Facebook message of herself attending a Sunday church service, mixing physical exhibitionism and online visibility.[1] Furthermore, analysing a specific social concept, privacy, in the multiple urban spaces that informants operate in allowed me to seek parallels, contradictions, and symbolic interactions between the fields themselves, for instance, between a Facebook newsfeed and a town's main street.

There is a long tradition of investigating Africa as a unique and incomparable phenomenon that denies the position of its inhabitants as valid global actors who participate in a universal frame of meanings such as globalisation, digitisation, cosmopolitanism, and modernisation. According to Ferguson (2006), scholars of globalisation tend to either present Africa as a negative case study of global transformations or exclude it from their analysis altogether. I place this research within an ever-growing body of literature that aims to portray Africa as a global centre in its own right, and not as the margins of a 'bigger' story or an impoverished place that needs 'saving' (Comaroff and Comaroff, 2015). Research under this category de-familiarises and disturbs previous readings of Africa by exploring *themes of sameness* (Mbembe, 2001) and insisting on its important role for the understanding of globalisation, neoliberalism, and digisiation.

By stepping away from the 'popular' Africa-related topics of poverty, magic rituals, disease, famine, crisis, and war, one can break the repetitive (and at times simplistic) divisions between geographical locations and research topics that often result in the exclusion of Africa from studies about global flows (Appadurai, 1986; Ferguson, 2006). In other words, by exploring global issues such as middle class, urban life, digital technologies, and neoliberal consumption through an African perspective, I aim to confront those aspects of globalisation that 'might otherwise be passed over or left unresolved' (Ferguson, 1999: 29) while challenging dominant narratives of victimhood and suffering in anthropological readings of Africa (Robbins, 2013).

1.2 Three theoretical frameworks (literature review)

1.2.1 Studying privacy

Privacy is a much-debated term in the crossroads between psychology, behavioural sciences, law, sociology, and political theory. As a result,

Introduction 5

research on privacy remains relatively undeveloped because it is conducted in sub-disciplines that 'rarely speak to each other' (Anthony, Campos-Castillo and Horne, 2017). Overall, current research on privacy is predominantly studied as part of the political, legal, and intellectual history of the Western nation-state and reflects on one of the 'grand dichotomies of Western thought' (Weintraub, 1997). At other times scholars present it as a universal cognitive concept that transcends history and geography with mild cultural variations (Altman, 1977). Much of this literature comes from law and computer science – 'each of which has its own reasons for presuming a universal subjectivity' (Marwick and boyd, 2018: 1159).

In accordance with its rich scholarly tradition on public/private divisions, sociology offers a larger body of work on privacy rather than on anthropology. Sociologists examined privacy concerning class and inequality (Warren and Laslett, 1977; Kasper, 2007), stigma, and secrets among urban communities (Simmel, 1906; Goffman, 1986), and, more recently, privacy in the age of information and communication technologies (Nissenbaum, 2004; boyd, 2008). The most significant sociological contribution to the study of privacy comes from more extensive scholarship in political theory and history about public and private spheres (Habermas, 1989; Ariès, Duby and Perrot, 1990; Arendt, 2013; Sennett, 2017). This influential scholarly work analysed and explained social and political order according to contemporary and historical divisions between privacy and publicity, such as between the state and 'civil society' (Habermas, 1989). However, its often binary divisions, for instance, between 'the house' and 'the polis' in Arendt's work, tend to be inconsistent and overdeterministic. Whilst some scholars contrast 'public' governments and politics with 'private' economic markets, others contrast that same economic market with private domestic life (Weintraub, 1997). Therefore, it is unclear which sphere is the 'public' or 'impersonal' opposite of the intimate and individual home.

This confusion increases when addressing feminist scholarship about the private/public distinction, as it confronts the 'intimate' domestic sphere as a site of male power and oppression in its own right (Pateman, 1983; Landes, 2003; Meehan, 2013). The supposedly 'private' family institution constantly intertwines love and money, emotions and economy, biology and politics, making it 'public' in many ways (Gal, 2002: 78). Feminist critique challenged the conventional male-oriented divisions between private and public spheres and eagerly critiqued the post-enlightenment theories of social order. However, while exposing the ideological and political contradictions of previous sociological theories, the feminist critique often replaced these dichotomies with new ones, still presenting them as super-structures that explain, organise, and determine the world we live in (Gal, 2002).

Another inconsistency in the academic discussion of private/public is between its meaning as a visual category – all that is hidden versus all that is revealed – and its overlapping yet profoundly different meaning as a social category – all that is individual versus all that is collective (Weintraub, 1997). This inconsistency may explain the division in the literature between scholars who focus on private and public property (material and intellectual) and

6 *Introduction*

those who focus on private and public communication. In the first instance, privacy is objectified either as physical 'things' that can be hidden or as personal information that can be kept in secret. In the second instance, alternatively, privacy is an index of individuality, solitude, and social withdrawal (Nippert-Eng, 2010). Any use of the term privacy, therefore, may address the hidden parts of a person's body, home, or biography (Madanipour, 2003) but also any activities that are done in isolation (e.g., going to the toilet).

The latter meaning – privacy as a social category – was notably developed by Erving Goffman (1956) in his dramaturgical theory of 'front stage' versus 'backstage.' Although Goffman did not focus on the term privacy per se, his main contribution is in directing our gaze to how everyday life can be divided into a series of performances and their 'knowingly contradicted' back regions. These 'back regions' must be kept hidden from their particular audiences. For instance, a teenage girl will wear different clothes, drink different beverages, tell different jokes, and even move her body differently when attending family events versus hanging out with her friends. What is more, she will use her bedroom as a 'backstage' to transform and prepare herself accordingly. As I will demonstrate in Chapter 5, in a discussion about the materiality of private houses, middle-class Ghanaians operate according to spatial and temporal boundaries that separate audiences from each other and guide the content of each performance.

Goffman's dramaturgical model seems to offer a more nuanced and grounded approach than Arendt's and Habermas' rigorous divisions of political theory. This shift to micro-situations made him a popular reference point in studies of privacy, offline and online (Schroeder, 2001; Lewis, Kaufman and Christakis, 2008; Hogan, 2010). His particular point about the potential collapse of boundaries between frontstage and backstage becomes ever more relevant in the digital age, as information and communication technologies lead to an overlap amongst different audiences in shared virtual spaces. For instance, Facebook became a space where people 'perform' to their colleagues, friends, and family all at once, which requires new social codes and raises new social dilemmas (Lange, 2007; Debatin et al., 2009; Vitak, 2012; Guta and Karolak, 2015; Sinanan, 2017; Spyer, 2018). A key term regarding this ever-shifting socio-technical environment is 'networked privacy' which requires one to analyse privacy as an ongoing negotiation between technological features, social networks, and individual desires (Marwick and boyd, 2014; Cho and Filippova, 2016).

Despite his unquestionable contribution, Goffman was critiqued for reproducing the binaries of private/public in his frontstage and backstage metaphor. Furthermore, while his model is useful for describing physical space and face-to-face interactions, it seems outdated when addressing many (written and visual) digital interactions, as they often remain archived or presented long after their original occurrence, demanding new theoretical frameworks. Hogan (2010) addresses this contemporary departure from Goffman by explaining that technology is moving from mediums of conversations (e.g., chats) to mediums of presentation (e.g., timelines, photo

Introduction 7

galleries, and profiles). As a result, she argues, there is a growing need to re-define the previous distinction between public/private as a spectrum rather than a dichotomy in a digital age (Ford, 2011).

Another significant contribution in that frontier is Lange's (2007) distinction between two modes of video content sharing on YouTube: 'privately public' and 'publicly private.' While the former type of videos features micro-celebrities and public personas that conceal their faces and identities, the latter term refers to public content that is inaccessible to the public and limited to an enclosed social group through privacy settings or 'strategic tagging.' Lang was inspired by approaches in linguistic anthropology such as Gal's (2002) 'fractal recursions,' which offered a highly contextual and flexible framework that views private/public as constantly negotiable and relative cultural categories. For instance, a house is private when compared to the street, but its living room is public when compared to its bedrooms (Gal, 2002: 82). These infinite divisions and subdivisions are useful to describe any social or ethnographic situation in which distinctions between private and public become symbolic, semiotic, and discursive actions.

A profoundly different yet equally influential body of literature on privacy comes from the fields of social psychology and behavioural science. Unlike the dualistic super-structures of sociology and political theory, these works offered an analysis of privacy as a cognitive (at times evolutionary) social concept with fixed (yet dynamic) characteristics (Westin, 1967; Schwartz, 1968; Altman, 1975; Petronio, 2002). Altman, perhaps the most well-known social psychologist dealing with privacy, defined it as 'a selective control of access to the self' with mild cultural variations (Altman, 1975, 1977).[2] Petronio's (2002) theory of CPM (communication privacy management) suggested the metaphor of thick and thin boundaries to illustrate that privacy management is a communicative act of gaining individual and collective control over information.

Inspired by this body of literature, Nippert-Eng (2010) conducted formal interviews with middle- and upper-class Americans about their daily attempts to achieve and control privacy. Nippert-Eng's (2010) main contribution is by grounding the often-generic models of social psychology in vivid and often comic situations where people create 'islands of privacy' in their wallets, mobile phones, bedrooms, and minds. What's more, she shifts our observation from super-structures of private and public realms to actual daily communication. However, like the classic literature in social psychology, this focus on micro-interactions sometimes harms her ability to contextualise the particular situations she describes sociologically. Furthermore, using elicitation methods regarding privacy overly relies on self-awareness and individual agency; as this book will show, privacy practices are often intuitive and deeply embodied.

Therefore, while this disciplinary alternative to super-structures using analysis of open and closed interactions is of high value (especially for anthropology), the risk of de-contextualising means much of the data about privacy is predominantly Eurocentric. Westin's classical text *Privacy and Freedom* (1967), for instance, links law studies and behavioural science by linking the claim

8 *Introduction*

for privacy with modernity, civil rights, and individual freedom. Thus, like the political theory of public/private spheres (and perhaps even more), these theories of privacy are strongly connected to Western democracies and their liberal foundations. In other words, they theorise 'the right to be left alone.'

The digital age brought a great new interest in privacy, but it is still predominantly studied and perceived as an individual right that each civilian is entitled to and is expected to fight for (Warren and Brandeis, 1890; Schoeman, 1984; Wacks, 2015). Following a 'model of liberal self-hood' (Marwick and boyd, 2014), it is often measured legally and morally as information owned by an individual who tries to control the nature and scope of its distribution (Petronio, 2002; Nippert-Eng, 2007). Due to its close bond with European notions of the 'autonomous self,' there is a need to re-discover it in other contexts where different ideas of personhood (often more collective or hybrid) are negotiated with these Western values of individualism, liberalism, and ownership (Comaroff and Comaroff, 2001).

As privacy is perceived and studied in the US as an individual civil, legal, and natural right, it comes as no surprise that the emergence of digital technologies, surveillance cameras, 'big data' accumulation, GPS tracking, face recognition, biometric tracking, and even social media is often perceived by journalists, academics, politicians, and activists as a serious threat to privacy. Both public and academic discourse are dealing with the 'loss,' 'death,' or 'danger' of privacy extensively in recent years (Nissenbaum, 2004; Wicker, 2013; Igo, 2015). This critique described by Wacks (2015) as an 'Orwellian horror of relentless scrutiny' often assumes that 'the right to privacy' is not culturally and politically specific but a source of global concern.

In addition, while the Western upper and middle class enjoy higher levels of privacy, it is often stripped off marginal groups such as teenagers, political activists, and lower-income populations who may become the main targets of sophisticated surveillance technologies or are forced to give away information in exchange for certain services (Marwick and boyd, 2018). In their study of India's national identification system, Srinivasan et al. (2018) show that collectivist, non-Western, and financially impoverished societies face different dilemmas regarding privacy such as unveiling their faces for photo IDs, providing personal mobile numbers known only to family members, and enclosing sensitive medical information. Literature about aboriginal communities in Australia also shows that the encounter with colonialism and nation-states posed a severe risk to indigenous notions of secrecy and collective intellectual property (Michaels, 1991; Geismar, 2012).

To sum, while focusing on the imagined relationship between the 'private' individual and the 'public' state or corporation, the journalistic and academic discourse about the death of privacy tends to marginalise the daily experience of privacy within communities, cities, and households. For instance, how do parents have sexual relations when they share a bedroom with their children (van der Geest, 2008)? What is the private nature of toilets when they are communally shared (Chalfin, 2014)? Ethnographers who shift their gaze into a nuanced and daily perception of privacy without

Introduction 9

neglecting its structural and contextual influences often find a more complex picture whereby people experience new forms of privacy, sometimes for the first time in their lives (Miller et al., 2016; Wang, 2016). What is more, a grounded, detailed, and sensitive exploration of privacy can demonstrate how it is practised across societies and under various transformations, especially in the digital age.

1.2.2 Digital anthropology

While journalists, academics, and politicians often see the emergence of the internet as a novel, revolutionary, or even dangerous departure from previous behaviours and conventions, anthropologists studying digitisation encourage a dialectic examination of the internet within particular case studies and social contexts. In other words, as an ethnographer discovers the life-worlds of certain communities, expanding the field to the online is a 'natural' ethnographic procedure. According to this approach, the online becomes a focal point that highlights, extends, and challenges pre-existing empirical and theoretical frameworks, but it is still part of the same 'mediated' world that people lived in beforehand (Miller and Horst, 2012).

In their pioneering ethnography of the internet in Trinidad, Miller & Slater challenged a popular assumption in academia and journalism – that the internet is a monolithic or placeless 'cyberspace' with universal properties. Their contextual approach aimed to break the dichotomy between 'virtual' and 'real' in internet studies by phrasing an alternative set of questions:

> We are not simply asking about the 'use' or the 'effects' of a new medium: rather, we are looking at how members of a specific culture attempt to make themselves at home in a transforming communicative environment, how they can find themselves in this environment and at the same time try to mould it in their own image.
>
> (Miller and Slater, 2001: 1)

This call for ethnography of the internet established a young sub-discipline in Anthropology dedicated to the unique relationship between culture, society, and binary code technology, also known as digital anthropology. Some scholars called to see online spaces as cultural worlds 'in their own right,' disproving the traditional requirement for physical contextualisation (Lysloff, 2003; Boellstorff, 2012; Coleman, 2014). Others explored the essentially local properties of these global technologies examining topics such as the domestication of digital devices and how it influences family dynamics (Horst, 2012; Madianou and Miller, 2012; Broadbent, 2013; McDonald, 2015), the influence of digital technologies on politics and activism (Gerbaudo, 2012; Postill, 2014; Bonilla and Rosa, 2015), the incorporation of mobile phones in daily lives (Slater and Kwami, 2005; Horst and Miller, 2006; Tacchi and Chandola, 2015), and the way people around the world use social media (McKay, 2010; Miller, 2011; Marwick and boyd, 2014).

10 *Introduction*

Of particular relevance to this study is the *Why We Post* project – a collection of ethnographies comparing the use of social media across nine field sites (Costa, 2016; Haynes, 2016; McDonald, 2016; Miller, 2016; Nicolescu, 2016; Wang, 2016; Sinanan, 2017; Venkatraman, 2017; Spyer, 2018). These studies have established the claim that social media and digital technologies are used differently across various cultural regions. The ethnographers did not describe their findings as technological 'appropriation,' which assumes a pre-determined or 'normal' way of using social media, but as a presented field in its own right even when it challenged familiar readings of social media as an expression of 'Western' individualism. The ethnographies in the project examine social media concerning a range of topics such as education, work, gender, politics, and online/offline relationships.

The project is ironically titled 'How the world changed social media' (Miller et al., 2016) to emphasise the human agency and cultural engine behind visual and material technologies. Social media, as the introductory volume argues, has ended the previous dichotomy between public broadcast media (e.g., television, radio) and private dyadic media (e.g., letters, telephones). Instead, it introduced a variety of platforms and functions that allow (at least) two types of 'scalable sociality': from most private to most public content distribution and from smallest to largest group/audience interaction (Miller et al., 2016: 5). This new cultural space poses an exciting opportunity for anthropologists to explore issues that sociologists and psychologists have often deemed irrelevant in what they saw as an increasingly globalised and individualised world – small-scale communities, regional comparisons, normativity, and cultural identity.

The issue of privacy was a common theme in the *Why We Post* project, especially in field sites such as China, Italy, southeast Turkey, England, Trinidad, India, and Brazil. The repeating argument in these monographs is that people in close-knit communities are less worried about governmental and corporate monitoring of private digital data (as predominantly described in contemporary literature about privacy). Instead, they occupy and interpret social media with regard to direct kin and kith, negotiating issues of identity, honour, and community. In his ethnography of social media in Brazil, for instance, Spyer (2018: 62) contrasts two types of online domains: 'lights on' refers to highly visible and public display of one's self as ideal moral, modern, and Christian subject, while 'lights off' describes secret activities such as online gossip or 'politically incorrect' content.

Although these findings complement the claims in this study, Spyer (and the *Why We Post* project at large) explores these themes with the aim of better understanding social media while my aim and scope are to understand a more abstract anthropological concept – privacy. In other words, while this collection of ethnographies delivers on its promise to promote 'holistic contextualisation' of social media, its primary object of study is still 'digital-centric.' This study, alternatively, promotes 'non-digital centric-ness' (Pink et al., 2015: 7) by examining social media as another urban space that

Introduction 11

reflects and challenges Ghanaian norms around privacy. Also, this book adds an African perspective to the *Why We Post* project, which has left the African continent out of its global comparison.

Finally, it is essential to address the strong influence of material culture studies on digital anthropology. Although virtual worlds and digitisation supposedly eliminate materiality through the reduction of papers and objects to virtual 'bits' (Blanchette, 2011), digital anthropologists tend to stress the material properties of these technologies by addressing their physical surroundings (Horst, 2012; Pink and Mackley, 2012), online visual language (Miller, 2000; McKay, 2010; Miller and Sinanan, 2017), and the importance of infrastructure (Burrell, 2012; Broadbent, 2013; Ben Elul, 2020).

Questions about place-making, geographic context, and the indexical relations of online/offline worlds (Postill, 2008; Boellstorff, 2008; Gerbaudo, 2012) make material culture ever more relevant to digital anthropology. Furthermore, trying to make sense of materiality in a digital age is one of the unique contributions of anthropologists to internet studies. As Horst and Miller (2012: 24) suggest in their introduction to *digital anthropology*, digitisation has three principles of materiality:

> First, there is the materiality of digital infrastructure and technology. Second, there is the materiality of digital content, and, third, there is the materiality of digital context.

In other words, digital spaces always rely on material infrastructure (e.g., institutions, bits, cables) but they also use material 'metaphors' in their designed content (e.g., Facebook 'walls,' chat 'rooms,' and 'garbage bins' for 'deleted' files). Finally, digital tools are always used and consumed within a material environmental context (e.g., bedrooms, vehicles, nightclubs), which alters the social experience around it. For instance, in her ethnography of internet cafés in Accra, Burrell (2012: 91) describes the social and material context of these technologies, arguing that the café's 'bland, often windowless rooms' were designed to prevent interactions and provide privacy. This last point is highly relevant to this study, as digital devices (especially mobile phones) become 'enclaves' of privacy whether we are entirely alone or surrounded by people. This form of disengagement from physical spaces can be liberating, especially in closely knit urban contexts (Guta and Karolak, 2015; Wang, 2016; Spyer, 2018).

The material approach to digitisation is inspired by scholars of material culture such as Bourdieu (1984), Latour (1993), Miller (2008), Appadurai (1988), Douglas and Isherwood (1996) who established the notion that objects, artefacts, and materials are essential actors in the construction of social experience and, hence, to its deep understanding. According to Miller (2008), objects have a certain 'humility,' which means social scientists often overlook their contribution to our social worlds. Incorporating materiality in ethnographies, therefore, draws our attention to the unspoken layers of meaning and

12 *Introduction*

sociality. This book takes a material culture approach to privacy and urban life by addressing the materiality of darkness as a concealing mechanism, the physical properties of houses as agents of privacy, and the design interface of mobile phone applications and digital software concerning online privacy.

The interdependency between the material and the immaterial, the actual and the virtual, may also explain the ambiguous relations of various religious congregations to the digital sphere. Miller and Horst (2012) point out that Catholics are notorious for visualising and materialising religious concepts (e.g., icons, portraits, and ceremonial objects) while Protestants tend to oppose any form of material mediation. However, when it comes to digitisation, the former group avoided it altogether while the latter became enthusiastic promoters of religious internet content. How come digital media seems more mediated than previous mediums (such as sculptures) to Catholics? How come some Protestants see digital spaces as completely immaterial and therefore unmediated?

These questions must be answered through a detailed and nuanced exploration of particular case studies. For instance, in contemporary urban African life, the parallels and exchanges between theology and digitisation are essential for the religious public sphere promoted by evangelist Christianity (Meyer and Moors, 2005). Digital media is often seen as a Godly blessing thanks to its ability to spread the gospel around the world in unprecedented ways while potentially weakening local religions and cosmologies (Miller and Slater, 2001: 187). According to Burrell (2012: 167) the parallel line between religion and technology in urban Ghana is the potential of both to fulfil the same desires:

> In a sense, the Internet was merely the newest religion, competing with churches, mosques, and shrines for followers and offering some of the same tangible rewards. These rewards included migration opportunities, healing, monetary wealth, business success as well as the opportunity for fellowship.

Much like the scholarly debate about digitisation, some anthropologists of Christianity saw the church as a European/Colonial entity overtaking previous cosmologies, while others examined the continuities and interactions between local cultures and Christian reformation (van Dijk, 1997; Meyer, 1999; Robbins, 2004a; Comaroff and Comaroff, 2008b). By bringing these two domains together, I ask, how are new realms of privacy and publicity carved out within this ambiguous religious-digital sphere?

1.2.3 Pentecostalism and the anthropology of Christianity

According to Gordon and Hancock (2005) 'Pentecostalism is the fastest growing sector of Protestant evangelicalism, particularly in Africa and Latin America.' As a global product 'exported' mostly from the US, the Pentecostal church in Ghana (and Protestant Christianity at large)

Introduction 13

operates mainly in urban centres such as Accra, Tema, Kumasi, and Cape Coast but also among rural communities and the diaspora.[3] The church and the public discourse around it are highly relevant to this study due to its tendencies to create and reinforce the dichotomies between demonic/holy, past/future, and individual/family. This binary discourse has a profound influence on how privacy is perceived and practised in urban Ghana.

In his classic text *The Protestant Ethic and the Spirit of Capitalism*, Max Weber argued that Protestant ethics became agents of modernity, capitalism, and wealth due to the privatisation of faith and the liberation of the individual from religious institutions (Weber, 1930). These changes, he argued, brought a spirit of achievement and material success to the Western world, as people became more concerned with their current lives, rather than their afterlives. Unlike Marx, Weber claimed that wealthy, modern, and democratic societies are not the result of class system but the fruits of Protestant reformation. According to Comaroff and Comaroff (2008a), this reformation led profound changes in European personhood that later developed (or 'secularised') into bourgeois ideology. Some of these changes included the establishment of individualism, as 'the person seemed to have been cut free at last from enchanted entanglements, his soul transformed into an inward probing consciousness with the potential for knowing the world and for making a place within it for himself' (2008a: 62).

These Protestant ethics and virtues were brought by missionaries to Sub-Saharan Africa through a process of cultural translation into local terminologies and cosmologies (Meyer, 1999; Comaroff and Comaroff, 2008b). In his study of Pentecostalism in Zimbabwe, for instance, Maxwell (1998) describes how local pastors combat 'the spirit of poverty' and spread the 'prosperity gospel' by re-socialising African urbanites as upwardly mobile modern individuals. A similar process occurs in present-day Ghana, where these Pentecostal ethics are one of the significant forces that re-shape consumption patterns, individual aspirations, middle-class lifestyle, and ethical conduct (Meyer, 1998; Gifford, 2004).

According to Meyer, who researched the spread of Pentecostalism among the Ewes of Ghana, members of these churches often express their need to 'make a complete break with the past' (Meyer, 1998). This marks a dramatic departure from state ideologies of national heritage and cultural preservation promoted by Ghana's first president Kwame Nkrumah. By cultivating cosmopolitan, individual, and nuclear family value systems, Pentecostalism becomes an integral component of postcolonial modernity and often includes severing ties with ancestral spirits, extended kin, and rural communities (van Dijk, 1997; Marshall-Fratani, 1998). Joining a Pentecostal church as new members is led by a narrative of being 'born again' and making a fresh start, sometimes with the aid of shared international practices such as baptism, speaking tongues, and healing rituals.

Pentecostal reform also incorporates a highly sophisticated surveillance system with strong moral standpoints regarding family, economy, and

14 *Introduction*

tradition. As Meyer (1998) shows, even the questionnaires urban Ghanaians fill out when joining a Pentecostal church include questions about tribal body incisions and their meaning, names of family shrines, ownership of ancestral artefacts, 'possible chieftaincy conflicts in the family and special stories concerning one's upbringing.' In this sense, the church becomes a type of 'big brother' that penetrates the most intimate corners of people's life. This book describes how this surveillance system influences digital practices as well as physical urban practices.

Unlike many previous Christian attitudes towards local cosmologies, which usually dismissed them as mere superstitions and practically ignored their relevance to peoples' daily lives, Pentecostal pastors regularly acknowledge and discuss local rituals, ceremonies, and faiths. However, this acknowledgement is usually a tool to stress the urgency of 'breaking free' and severing ties with such 'demonic' or 'pagan' pathologies. The demand to re-socialise oneself contains a demand to shed the burden of the past and advance towards modernity and redemption. The literature on Pentecostalism in Africa suggests that this process is not linear but ongoing, repeating, and paradoxical (Gifford, 1998; Corten and Marshall-Fratani, 2001; Robbins, 2003; Meyer, 2004a; Engelke, 2010; Daswani, 2013).

Referring back to Weber's Protestant ethics and capitalist spirit, Pentecostalism offers an alternative post-national vision to its followers: a promising global village of modern cosmopolitans (or 'a kingdom of God') sharing a wholesome type of kinship as human beings (Corten and Marshall-Fratani, 2001; Gifford, 2015). This vision is essentially anti-nostalgic, emphasising the future and its promising prosperity as a central point of reference. However, the churches also combine fierce criticism about Africa's theological past (and rural present) as the biggest enemy of wealth, prosperity, and growth. This duality, which often becomes the duality between private and public realms, resonates well with economically aspiring individuals. As Meyer phrased it:

> These churches had tremendous appeal especially for young people, who seek to eschew gerontocratic hierarchies and aspire to progress in life (the upwardly mobile), yet think (realistically, perhaps) that this goal can be achieved only through a God-given miracle.
>
> (2004: 460)

While the first wave of Protestantism (as discussed by Weber) idealised humbleness and rejected materiality, its Pentecostal continuation presents consumerism and prosperity as visible expressions of one's spiritual virtues. Middle-class worshippers and their pastors present elegant clothes, digital gadgets, and stylish cars as tangible proofs of success. However, friends, colleagues, and relatives judge the way one achieves his wealth according to ethical speculations and religious interpretations that may deem someone's success as a result of witchcraft, greediness, or materialism (van Dijk, 2003a). The road to wealth and success requires overcoming envious relatives and jealous friends and detaching from all those who 'pull us down'

Introduction   15

financially and spiritually. This collective belief breeds tension between traditional systems of sharing and displaying wealth to contemporary practices of hiding it (Maxwell, 1998; van Dijk, 2003b).

The dualistic worldview of Pentecostalism reinforces the dualism of private and public as people push certain parts of their lives into secret and invisible corners to avoid judgement or even worse – jealousy. In his research on the Ghanaian Pentecostal diaspora, van Dijk (2003b) shows that the church produces a distinct urban identity that often includes rejection and stereotyping of surrounding societies, neighbours, and friends. van Dijk analysed Ghanaian-owned beauty salons in Botswana as 'bodily contact-zones' between Ghanaians and 'strangers,' stressing that Pentecostalism constructs a state of fear and suspicion towards outsiders, often expressed in accusation of witchcraft and routine ritual sanctifications.

The majority of informants in this study attend Pentecostal churches and even those who do operate within its public sphere in family events, street campaigns, radio and television broadcasts, and social media posts.[4] According to the 2010 Ghana Population Census, 28.3% out of 24.65 million Ghanaians belong to the Pentecostal/Charismatic religious affiliation, and it is safe to assume that these numbers have increased sharply since. In that sense, Pentecostalism in Africa is not merely a private individual preference but has a robust public presence that influences many city dwellers. In the words of Gilford (2004: 34), 'nobody in Ghana is unaware of the shift.'

There are no sharp boundaries between the different types of churches in Africa, as most of them currently take some inspiration from Charismatic styles of worship (Meyer, 2004a; Omenyo, 2005; Engelke, 2010). Therefore, an urban middle-class household in Ghana is highly exposed to Pentecostal values and preaching, whether the household members are Pentecostal or of another denomination. However, this study does not fully apply to the experience of orthodox, Traditionalists, or Muslim Ghanaians nor can it apply to the case of rural or working-class groups in Ghana. This research took no comparative agenda (beyond the inherently comparative nature of the anthropological endeavour) and focused on urban Pentecostals.

Churches in Ghana demonstrate Gal's (2002) idea of recursive and semiotic divisions between public and private spheres: the withdrawal from chaotic and uncertain urban life into churches as protective 'social capsules' reflect a new type of private sphere but the collective and visible style of these churches makes them a stage for the display of modernity, success, and wealth (Marshall-Fratani, 1998). The 'publicness' of Christianity, therefore, is reproduced in a recursive manner on global, urban, domestic, and individual scales. Pentecostal discourse and culture are present in cinema, television, radio broadcasts, street adverts, large-scale public gatherings and conferences, and spontaneous street preaching. It is also evident in small and daily conventions such as praising God during conversations; *Nyame Adom*, for instance, is Twi for 'By the grace of God.' Naming small businesses with Christian/biblical idioms such as 'Thank You Jesus Barbershop,' 'God Will provide Food Joint,' or 'Psalm 23 carpenters' is also very common.

16 *Introduction*

The debate about Pentecostalism strongly relates to topics of globalisation, localisation, and transnational commodities (Appadurai, 1996). While some scholars saw Pentecostal practices of healing, speaking tongues, and baptism as a type of cultural evolution or continuation of local African traditions (Asamoah-Gyadu, 2005), the latest literature claims these are actually standard universal practices, spread by international Pentecostal churches around the globe (Corten and Marshall-Fratani, 2001). Either way, these debates reflect the dialectical relations between Pentecostalism and African cosmologies, continually shifting between practices of globalisation (which require rejection and denial of local culture) to practices of localisation (which demand unique narratives and cultural recognition).

By pointing out the globalised nature of Pentecostalism, scholars urge us to acknowledge discontinuity and rupture as a valid anthropological process (Robbins, 2003). Unlike the movement of African Independent churches that aimed to incorporate African rituals and traditions within Christian values, Pentecostal values operate by rejecting them and hence creating dualistic schemas of good/bad, private/public, and sinful/holy. They also set strict moral codes around traditional culture, drinking, sexuality, drug use, adultery, or any rude behaviour, which profoundly influence how people compose themselves in public spheres (Robbins, 2003, 2004b; Meyer, 2004a; Engelke, 2010).

While these clear divisions between public and private spheres explain the incredible popularity of Pentecostal churches in West Africa and other non-European Christian countries, they often create ruptures between persons and their family, their neighbours, and their histories. The ruptures, boundaries, and paradoxes described in the Africanist literature about Pentecostalism are a critical theoretical framework in this research and set an important reference point for the exploration of privacy. Moreover, this unique intersection between Anthropology of Christianity and the ethics of privacy 'takes moments of uncertainty as opportunities for understanding the dynamics and complexities of human evaluation and decision-making processes'(Daswani, 2013: 468).

References

Altman, I. (1975) *The Environment and Social Behavior: Privacy, Personal Space, Territory, and Crowding.* Monterey: Brooks/Cole Publishing.

Altman, I. (1977) 'Privacy Regulation: Culturally Universal or Culturally Specific?', *Journal of Social Issues*, 33(3), pp. 66–84. doi: 10.1111/j.1540–4560.1977.tb01883.x.

Anthony, D., Campos-Castillo, C. and Horne, C. (2017) 'Toward a Sociology of Privacy', *Annual Review of Sociology*, 43(1), pp. 249–296.

Appadurai, A. (1986) 'Theory in Anthropology: Center and Periphery', *Comparative Studies in Society and History*, 28(2), pp. 356–361.

Appadurai, A. (ed.). (1988) *The Social Life of Things: Commodities in Cultural Perspective.* Cambridge: Cambridge University Press.

Introduction 17

Appadurai, A. (1996) 'Global Ethnoscapes: Notes and Queries for a Transnational Anthropology', in Appadurai, A. (ed.) *Modernity at Large.* Minneapolis: University of Minnesota Press, pp. 48–65.

Arendt, H. (2013) *The Human Condition: Second Edition.* Chicago, IL: University of Chicago Press.

Ariès, P., Duby, G. and Perrot, M. (1990) *A History of Private Life: From the Fires of Revolution to the Great War.* London: Harvard University Press.

Asamoah-Gyadu, J. K. (2005) '"Christ is the Answer': What is the Question?" A Ghana Airways Prayer Vigil and its Implications for Religion, Evil and Public Space', *Journal of Religion in Africa*, 35(1), pp. 93–117. doi: 10.1163/1570066052995834.

Ben Elul. E, 2020. 'Noisy Polymedia in Urban Ghana: Strategies for Choosing and Switching Between Media under Unstable Infrastructures', *New Media & Society.* doi: 10.1177/1461444820925047.

Blanchette, J. -F. (2011) 'A Material History of Bits', *Journal of the American Society for Information Science and Technology*, 62(6), pp. 1042–1057.

Boellstorff, T. (2008) *Coming of Age in Second Life: An Anthropologist Explores the Virtually Human.* Princeton, NJ: Princeton University Press.

Bonilla, Y. and Rosa, J. (2015) '#Ferguson: Digital Protest, Hashtag Ethnography, and the Racial Politics of Social Media in the United States', *American Ethnologist*, 42(1), pp. 4–17. doi: 10.1111/amet.12112.

Bourdieu, P. (1984) *Distinction: A Social Critique of the Judgement of Taste.* Cambridge: Harvard University Press.

boyd, D. (2008) 'Facebook's Privacy Trainwreck', *Convergence*, 14(1), pp. 13–20. doi: 10.1177/1354856507084416.

Broadbent, S. (2013) 'Approaches to Personal Communication', in Horst, H. and Miller, D. (eds) *Digital Anthropology.* London; New York: Berg Publishers, pp. 127–142.

Burrell, J. (2012) *Invisible Users: Youth in the Internet Cafés of Urban Ghana.* Cambridge, MA: MIT Press.

Chalfin, B. (2014) 'Public Things, Excremental Politics, and the Infrastructure of Bare Life in Ghana's City of Tema', *American Ethnologist*, 41(1), pp. 92–109. doi: 10.1111/amet.12062.

Cho, H. and Filippova, A. (2016) 'Networked Privacy Management in Facebook: A Mixed-Methods and Multinational Study', in *Proceedings of the 19th ACM Conference on Computer-Supported Cooperative Work & Social Computing.* New York: ACM (CSCW '16), pp. 503–514. doi: 10.1145/2818048.2819996.

Coleman, G. (2014) *Hacker, Hoaxer, Whistleblower, Spy: The Many Faces of Anonymous.* New York: Verso.

Comaroff, J. L. and Comaroff, J. (2001) 'On Personhood: An Anthropological Perspective from Africa', *Social Identities*, 7(2), pp. 267–283.

Comaroff, J. and Comaroff, J. L. (2008a) 'Occult Economies and the Violence of Abstraction: Notes from the South African Postcolony', *American Ethnologist*, 26(2), pp. 279–303. doi: 10.1525/ae.1999.26.2.279.

Comaroff, J. and Comaroff, J. L. (2008b) *Of Revelation and Revolution, Volume 1: Christianity, Colonialism, and Consciousness in South Africa.* Chicago, IL: University of Chicago Press.

Comaroff, J. and Comaroff, J. L. (2015) *Theory from the South: Or, How Euro-America Is Evolving toward Africa.* London: Routledge.

18   *Introduction*

Corten, A. and Marshall-Fratani, R. R. (eds) (2001) *Between Babel and Pentecost: Transnational Pentecostalism in Africa and Latin America*. Bloomington: Indiana University Press.

Costa, E. (2016) *Social Media in Southeast Turkey*. London: UCL Press.

Daswani, G. (2013) 'On Christianity and ethics: Rupture as ethical practice in Ghanaian Pentecostalism', *American Ethnologist*, 40(3), pp. 467–479. doi: 10.1111/amet.12033.

Debatin, B. et al. (2009) 'Facebook and Online Privacy: Attitudes, Behaviors, and Unintended Consequences', *Journal of Computer-Mediated Communication*, 15(1), pp. 83–108. doi: 10.1111/j.1083–6101.2009.01494.x.

Douglas, M. and Isherwood, B. C. (1996) *The World of Goods: Towards an Anthropology of Consumption : With a New Introduction*. London: Routledge.

Engelke, M. (2010) 'Past Pentecostalism: Notes on Rupture, Realignment, and Everyday Life in Pentecostal and African Independent Churches', *Africa*, 80(2), pp. 177–199. doi: 10.3366/afr.2010.0201.

Ferguson, J. (1999) *Expectations of Modernity: Myths and Meanings of Urban Life on the Zambian Copperbelt*. University of California Press.

Ferguson, J. (2006) *Global Shadows: Africa in the Neoliberal World Order*. Durham, NC: Duke University Press.

Ford, S. M. (2011) 'Reconceptualizing the Public/Private Distinction in the Age of Information Technology', *Information, Communication & Society*, 14(4), pp. 550–567. doi: 10.1080/1369118X.2011.562220.

Gal, S. (2002) 'A Semiotics of the Public/Private Distinction', *Differences: A Journal of Feminist Cultural Studies*, 13(1), pp. 77–95.

Geismar, H. (2012) 'Museum+Digital=?', in Miller, D. and Horst, H. (eds) *Digital Anthropology*. London: Berg, pp. 266–287.

Gerbaudo, P. (2012) *Tweets and the Streets: Social Media and Contemporary Activism*. London: Pluto Press.

Gifford, P. (1998) *African Christianity: Its Public Role*. London: C. Hurst & Co. Publishers.

Gifford, P. (2004) *Ghana's New Christianity: Pentecostalism in a Globalising African Economy*. London: C. Hurst & Co. Publishers.

Gifford, P. (2015) *Christianity, Development and Modernity in Africa*. London: Hurst.

Goffman, E. (1956) *The Presentation of Self in Everyday Life*. New York: Doubleday.

Goffman, E. (1986) *Stigma: Notes on the Management of Spoiled Identity*. Reissue edition. New York: Touchstone.

Gordon, T. and Hancock, M. (2005) '"The Crusade Is the Vision": Branding Charisma in a Global Pentecostal Ministry', *Material Religion*, 1(3), pp. 386–404. doi: 10.2752/174322005778054023.

Guta, H. and Karolak, M. (2015) 'Veiling and Blogging: Social Media as Sites of Identity Negotiation and Expression among Saudi Women', *Journal of International Women's Studies*, 16(2), pp. 115–127.

Habermas, J. (1989) *The Structural Transformation of the Public Sphere*, trans. Thomas Burger, Cambridge: MIT Press, 85, pp. 85–92.

Haynes, N. (2016) *Social Media in Northern Chile*. London: UCL Press.

Hogan, B. (2010) 'The Presentation of Self in the Age of Social Media: Distinguishing Performances and Exhibitions Online', *Bulletin of Science, Technology & Society*, 30(6), pp. 377–386. doi: 10.1177/0270467610385893.

Introduction 19

Horst, H. (2012) 'New Media Technologies in Everyday Life', in Miller, D. and Horst, H. (eds) *Digital Anthropology*. Oxford: Berg, pp. 61–79.

Horst, H. and Miller, D. (2006) *The Cell Phone: An Anthropology of Communication*. New York: Berg.

Igo, S. E. (2015) 'The Beginnings of the End of Privacy', *The Hedgehog Review*, 17(1). Available at: http://www.iasc-culture.org/THR/THR_article_2015_Spring_Igo. php (Accessed: 13 December 2017).

Kasper, D. V. S. (2007) 'Privacy as a Social Good', *Social Thought & Research*, 28, pp. 165–189.

Landes, J. B. (2003) 'Further Thoughts on the Public/Private Distinction', *Journal of Women's History*, 15(2), pp. 28–39. doi: 10.1353/jowh.2003.0051.

Lange, P. G. (2007) 'Publicly Private and Privately Public: Social Networking on YouTube', *Journal of Computer-Mediated Communication*, 13(1), pp. 361–380. doi: 10.1111/j.1083–6101.2007.00400.x.

Latour, B. (1993) *We Have Never Been Modern*. Cambridge, MA: Harvard University Press.

Lewis, K., Kaufman, J. and Christakis, N. (2008) 'The Taste for Privacy: An Analysis of College Student Privacy Settings in an Online Social Network', *Journal of Computer-Mediated Communication*, 14(1), pp. 79–100. doi: 10.1111/j.1083–6101.2008.01432.x.

Lysloff, R. T. A. (2003) 'Musical Community on the Internet: An On-Line Ethnography', *Cultural Anthropology*, 18(2), pp. 233–263. doi: 10.1525/can.2003.18.2.233.

Madanipour, A. (2003) *Public and Private Spaces of the City*. London: Routledge.

Madianou, M. and Miller, D. (2012) *Migration and New Media: Transnational Families and Polymedia*. Abingdon, Oxon; New York: Routledge

Marshall-Fratani, R. (1998) 'Mediating the Global and Local in Nigerian Pentecostalism', *Journal of Religion in Africa*, 28(3), pp. 278–315. doi: 10.2307/1581572.

Marwick, A. E. and boyd, D. (2014) 'Networked Privacy: How Teenagers Negotiate Context in Social Media', *New Media & Society*, 16(7), pp. 1051–1067. doi: 10.1177/1461444814543995.

Marwick, A. E. and boyd, D. (2018) 'Privacy at the Margins: Understanding Privacy at the Margins—Introduction', *International Journal of Communication*, 12, pp. 1157–1165.

Maxwell, D. (1998) '"Delivered from the Spirit of Poverty?": Pentecostalism, Prosperity and Modernity in Zimbabwe', *Journal of Religion in Africa*, 28(3), pp. 350–373. doi: 10.2307/1581574.

Mbembe, A. (2001) 'Ways of Seeing: Beyond the New Nativism. Introduction', *African Studies Review*, 44(2), pp. 1–14. doi: 10.2307/525572.

McDonald, T. (2015) 'Affecting Relations: Domesticating the Internet in a South-Western Chinese Town', *Information, Communication & Society*, 18(1), pp. 17–31. doi: 10.1080/1369118X.2014.924981.

McDonald, T. (2016) *Social Media in Rural China*. London: UCL Press

McKay, D. (2010) 'On the Face of Facebook: Historical Images and Personhood in Filipino Social Networking', *History and Anthropology*, 21(4), pp. 479–498. doi: 10.1080/02757206.2010.522311.

Meehan, J. (2013) *Feminists Read Habermas (RLE Feminist Theory): Gendering the Subject of Discourse*. New York: Routledge.

20 Introduction

Meyer, B. (1998) '"Make a Complete Break with the Past." Memory and Post-Colonial Modernity in Ghanaian Pentecostalist Discourse', *Journal of Religion in Africa*, 28(3), pp. 316–349. doi: 10.2307/1581573.

Meyer, B. (1999) *Translating the Devil: Religion and Modernity among the Ewe in Ghana*. Trenton, NJ: Africa World Pr.

Meyer, B. (2004a) 'Christianity in Africa: From African Independent to Pentecostal-Charismatic Churches', *Annual Review of Anthropology*, 33(1), pp. 447–474. doi: 10.1146/annurev.anthro.33.070203.143835.

Meyer, B. (2004b) '"Praise the Lord": Popular Cinema and pentecostalite Style in Ghana's New Public Sphere', *American Ethnologist*, 31(1), pp. 92–10. doi: 10.1525/ae.2004.31.1.92.

Meyer, B. (2012) 'Religious and Secular, "Spiritual" and "Physical" in Ghana', in Bender, C. and Taves, A. (eds) *What Matters? Ethnographies of Value in a (Not So) Secular Age*. New York: Columbia University Press (SSRC), pp. 86–118.

Meyer, B. and Moors, A. (2005) *Religion, Media, and the Public Sphere*. Bloomington: Indiana University Press.

Michaels, E. (1991) 'A Primer of Restrictions on Picture-Taking in Traditional Areas of Aboriginal Australia', *Visual Anthropology*, 4(3–4), pp. 259–275. doi: 10.1080/08949468.1991.9966564.

Miller, D. (2000) 'The Fame of Trinis: Websites as Traps', *Journal of Material Culture*, 5(1), pp. 5–24. doi: 10.1177/135918350000500101.

Miller, D. (2008) *The Comfort of Things*. First Edition. London: Polity Press.

Miller, D. (2011) *Tales from Facebook*. London: Polity Press.

Miller, D. (2016) *Social Media in an English Village*. London: UCL Press. doi: 10.14324/111.9781910634431.

Miller, D. and Horst, H. (eds) (2012) *Digital Anthropology*. First Edition. London: Berg Publishers.

Miller, D. and Sinanan, J. (2017) *Visualising Facebook: A Comparative Perspective*. London: UCL Press.

Miller, D. and Slater, D. (2001) *The Internet: An Ethnographic Approach*. First Edition. Oxford; New York: Bloomsbury Academic.

Miller, D. et al. (2016) *How the World Changed Social Media*. London: UCL Press.

Nicolescu, R. (2016) *Social Media in Southeast Italy*. London: UCL Press.

Nippert-Eng, C. (2007) 'Privacy in the United States: Some Implications for Design', *International Journal of Design*, 1(2). Available at: https://search.proquest.com/openview/81f09f1bf8d166c1c24d8d898f5bf0d5/1?pq-origsite=gscholar&cbl=466416 (Accessed: 14 December 2017).

Nippert-Eng, C. (2010) *Islands of Privacy*. Chicago, IL: University of Chicago Press.

Nissenbaum, H. (2004) 'Privacy as Contextual Integrity Symposium – Technology, Values, and the Justice System', *Washington Law Review*, 79, pp. 119–158.

Omenyo, C. N. (2005) 'From the Fringes to the Centre: Pentecostalization of the Mainline Churches in Ghana', *Exchange*, 34(1), pp. 39–60. doi: 10.1163/1572543053506338.

Pateman, C. (1983) 'Feminist Critique of Public/Private Dichotomy', in Gaus, G. F. and Benn, S. I. (eds) *Public and Private in Social Life*. London : Croom Helm; New York : St. Martin's Press. Available at: https://trove.nla.gov.au/version/46390557 (Accessed: 9 April 2018).

Patterson, A. H. and Chiswick, N. R. (1981) 'The Role of the Social and Physical Environment in Privacy Maintenance among the Iban of Borneo', *Journal of Environmental Psychology*, 1(2), pp. 131–139. doi: 10.1016/S0272-4944(81)80003-5.

Petronio, S. (2002) *Boundaries of Privacy: Dialectics of Disclosure*. Albany: State University of New York Press.

Pink, S. and Mackley, K. L. (2012) 'Video and a Sense of the Invisible: Approaching Domestic Energy Consumption through the Sensory Home', *Sociological Research Online*, 17(1), pp. 1–19. doi: 10.5153/sro.2583.

Pink, S. et al. (2015) *Digital Ethnography: Principles and Practice*. London: SAGE Publications.

Postill, J. (2008) 'Localizing the Internet beyond Communities and Networks', *New Media & Society*, 10(3), pp. 413–431. doi: 10.1177/1461444808089416.

Postill, J. (2014) 'Freedom Technologists and the New Protest Movements a Theory of Protest Formulas', *Convergence: The International Journal of Research into New Media Technologies*, 20(4), pp. 402–418. doi: 10.1177/1354856514541350.

Postill, J. and Pink, S. (2012) 'Social Media Ethnography: The Digital Researcher in a Messy Web', *Media International Australia*, 145(1), pp. 123–134. doi: 10.1177/1329878X1214500114.

Robbins, J. (2003) 'On the Paradoxes of Global Pentecostalism and the Perils of Continuity thinking', Religion, 33(3), pp. 221–231. doi: 10.1016/S0048-721X(03)00055-1.

Robbins, J. (2004a) *Becoming Sinners: Christianity and Moral Torment in a Papua New Guinea Society*. Oakland: University of California Press.

Robbins, J. (2004b) 'The Globalization of Pentacostal and Charismatic Christianity', *Annual Review of Anthropology*, 33, pp. 117–143.

Robbins, J. (2013) 'Beyond the Suffering Subject: Toward an Anthropology of the Good', *Journal of the Royal Anthropological Institute*, 19(3), pp. 447–462. doi: 10.1111/1467–9655.12044.

Schoeman, F. (1984) 'Privacy: Philosophical Dimensions', *American Philosophical Quarterly*, 21(3), pp. 199–213.

Schroeder, R. (2001) *The Social Life of Avatars: Presence and Interaction in Shared Virtual Environments*. New York: Springer Science & Business Media.

Schwartz, B. (1968) 'The Social Psychology of Privacy', *American Journal of Sociology*, 73(6), pp. 741–752. doi: 10.1086/224567.

Sennett, R. (2017) *The Fall of Public Man (40th Anniversary Edition)*. New York: W. W. Norton & Company.

Simmel, G. (1906) 'The Sociology of Secrecy and of Secret Societies', *American Journal of Sociology*, 11(4), pp. 441–498.

Sinanan, J. (2017) *Social Media in Trinidad*. London: UCL Press.

Slater, D. and Kwami, J. (2005) 'Embeddedness and Escape: Internet and Mobile Use as Poverty Reduction Strategies in Ghana', *Information Society Research Group (ISRG) Report*. Available at: http://www.researchgate.net/profile/Janet_Kwami/publication/228635823_Embeddedness_and_escape_Internet_and_mobile_use_as_poverty_reduction_strategies_in_Ghana/links/00b7d530253d3b70b1000000.pdf (Accessed: 6 July 2015).

Spyer, J. (2018) *Social Media in Emergent Brazil*. London: UCL Press.

Srinivasan, J. et al. (2018) 'Privacy at the Margins: The Poverty of Privacy: Understanding Privacy Trade-Offs from Identity Infrastructure Users in India', *International Journal of Communication*, 12(0), p. 20.

Tacchi, J. and Chandola, T. (2015) 'Complicating Connectivity: Women's Negotiations with Smartphones in an Indian Slum', in Hjorth, L. and Khoom, O. (eds.) *Routledge Handbook of New Media in Asia*. New York: Routledge, pp. 191–200.

van der Geest, S. (2008) 'Life after dark in Kwahu Tafo, Ghana', *Etnofoor*, 20 (2), pp. 23–39. Available at: https://hdl.handle.net/11245/1.299891

22 *Introduction*

van Dijk, R. (1997) 'From Camp to Encompassment: Discourses of Transsubjectivity in the Ghanaian Pentecostal Diaspora', *Journal of Religion in Africa*, 27(2), pp. 135–159. doi: 10.2307/1581683.

van Dijk, R. (2003a) 'Localisation, Ghanaian Pentecostalism and the Stranger's Beauty in Botswana', *Africa*, 73(4), pp. 560–583. doi: 10.3366/afr.2003.73.4.560.

van Dijk, R. (2003b) 'Religion, Reciprocity and Restructuring Family Responsibility in the Ghanaian Pentecostal Diaspora', in Bryceson, D. F. and Vuorela, U. (eds) *The Transnational Family: New European Frontiers and Global Networks*. First Edition. New York: Berg, pp. 173–196.

Venkatraman, S. (2017) *Social Media in South India*. London: UCL Press.

Vitak, J. (2012) 'The Impact of Context Collapse and Privacy on Social Network Site Disclosures', *Journal of Broadcasting & Electronic Media*, 56(4), pp. 451–470. doi: 10.1080/08838151.2012.732140.

Wacks, R. (2015) *Privacy: A Very Short Introduction*. Second Edition. Oxford, New York: Oxford University Press (Very Short Introductions).

Wang, X. (2016) *Social Media in Industrial China*. London: UCL Press.

Warren, C. and Laslett, B. (1977) 'Privacy and Secrecy: A Conceptual Comparison', *Journal of Social Issues*, 33(3), pp. 43–51. doi: 10.1111/j.1540–4560.1977.tb01881.x.

Warren, S. D. and Brandeis, L. D. (1890) 'The Right to Privacy', *Harvard Law Review*, 4(5), pp. 193–220. doi: 10.2307/1321160.

Weber, M. (1930) *The Protestant Ethic and the Spirit of Capitalism: and Other Writings*. London: Penguin.

Weintraub, J. (1997) 'The Theory and Politics of the Public/Private Distinction', in Kumar, K. (ed.) *Public and Private in Thought and Practice: Perspectives on a Grand Dichotomy*. Chicago: University of Chicago Press, pp. 1–39.

Westin, A. F. (1967) *Privacy and Freedom*. New York: Ig Publishing.

Wicker, S. B. (2013) *Cellular Convergence and the Death of Privacy*. First Edition. New York: Oxford University Press.

Notes

1 Facebook is a free American social media platform founded in 2004. As of December 2018, there were 5,424,000 Facebook users in Ghana, 18.1% of its entire population (NapoleonCat.com).

2 Altman's notion that privacy can be culturally constructed encouraged several scholars in social psychology to examine it in pre-industrial non-Western settings (see Patterson and Chiswick, 1981).

3 According to the 2010 Ghana Population Census, 28.3% out of 24.65 million Ghanaians belong to the Pentecostal/Charismatic religious affiliation.

4 Scholars of Christianity in Ghana have noted the fluid boundaries between different denominations such as AIC (African-initiated church) and Pentecostalism, as well as the undeniable influence of Pentecostalism over mainline churches (Gifford, 1998; Meyer, 2004b; Meyer and Moors, 2005).

2 Method and reflection

This ethnographic research was conducted over a period of three years (2014–2017) in multiple data gathering sites, both physical and digital. The research process was not a linear transition from fieldwork to theory and writing but a constant intersection between all 'stages,' going back and forth as needed to develop a coherent theoretical case (Wagon, 1992). I was moving between various mediums, scholarly work, graphic materials, social media conversations, and face-to-face encounters throughout the entire process.

My main (physical) field site was Tema, a city in the region of Greater Accra (Ghana).[1] I spent seven months living with a local family in Tema (four months in October 2015 and three months in February 2016). Tema is an especially useful site for the study of middle-class Ghanaians due to its history as a new town constructed in the early 1960s to attract young professionals and nuclear families who were employed in the nearby harbour and factories (Jackson and Oppong, 2014).

As a planned city with modern infrastructure, running water, and electricity, Tema became a promising destination for skilled rural migrants from Ghana and neighbouring countries to begin a new modern life in Africa's rising democracy. Therefore, the middle class is the original (and somewhat artificial) demographic of the city. As a vibrant urban centre, Tema also has a high concentration of Pentecostal churches that encourage narratives of social mobility, future aspirations, and detachment from life back in the village.

Tema has a grid street plan with roads and streets divided into small neighbourhoods known as 'Communities.' Most of the time I was based in central, well-established, and relatively busy 'communities' but I do not mention specific neighbourhoods to protect the anonymity of informants. I also spent time in nearby neighbourhoods varying from older and neglected parts of town to upcoming neighbourhoods and gated communities with spacious private houses (often called 'new lands'). I was mixing scheduled interviews and informal conversation, while also observing a wide variety of people such as family members, elders, students, religious leaders, vendors, taxi drivers, academics, etc. I interviewed about 30 people for this study but conducted informal, unstructured conversations and observations with dozens of others, both online and offline.

DOI: 10.4324/9781003187424 -2

24 *Method and reflection*

The informants come from a range of middle-class backgrounds: young professionals, small business owners, students, upcoming pastors, and more. Most were of either the first or second generation to live in the city, still carrying strong links to their hometowns. As modern urbanites, who typically attend school, the people of Tema use English as their primary (written and spoken) language, which gave me easy access to conversations and interviews. However, they also use a variety of native languages (e.g., Twi, Ga, and Ewe) especially for private family conversations, slang, or unique proverbs. This lingual interplay can be seen as yet another tension between tradition and modernity, as well as private and public behaviour. Some middle-class members see fellow urbanites that do not speak or read fluent English as 'misplaced' in the city or simply 'backwards.'

I conducted participant observations in a variety of locations such as houses, yards, shops, bars, churches, schools, and streets. I spent long evenings in nightlife spots such as bars and clubs, in the company of pub goers chatting about politics, religion, and family. I also regularly visited private houses, especially their front yards and verandas, where I helped in household chores, held conversations, or just devoted time for 'deep hanging out' (Geertz, 1998). This 'traditional' fieldwork was accompanied by long-term observations and interactions in online spaces, also known as digital ethnography (Pink et al., 2015; Barendregt, 2017).

I observed and followed various social media platforms, including Facebook, WhatsApp, Instagram,[2] and Snapchat, where I interacted with informants in multiple manners. According to Pink et al. (2015: 44), digital ethnography is particularly useful for the study of practices — in my case privacy practices – because it offers a two-dimensional look into what people do alongside what they report doing. In other words, social media is a cultural practice but also a place where people exhibit their desired practices. Howard and Mawyer (2015: 7) add that digital ethnography extends 'nondigital sites of human engagement in new ways by dis-establishing space-time boundaries for structured and unstructured social interactions.'

Conducting a digital ethnography allowed me to maintain ongoing contact with informants even when I was away from the geographical field and to document the rapid technological developments they adjusted to. For instance, in 2017 both Instagram and Facebook added a feature known as 'Stories' to their applications. These features are inspired by Snapchat 'Stories' and encourage users to broadcast ephemeral photos and videos of their daily lives. According to my observation of this process, while Ghanaians adopted Instagram stories enthusiastically, they mostly left their Facebook stories unused; this provided me not only with rich first-hand visual data but also with insights about the division of social media platforms into private and public spaces.

Describing the methodological procedures of this study is in some ways very simple and straightforward and in other ways incredibly enigmatic and

Method and reflection 25

complex. The reason for this paradox is that I claim to study exactly what was hidden from me – the private, invisible, and secret aspects of people's lives. I aspired to provide a glimpse into what happens beyond the 'naked eye' of public interactions and beyond my reach as a foreign researcher, while maintaining all the ethical guidelines of ethnographic research.[3] As mentioned, all the names of people, places, and particular details of events in this study were changed and anonymised due to the sensitive topic of privacy.

Previous scholarly work in Ghana often refers to issues of discreteness, shyness, lies, rumours, and secrets – what Coe phrased as a 'Ghanaian aesthetic of indirection' (Coe, 2008).[4] Clear divisions between private and public spaces often come up as related empirical findings (van der Geest, 1998; Chalfin, 2004, 2014; McDonnell, 2010), while challenges during interviews and fieldwork are often explained as a result of Ghanaian discreteness and evasiveness (Bleek, 1987; Coe, 2008; Dankwa, 2009; Burrell, 2012). For instance, by comparing medical surveys with ethnographic knowledge, Bleek (1987) was able to 'expose' how informants had 'lied lavishly' to nurses about issues of abortions, marriage, and health to protect their good name and maintain privacy.[5]

While HIV, abortions, and other medical issues are indeed extreme examples where one might wish to protect his or her privacy, the main point to be drawn is that impression management in Ghana is often collective, aiming to prevent shaming or disgrace (in Twi: *animguase*). According to the Akan proverb *Feree ne animguasee dee fanyinam owuo* it is better to die than to be ashamed. This protection of family honour is seen in how elders in Ghana praise their 'successful children' even if they neglect them financially and medically (van der Geest, 2000) or in the immense importance of funerals and other festivities as vehicles of collective reputation (Witte, 2001; Mazzucato, Kabki and Smith, 2006). The fear of being stigmatised or shamed means 'as long as one is not certain about the trustworthiness of the other person, it is prudent to keep certain things secret, which may include lying' (van der Geest and Mensah Dapaah, 2012).

It is unclear whether anthropologists who are seen as strangers face more suspicion and distance than native researchers, who reported even more suspicion towards their position as an 'insider' (Clifford and Marcus, 1986; Weinreb, 2006; Aberese-Ako, 2017). Nonetheless, my first attempts to understand such an introverted field felt like a failure; I was stuck in a highly composed and artificial public terrain, conducting interviews that often felt disingenuous. I was trying to penetrate both metaphorical and physical boundaries that other urbanites knew very well (Petronio, 2002) and, as a result, I was seen as the *Obroni* ('visitor' or 'foreigner') who asks too many questions. What has changed then?

Through in-depth and continuous exploration of multiple fields and an analysis of my own personal experience, I decided to shift my focus from trying to cross boundaries to trying to map them. In other words, instead

26 *Method and reflection*

of trying to disturb people's privacy I observed how people managed their identity by dividing their practices and information into private and public realms. To borrow Nippert-Eng's (2010) metaphor in her ethnographic work on perceptions of privacy among Chicago's middle class, if publicity is an ocean and privacy is an island, I became interested in 'the beach,' where they both meet and intercept. These meeting points between private and public, connected and autonomous, concealed and visible, are dynamic, dialectic, balanced, and tensed all at once (Petronio, 2002).

The process of mapping privacy practices included an honest reflection about my own ways of maintaining privacy. I mainly tried to assess which aspects of myself are expressed in the field and which are suppressed and silenced. I was inspired by Behar's (1997) spirited discussion about reflexivity and vulnerability and her call to challenge the pivotal convention in Anthropology in which the researcher is always more potent than the informants. Behar invites social scientists to find their own 'weak spots,' and even their moments of suffering, while doing fieldwork. By doing so, she argues, the observer investigates his or her personal involvement in the field and reaches a more profound truth. Resisting the role of the ethnographer as the ultimate privileged and powerful agent requires a process of self-exploration; it starts by asking 'what aspects of the self are the most important filters through which one perceives the world and, more particularly, the topic being studied' (Behar, 1997: 13).

Anthropologists who studied their own people, and mainly female anthropologists who conducted ethnographies with women, used the term 'halfies' to express their position as an 'insider' and 'outsider' at the same time (Goldstein-Gidoni, 2000; Halstead, 2001; Subedi, 2006; Halstead, Hirsch and Okely, 2008). Halstead (2001) describes how her hosts constantly shifted their perception of her, from a respectable Western researcher in some situations to a fellow East Indian woman in others. Halstead theorised this 'framing' process as a postcolonial notion of identities as flowing and flexible, changing with each context and situation. In my case, it is not the differences and commonalities with my informants that I wish to discuss but my subjective position in the field, and how my identity is interpreted in an unfamiliar environment that praises discreteness yet values a good reputation.

There are (at least) two aspects of myself that influenced how I was framed and observed in the field: my gay identity and my Jewish identity. These two 'filters'– one touches issues of gender and sexuality and the other relates to religion and ethnicity – were at times parallel and at times contradictory, for they both express my profound difference and marginality as a researcher in this specific field. Both 'filters' are possible to hide or lie about, unlike a Black identity for instance, which is 'overdetermined from the outside' (Fanon, 2008: 95). However, while these identities have the benefit of staying private, one of them was publicly disclosed and spoken while the other was kept entirely hidden.

Method and reflection 27

1.1 Back to the closet – a gay researcher undercover

A few weeks before my first fieldwork trip to Ghana I received a message from Ama, a key informant and dear friend who connected me to her family members in Tema. 'My cousin Louisa knows you are gay somehow. She told me it is best if you keep it private when you are in Ghana.' Apparently, Louisa asked for my name and found my Facebook profile, where she saw photos of my spouse and connected the dots. From that point on I decided to make my profile (and my identity) private. Furthermore, I opened a new Facebook profile for my Ghana contacts, where I had minimal personal information.[6] This 'fake' profile turned out to be useful methodologically because it created a virtual field containing only my informant's social media profiles. Whenever I logged into this unique Facebook profile, I actually entered Ghana's Facebook.

Outside Ghana, friends and colleagues often inaccurately assumed that my decision to keep my sexual identity discrete was for safety, imagining a hostile or aggressive society that might harm me if they discover my sexuality. On the most elementary level, homosexuality is often considered an 'unnatural carnal act,' which is prohibited under the Consolidation of Criminal Code, 1960 (Act 29), Chapter 6, section 102. This law was first introduced and enforced by the British colony but remains current to this day. However, as Ghana is a liberal democracy, and as the law does not explicitly refer to same-sex activity between men, there is currently no active state persecution or imprisonment.

Ghana can be a very homophobic place, fuelled by anti-gay religious leaders, politicians, mass media, and popular literature. These forces attack homosexuality from two angles: the Christian conservative discourse of American Pentecostal churches on the one hand and the 'Africanist' perception of homosexuals as Western imperialists who introduce this 'un-African' act to local men (Dunton, 1989; Essien and Aderinto, 2009). Consequently, many tourist guides and internet forums emphasise that White tourists should be especially careful about this homophobic climate, as it can often be used for bribes, blackmails, or even robberies.

Several LGBT activists in Ghana launched a website dedicated to exposing local men who seduce gays via dating applications and chats to meet with them. Once they meet and go to a private place, these 'hunters' either blackmail the gay men they met or cooperate with policemen to demand a bribe. This website reflects the internet as an essential and dangerous platform for public shaming, especially when it comes to sexuality and secret identities. In a sense, LGBT identity in Ghana reflects broader anxieties about privacy as 'blackmail can be committed by strangers, acquaintances, employers, colleagues, friends, or even family –virtually anyone who might have access to information that another person wants to keep secret' (Thoreson, 2011: 13).

Despite this alarming climate, often critiqued by human rights activists from inside and outside Africa (Solace Brothers Foundation et al., 2016),

28 *Method and reflection*

and without downplaying its importance, my ethnographic experience placed the 'danger' of exposing my sexual identity for a much more trivial reason. My discretion (and often lies) was about maintaining a respectable position in a conservative community, to avoid unnecessary conflicts and awkward situations. Mostly, it was about assuring my role as a positive figure so that potential informants who might feel critical about my 'lifestyle' will not reject my presence in their daily lives.

According to Norman et al., the social norm around courtship, marriage, and sexual behaviours 'remains largely conventional in the urban centres and parochial in the rural areas' (2016: 13). This need to subvert one's self to communal norms and convention felt stronger than ever. Individualistic, overly liberal or rebellious behaviour was not something I had the privilege of practising, especially if I wished to be invited to family gatherings, get introduced to elders and youth, or get access to people's homes.

Therefore, it was not a sense of physical danger that made me hide my identity, nor was it an attempt to deceive my informants, but a growing understanding of how members of the community operate by keeping certain personal aspects out of sight. These secrets and lies are often entirely individual but once disclosed to even one person they become shared knowledge, co-owned by two parties who depend on each other to maintain the secret (Petronio, 2002). In my case, the information was co-owned by Ama, Louisa, and me. We had to keep a secret before, during, and after my arrival, even from close family members and informants. Similar secrets were shared between me and other informants on various topics, but this particular secret was mine, and, ironically, the publication of this text undermines it.

Literature by and about LGBT anthropologists tends to encourage coming out of the closet in the field, pointing at the benefits of the process concerning establishing intimacy and honesty with informants (Williams, 1993; Lewin and Leap, 1996; Jackson, 1998). Apart from the clear social mission to 'liberate' both anthropologists and informants from misconceptions about homosexuality, coming out is often discussed as a methodological virtue that produces better research.[7] Describing his experience of studying the native American culture of 'two-spirits' and cross-gender, Williams states:

> Many lesbian and gay ethnographers have been unnecessarily closeted and overly cautious during their fieldwork, and I am dismayed that even some of those who are open about themselves at their university have so little self-esteem that they will lie to their informants.
>
> (1996: 74)

While I understand the logic behind Williams' claims, and even though he deliberately included the case of coming out in 'non-Western cultures' (Williams, 1993), his research topic focuses on homosexual identities and sexuality. Research topics can set a crucial difference especially if the informants are gay themselves and will probably feel more comfortable in

Method and reflection 29

the company of a gay researcher. Besides, Williams and other LGBT scholars set out to challenge the old code in anthropology whereby the ethnographer is 'de-sexualised' and must refrain from sexual activity in the field (Kulick and Willson, 1995; Shokeid, 2014).

My case was different; I did not study topics of homosexuality or sexuality beyond their position as 'private' issues. In fact, it was beyond the scope of this study to analyse issues of gender in Ghana at large. Due to the profoundly different gender experience, performance, and division of labour in Africa, and especially in Ghana where matrilineal structures and Christian values profoundly change the position of men and women, this sort of analysis would have required a different set of research questions and theoretical frameworks (Gill, 1990; Oyewùmí, 2003; Miescher, 2005; Oyewumi, 2005; Wong, 2006; Cole, Manuh and Miescher, 2007; Dankwa, 2009). As Oyewumi (2005: 16) asks while critiquing the use of universal gender categories in a study about social-class formations in Accra: 'Women? What women? Who qualifies to be women in this cultural setting, and on what bases are they to be identified?' due to these complexities, I chose a mixture of men and women and did not place gender as the main focal point of this study.

Furthermore, I was strongly advised by the few informants who did know about my identity that I should refrain from telling people I am gay. Also, I was often reminded of the negative attitudes towards homosexuality when informants felt comfortable enough to voice them in our conversations. Even though the actual criminal restrictions were not an alarming issue for me, staying closeted proved to be the right choice because I ended up studying practices of privacy. My participant observation became much more productive and nuanced once I realised that I was actually devoting myself to a much larger game of secrecy, lying, and hiding. This game was not only socially acceptable and expected but also crucial to the harmony and balance of public interactions (Altman, 1975; Bok, 1999).

Nonetheless, coming from a very accepting and liberal environment, having to lie about my life back home was far from easy. One lie led to another and at some point I even had to pretend I had a fiancée, with the aim of politely refusing flirtatious women.[8] As Lewin and Leap (1996: 12) wrote in their edited collection of articles about LGBT anthropology:

> Secrecy and passing tend to have a painful effect on the individual's self-esteem... the personal history that includes a period of concealing one's orientation from oneself makes clear how painful it can be to realise that one belongs to a despised category.

This painful effect was evident whenever I had to lie about my history or listen politely to homophobic discussions at church, restaurants, or domestic spaces. However, this also meant that people did not censor themselves in my presence and I got to document their critique with an open mind.

30 *Method and reflection*

To sum, scholars dealing with privacy described how stigmatised or anomalous individuals, who are often 'disqualified from full social acceptance,' choose to hide their identity/condition in defence of their position in a community (van der Geest and Mensah Dapaah, 2012; Goffman, 1986; Hjorth, Pink and Horst, 2018). Sharing or disclosing sensitive information may have outcomes worse than keeping it hidden, even if only at certain times or in specific contexts (Miall, 1989; Petronio, 2002). In fact, it might be necessary for the maintenance of social order and the existence of long-term relationships (Simmel, 1906). Unlike other documented cases of LGBT ethnographers disclosing their identity, in my case keeping it hidden was more useful strategically and methodologically.

For example, realising the crucial implications of my public social media posts and hence my social media identity to the extent of opening a unique Facebook profile helped me define social media as a vulnerable zone of judgement and as a threat to my own privacy. Therefore, it comes as no surprise that non-fiction literature about African gays and lesbians often deals with secrecy, invisibility, and bi-sexuality as a way of avoiding ostracising (Mwachiro, 2014; Azuah, 2016).

As I placed my concealment in a cultural context, I realised that everyone I met was inside some sort of closet. The people concerned about class versus their economic status, the religious persona they express versus their sins, the family life they present versus their secret affairs, the exterior of their houses versus the interior, and their past versus their future were all types of 'closets.' Thus, interpreting the act of hiding as purely 'oppressive' misses out the nuances and possibilities that such hiding allows. As Dankwa (2009: 202) showed in her study of same-sex relations among urban Ghanaian women, by celebrating and reinforcing secrecy rather than fighting for public legitimacy in liberal terms, women allow their family members to remain casual about their 'non-normative' behaviour, while staying active in familial and religious life.

Similarly, in his ethnography of queer cultures in Indonesia, Boellstorff (2005) states that gay men often marry women and build traditional homes. Heterosexual marriage, he argues, is not incompatible with gay identity because there is no expectation for an 'integrated self, out of its closet and always the same.' This makes room for 'distinct subjectivities' whereby one may be openly gay in gay spaces but closeted at home, work, or the mosque (Boellstorff, 2005: 116). These 'cultures of silence' (Arnfred, 2005) obtained by discreteness are integral to this study. As a young Ghanaian gay artist told me:

> It is not part of our culture to be very outspoken and loud about who we are… the community tends to accept those who don't abandon their duties and obligations to the family – they will be more tolerant of what they do away from social life.

In other words, as long as no one is shaming the reputation of the *Abusua* his or her discrete and private practices will be more tolerated. Privacy is

Method and reflection   31

strongly associated with honour, status, and community. My own experience of concealing versus sharing taught me much about the topic I explored. The other side of this dialectic tension is what people do perform, celebrate, and exhibit. In my case, it turned out to be another essential component of my identity – my Jewishness.

1.2 What Jesus really looked like – the Jewish anthropologist

Unlike my gay identity, which was concealed and privatised, my Jewish identity became a significant part of how I was perceived and presented in the field. Whenever people heard that I came from Israel they asked about my religion, and once they realised I was Jewish they could not stay indifferent; whether they thanked me for belonging to the 'true people of God' or opened theological debates with me about the acceptance of Jesus Christ as a messiah, I instantly became an object of curiosity. Even a simple visit to the post office or a short taxi ride would often end up in heated theological discussions about monotheism, Christianity, Israel, and Judaism.

Stepping into a profoundly Christian and religious field swept by the promising charm of Pentecostal and Charismatic churches, I was surprised to find out that my Jewishness was no more an anecdote but a defining feature of how I am seen. Moreover, in a country where Jesus is continuously portrayed as a White European (Meyer, 2010), my physical appearance, olive skin, and dark hair were often described as a more authentic image of Jesus Christ. This visual authenticity was highly appreciated as 'Pentecostal practice constitutes visual experience as an important medium of divine intervention in the life of the (biblically informed) viewer' (Gordon and Hancock, 2005).

Informants often imposed my Jewish identity on me – in the words of Halstead (2001) I was 'framed' as Jewish by my hosts – and this framing became a central 'filter' in our interactions and construction of knowledge. Gossip about my Jewishness spread between residents of the neighbourhood, I was invited to multiple churches as a respectable guest, and people consulted with me about religious issues and especially about my direct access to Hebrew – the original language of the Holy Scriptures. I was often asked via WhatsApp to explain the lingual meaning of biblical terms that cannot be fully captured in their English translation, such as *Eshet Hail* ('woman of valour') or *Ezer Kenegdo* (simply translated as 'his helper'). I was even consulted when an informant wanted to tattoo her arm with Hebrew writing and prevented an unfortunate typo.

In the Pentecostal/Charismatic discourse, due to its renewed focus on the biblical text as a source of inspiration, personhood, and knowledge, Jews get a special place. Jewish people are the first recipients of the divine prophecy, the living heroes of these stories and histories that are discussed at church and (somewhat stereotypically) are an excellent example of 'the prosperity gospel' that sees economic success as a sign of spiritual progress (Maxwell,

32 *Method and reflection*

1998). Therefore, my Jewishness became central to my mobility, networking, reputation, and power. Sometimes it proved much more valuable than other elements of my identity such as being an academic, non-African, male, or financially privileged.

Being Jewish in Ghana was mostly a positive experience. I often had to step out of my religious 'comfort zone' and attend rituals and prayers that I never saw before, particularly of the Pentecostal/Charismatic movements known for their transnational rituals that include speaking in tongues, prophecy, and dramatic public displays of faith (Gifford, 1998; Meyer, 2004a). My own religious habits often clashed with the (non-Kosher) local cuisine or the lack of access to any Jewish synagogues during holidays or Shabbat. However, it still stood in sharp contrast to my secret gay identity, granting me a sense of authority and self-esteem.

This self-esteem and its social benefits in a conservative and often judgemental community helped me realise the importance of owning a beautiful home, an elegant car, a new phone, or having a good job when it comes to urban middle-class life. If someone has a virtue or an asset, physical or intellectual, that can contribute to his or her mobility they must exhibit and project it whenever possible. Alternatively, they must hide any element that might harm their reputation because the 'entire package' or 'integrated self' is rarely entirely achievable. Honour and self-esteem are connected to spiritual and financial achievements that the Pentecostal church attributes to the Jewish people, but a sexual orientation that does not stand in line with nuclear family values cannot be celebrated in those same circles.

To conclude, like my homosexuality, my Jewish identity had no direct link to my research topic or ethnographic interest. It was the moral codes of the community that made me extroverted about my Jewishness and introverted about my gayness; curiously, this is an exact reversal of my experience in European cities, where, as an Israeli, I am advised to hide any signifiers of Jewishness in public space, but as a gay man I feel legitimised and free. Therefore, this 'filter' became yet another significant force that shaped my interaction and insights within the physical and virtual field. Both 'filters' – Jewish and gay – are parallel in how they attribute difference and marginality to my presence in the field yet contradict in how difference is interpreted by this particular community.

'It is by being othered that the anthropologist comes to see,' state Halstead et al. (2008: 17); it offers the researcher direct access into the perspectives of those being studied while 'finding a space of distance within the study.' Experiencing a crisis during fieldwork, as Halstead et al. argue, may be crucial to the construction of knowledge. While classic anthropologists such as Malinowski kept their personal hardships in a journal separate from their ethnography, contemporary ethnographers should reflect on their crisis, framing and positioning to express that both they and the field are constantly changing in the 'ethnographic present.'

Method and reflection 33

In this study, the ethnographic present was a constant game of conceal and reveal that stretches much further than my personal position as a foreign ethnographer. It is about a broader perception of privacy and vulnerability. In fact, locals are probably more constrained by these rules than I was. In her ethnography of Ghanaian hospitals, for instance, Aberese-Ako's (2017) research participants divided her multiple identities as a research student and hospital worker into personalities they trust and distrust. Surprisingly, it was her insider's identity as a Ghanaian working in the hospital that spurred suspicion while her outsider identity as a research student granted her certain respect. Eventually, she was even accused of spying on her own people.[9]

This parallel and contrast between my multiple identities, full of negotiations, vulnerability, and power structures (Behar, 1997; Halstead, 2001), developed into a deep and embodied ethnographic experience of privacy and publicity. In that sense, it goes beyond self-observed reflection into the actual methodological and theoretical procedures of this project and must not remain invisible. My own position in the field was dramatically influenced by parts of my identity that I had no control over. They determined the way I was perceived by informants, how I viewed them, and how I eventually write about our shared experience (Clifford and Marcus, 1986).

References

Aberese-Ako, M. (2017) '"I Won't Take Part!"': Exploring the Multiple Identities of the Ethnographer in Two Ghanaian Hospitals', *Ethnography*, 18(3), pp. 300–321. doi: 10.1177/1466138116673380.

Altman, I. (1975) *The Environment and Social Behavior: Privacy, Personal Space, Territory, and Crowding.* Monterey, CA: Brooks/Cole Publishing.

Arnfred, S. (2005) '"African Sexuality"/Sexuality in Africa: Tales and Silences', in Arnfred, S. (ed.) *Re-Thinking Sexualities in Africa.* Second edition. Sweden: Nordic Africa Institute, pp. 59–76.

Azuah, U. (2016) *Blessed Body: The Secret Lives of Lesbian, Gay, Bisexual and Transgender Nigerians.* Jackson: CookingPot Books.

Barendregt, B. (2017) 'Deep Hanging Out in the Age of the Digital; Contemporary Ways of Doing Online and Offline Ethnography', *Asiascape: Digital Asia*, 4(3), pp. 307–315. doi: 10.1163/22142312-12340082.

Behar, R. (1997) *The Vulnerable Observer: Anthropology that Breaks Your Heart.* Boston, MA: Beacon Press.

Bleek, W. (1987) 'Lying Informants: A Fieldwork Experience from Ghana', *Population and Development Review*, 13(2), pp. 314–322. doi: 10.2307/1973196.

Boellstorff, T. (2005) *The Gay Archipelago: Sexuality and Nation in Indonesia.* Princeton, NJ: Princeton University Press.

Boellstorff, T. (2008) *Coming of Age in Second Life: An Anthropologist Explores the Virtually Human.* Princeton, NJ: Princeton University Press.

Bok, S. (1999) *Lying: Moral Choice in Public and Private Life.* New York: Vintage Books.

34 *Method and reflection*

Burrell, J. (2011) 'User Agency in the Middle Range: Rumors and the Reinvention of the Internet in Accra, Ghana', *Science, Technology & Human Values*, 36(2), pp. 139–159. doi: 10.1177/0162243910366148.

Burrell, J. (2012) *Invisible Users: Youth in the Internet Cafés of Urban Ghana*. Cambridge, MA: MIT Press.

Chalfin, B. (2004) 'Border Scans: Sovereignty, Surveillance and the Customs Service in Ghana', *Identities*, 11(3), pp. 397–416. doi: 10.1080/10702890490493554.

Chalfin, B. (2014) 'Public Things, Excremental Politics, and the Infrastructure of Bare Life in Ghana's City of Tema', *American Ethnologist*, 41(1), pp. 92–109. doi: 10.1111/amet.12062.

Clifford, J. and Marcus, G. E. (1986) *Writing Culture: The Poetics and Politics of Ethnography: a School of American Research Advanced Seminar*. Berkeley: University of California Press.

Coe, C. (2008) 'The Structuring of Feeling in Ghanaian Transnational Families', *City & Society*, 20(2), pp. 222–250. doi: 10.1111/j.1548–744X.2008.00018.x.

Cole, C. M., Manuh, T. and Miescher, S. (2007) *Africa After Gender?* Bloomington: Indiana University Press.

Dankwa, S. O. (2009) '"It's a Silent Trade": Female Same-Sex Intimacies in Post-Colonial Ghana', *NORA - Nordic Journal of Feminist and Gender Research*, 17(3), pp. 192–205. doi: 10.1080/08038740903117208.

Dunton, C. (1989) '"Wheyting Be Dat?" The Treatment of Homosexuality in African Literature', *Research in African Literatures*, 20(3), pp. 422–448.

Essien, K. and Aderinto, S. (2009) '"Cutting the Head of the Roaring Monster": Homosexuality and Repression in Africa', *African Study Monographs*, 30(3), pp. 121–135. doi: 10.14989/85284.

Fanon, F. (2008) *Black Skin, White Masks*. Revised edition. Translated by R. Philcox. New York : Berkeley, CA: Grove Press.

Geertz, C. (1998) 'Deep Hanging Out', *The New York Review of Books*, 22 October.

Gifford, P. (1998) *African Christianity: Its Public Role*. London: C. Hurst & Co. Publishers.

Gill, L. (1990) '"Like a Veil to Cover Them": Women and the Pentecostal movement in La Paz', *American Ethnologist*, 17(4), pp. 708–721. doi: 10.1525/ae.1990.17.4.02a00060.

Goffman, E. (1986) *Stigma: Notes on the Management of Spoiled Identity*. Reissue edition. New York: Touchstone.

Goldstein-Gidoni, O. (2000) 'The Production of Tradition and Culture in the Japanese Wedding Enterprise', *Ethnos*, 65(1), pp. 33–55. doi: 10.1080/001418400360634.

Gordon, T. and Hancock, M. (2005) '"The Crusade Is the Vision": Branding Charisma in a Global Pentecostal Ministry', *Material Religion*, 1(3), pp. 386–404. doi: 10.2752/174322005778054023.

Halstead, N. (2001) 'Ethnographic Encounters. Positionings Within and Outside the Insider Frame', *Social Anthropology*, 9(3), pp. 307–321. doi: 10.1017/S0964028201000234.

Halstead, N., Hirsch, E. and Okely, J. (2008) *Knowing How to Know: Fieldwork and the Ethnographic Present*. Oxford: Berghahn Books.

Hjorth, L., Pink, S. and Horst, H. A. (2018) 'Privacy at the Margins: Being at Home with Privacy: Privacy and Mundane Intimacy Through Same-Sex Locative Media Practices', *International Journal of Communication*, 12(0), p. 19.

Method and reflection 35

Howard, A. and Mawyer, A. (2015) 'Ethnography in the Digital Age', in *Emerging Trends in the Social and Behavioral Sciences*. American Cancer Society, pp. 1–15. doi: 10.1002/9781118900772.etrds0119.

Jackson, I. and Oppong, R. A. (2014) 'The Planning of Late Colonial Village Housing in the Tropics: Tema Manhean, Ghana', *Planning Perspectives*, 29(4), pp. 475–499. doi: 10.1080/02665433.2013.829753.

Jackson, M. (1998) *Minima Ethnographica: Intersubjectivity and the Anthropological Project*. Chicago, IL: University of Chicago Press.

Kulick, D. and Willson, M. (1995) *Taboo: Sex, Identity, and Erotic Subjectivity in Anthropological Fieldwork*. London: Psychology Press.

Lewin, E. and Leap, W. (1996) *Out in the Field: Reflections of Lesbian and Gay Anthropologists*. Champaign: University of Illinois Press.

Maxwell, D. (1998) '"Delivered from the Spirit of Poverty?": Pentecostalism, Prosperity and Modernity in Zimbabwe', *Journal of Religion in Africa*, 28(3), pp. 350–373. doi: 10.2307/1581574.

Mazzucato, V., Kabki, M. and Smith, L. (2006) 'Transnational Migration and the Economy of Funerals: Changing Practices in Ghana', *Development and Change*, 37(5), pp. 1047–1072. doi: 10.1111/j.1467-7660.2006.00512.x.

McDonnell, T. E. (2010) 'Cultural Objects as Objects: Materiality, Urban Space, and the Interpretation of AIDS Campaigns in Accra, Ghana', *American Journal of Sociology*, 115(6), pp. 1800–1852. doi: 10.1086/651577.

Meyer, B. (2004a) 'Christianity in Africa: From African Independent to Pentecostal-Charismatic Churches', *Annual Review of Anthropology*, 33(1), pp. 447–474. doi: 10.1146/annurev.anthro.33.070203.143835.

Meyer, B. (2010) '"There Is a Spirit in that Image": Mass-Produced Jesus Pictures and Protestant-Pentecostal Animation in Ghana', *Comparative Studies in Society and History*, 52(1), pp. 100–130. doi: 10.1017/S001041750999034X.

Miall, C. E. (1989) 'Authenticity and the Disclosure of the Information Preserve: The Case of Adoptive Parenthood', *Qualitative Sociology*, 12(3), pp. 279–302. doi: 10.1007/BF00989287.

Miescher, S. (2005) *Making Men in Ghana*. Bloomington: Indiana University Press.

Mwachiro, K. (2014) *Invisible: Stories from Kenya's Queer Community*. Nairobi: Goethe-Institute Kenya and Native Intelligence.

Nippert-Eng, C. (2010) *Islands of Privacy*. Chicago, IL: University of Chicago Press.

Norman, I. D. et al. (2016) 'Homosexuality in Ghana', *Advances in Applied Sociology*, 06(01), pp. 12–27. doi: 10.4236/aasoci.2016.61002.

Oyewùmí, O. (2003) *African Women and Feminism Reflecting on the Politics of Sisterhood*. Trenton: Africa World Press.

Oyewumi, O. (2005) *African Gender Studies: A Reader*. London: Palgrave Macmillan US.

Petronio, S. (2002) *Boundaries of Privacy: Dialectics of Disclosure*. Albany: State University of New York Press.

Pink, S. et al. (2015) *Digital Ethnography: Principles and Practice*. London: SAGE Publications.

Shokeid, M. (2014) *Gay Voluntary Associations in New York: Public Sharing and Private Lives*. Philadelphia: University of Pennsylvania Press.

Simmel, G. (1906) 'The Sociology of Secrecy and of Secret Societies', *American Journal of Sociology*, 11(4), pp. 441–498.

36 *Method and reflection*

Solace Brothers Foundation et al. (2016) *Human Rights Violations Against Lesbian, Gay, Bisexual, and Transgender (LGBT) People in Ghana: A Shadow Report.* Geneva: 117th Session of the Human Rights Committee. Available at: https://tbinternet.ohchr.org/Treaties/CCPR/Shared%20Documents/GHA/INT_CCPR_CSS_GHA_24149_E.pdf (Accessed: 16 January 2019).

Srinivasan, J. et al. (2018) 'Privacy at the Margins| The Poverty of Privacy: Understanding Privacy Trade-Offs From Identity Infrastructure Users in India', *International Journal of Communication*, 12(0), p. 20.

Subedi, B. (2006) 'Theorizing a "halfie" Researcher's Identity in Transnational Fieldwork', *International Journal of Qualitative Studies in Education*, 19(5), pp. 573–593. doi: 10.1080/09518390600886353.

Thoreson, R. R. (2011) *Blackmail and Extortion of LGBT People in Sub-Saharan Africa.* ISBN: 978-1-884955-27-3. New York: International Gay and Lesbian Human Rights Commission, pp. 1–140. Available at: https://www.outrightinternational.org/sites/default/files/484-1.pdf.

van der Geest, S. (1998) 'Yebisa Wo Fie: Growing Old and Building a House in the Akan Culture of Ghana', *Journal of Cross-Cultural Gerontology*, 13(4), pp. 333–359.

van der Geest, S. (2000) 'Funerals for the Living: Conversations with Elderly People in Kwahu, Ghana', *African Studies Review*, 43(3), pp. 103–129.

van der Geest, S., Dapaah J., Kwansa B., and Spronk, R. (2012). 'The Dark Sides of Privacy: Stigma, Shame and HIV/AIDS in Ghana'. University of Amsterdam, Amsterdam Privacy Conference 2012 (APC 2012), Available at: SSRN: https://ssrn.com/abstract=2457968

Wagon, J. (1992) 'Making the Theoretical Case', in Ragin, C. C. and Becker, H. S. (eds) *What Is a Case?: Exploring the Foundations of Social Inquiry.* Cambridge: Cambridge University Press, pp. 121–137.

Weinreb, A. A. (2006) 'The Limitations of Stranger-Interviewers in Rural Kenya', *American Sociological Review*, 71(6), pp. 1014–1039. doi: 10.1177/000312240607100607.

Williams, W. L. (1993) 'Being Gay and Doing Research on Homosexuality in Non-Western Cultures', *Journal of Sex Research*, 30(2), pp. 115–120.

Williams, W. L. (1996) 'Being Gay and Doing Fieldwork', in Lewin, E. and Leap, W. (eds) *Out in the Field: Reflections of Lesbian and Gay Anthropologists.* Champaign: University of Illinois Press, pp. 70–85.

Witte, M. D. (2001) *Long Live the Dead!: Changing Funeral Celebrations in Asante, Ghana.* Amsterdam: Het Spinhuis.

Wong, M. (2006) 'The Gendered Politics of Remittances in Ghanaian Transnational Families', *Economic Geography*, 82(4), pp. 355–381. doi: 10.1111/j.1944–8287.2006.tb00321.x.

Notes

1 The Greater Accra Region includes Accra Metropolitan, Tema Metropolitan, Adenta Municipal, Ashaiman Municipal, Ledzokuku-Krowor Municipal, Ga East Municipal, Ga West Municipal, and Ga South Municipal districts.

2 Instagram is a photo and video sharing social media mobile phone application launched in 2010. The emphasis in this social media platform is on visual materials, encouraging users to create their own gallery, add professional

looking filters to their pictures, and tag their content using hashtags (#). As of September 2018, there were 1,393,700 Instagram users in Ghana, 4.6% of its entire population (NapoleonCat.com).

3 The words private and privacy appear 15 times in the "Ethical Guidelines for Good Research Practice" of the Association of Social Anthropologists of the UK and the Commonwealth (ASA). The sensitivity around issues of intrusion to private space, confidentiality, and anonymity, discreteness of field notes, and violations of privacy is a recurrent topic in this document.

4 Studies on health, illness, and particularly HIV/aids in Ghana have dealt with practices of hiding, lying, and maintaining privacy (van der Geest and Mensah Dapaah, 2012; Bleek, 1987; McDonnell, 2010). Interviews with HIV patients raised troubling stories on seeking medical care in distant hospitals, where no one can identify the patient, or worse, refusing treatment altogether to avoid shaming.

5 These findings differ from Srinivasan et al.'s (2018) study about the biometric survey in India, where people suspended their privacy concerns for the sake of state benefits.

6 As described in 5, opening multiple profiles or using fake names to conceal one's social media activity from unwanted eyes is a common local practice.

7 'Coming out' as a researcher may also appear as an ethical virtue. In his influential ethnography of the game Second Life, Tom Boellstorff states that although he interacted with informants as a virtual avatar in a digital universe (where people often change gender and identities), he kept his identity as a White openly gay male disclosed at all times. This face is disclosed under the ethical section of his methodological chapter (Boellstorff, 2008: 79).

8 This lie was also a suggestion by informants, presented as a perfectly standard procedure. However, it was not always useful because I was often told I am allowed to have a fiancée 'there' and a girlfriend 'here.'

9 While studying internet cafés in Accra, Jenna Burrell also faced suspicions and accusations of being a CIA spy by her informants. Burrell discloses that she was generating so much suspicion that one owner asked her to stop visiting his café. By not following the politics of indirection she was positioned as 'a hostile and duplicitous outsider from the perspective of the group' (Burrell 2011: 149).

3 Setting the field

People, place, language, and technology

March 6, 1957. After a long struggle against British colonialism, the British Gold Coast finally became the Republic of Ghana – the first independent nation-state in Sub-Saharan Africa. Dr. Kwame Nkrumah, the founding father of this young democracy and its very first president, had high hopes to fully develop Ghana economically and socially within seven years (Nkrumah, 1968). A significant part of this vision included the nationalisation, secularisation, and commercialisation of indigenous religions and traditional culture (mostly of the Akan people). This 're-articulation of roots' (Feld, 2012) occurred mainly through public broadcast media and education schemes, aiming to establish a collective heritage that unites Ghana's different ethnic groups and forms a modernised national identity (Heath, 1997; De Witte and Meyer, 2012).

Nkrumah's notion of retrieving knowledge and culture from the past in order to envision the future is best described through the *Sankofa* symbol (from the Akan phrase 'go back and take'). Portraying a bird looking backwards, while its feet are facing forward, this indigenous Adinkra[1] icon reflects the ideology of the time, shared by both government officials and mainline churches. Its visual language states that 'not a complete return to the past is aimed at, but a selective picking from long-standing traditions and past experience and wisdom' (De Witte and Meyer, 2012: 46). However, due to his socialist economic policies, anti-imperialist ideologies, and pan-Africanist political agendas, Nkrumah soon faced many rivals and opponents (Sherwood, 1993). In 1964, he turned his Convention People's Party (CPP) into a single-party state, posing a severe threat to Ghana's democratic vision.

On February 24, 1966, a group of military rebels from the National Liberation Council (NLC), supported by the CIA, overthrew and banished Kwame Nkrumah, who was in China at the time. This coup led Ghana to almost three decades of poverty, political instability, ethnic tensions, violence, inflation, mismanagement, and corruption (Hansen and Collins, 1980). It also included the expulsion of a million Ghanaians from Nigeria and a drop of 80% in Ghana's economy (Gifford, 1998: 59). After two oppressive military regimes of Generals Acheampong and Akuffo (1972–1979) and two military coups by Jerry Rawlings (1979 and 1981), Ghana finally established

DOI: 10.4324/9781003187424-3

People, place, language, and technology 39

its Fourth Republic in 1993, and restored its multiple-party democratic system (Williams, 2015).

During his 12-year presidency, and using substantial loans from the World Bank, it was Jerry Rawlings who led a dramatic Structural Adjustment Program (SAP) in Ghana, 'beginning its transition from a state-managed economy to a free-market system' (Williams, 2015: 368). This included the privatisation of former state-owned enterprises such as manufacturing, agriculture, and telecommunication (Bennell, 1997; Tsamenyi, Onumah and Tetteh-Kumah, 2010; Adams, 2011), neoliberal reforms in education, health care, water, and electricity (Williams, 2015: 368), rapid shift from production to consumption, and eventually the mass purchase of mobile phones and other communication technologies (Slater and Kwami, 2005; Bruijn et al., 2009; Burrell, 2012). During these years of newly found optimism, and as a backlash to Rawling's attempts to revive traditional African religions, more and more Ghanaians found the Pentecostal/Charismatic stream of Christianity (Daswani, 2013).

3.1 Tema new town: the promise of a city

As a new city founded by Kwame Nkrumah in 1961, Tema, the main site of my research, contains mostly first- and second-generation urbanites, descending from rural migrants and aspiring professionals. These 'new' urbanites, who arrived in Tema after the construction of its grand harbour and industrial sites, live under rapid technological, economic, social, and theological changes. The fall of colonialism and the rise of young African nation-states, such as Ghana, rapidly increased urbanisation and rural-urban migration (Meagher, 1995; Pieterse, 2009). Tema, an 'ordinary' city in West Africa, is a highly suitable site for the exploration of these transformations.

The urban planning of Tema relates to the export of British New Towns to all Commonwealth ex-colonies (Home, 2013). Top British architects and urban advisers such as Jane Drew, Maxwell Fry, and Alfred Alcock planned Tema throughout the 1950s and 1960s, as Ghana approached independence. 'The Volta River Hydroelectric and Resettlement Project' was part of Kwame Nkrumah's most promising development scheme, serving as a 'symbol of progress' for the entire nation (Jackson and Oppong, 2014). Set on the ruins of a small Ga fishing village whose inhabitants were painfully resettled nearby in Tema Manhean, Tema was to become a home for modern industrial cosmopolitan citizens, liberated from both the heavy baggage of British colonialism and the social structures of village life and ethnic divisions (Chalfin, 2014).

The constructers of Tema's industrial harbour project invited mostly upwardly mobile nuclear families from across the country to take part in a promising urban national vision; they offered a detailed housing scheme using a company-based rotation method whereby employees lived in small houses or larger two-storey houses according to their marital status, age, and position. Upon retirement, workers were expected to return to their villages or home-towns so the housing rotation could proceed. The houses were laid out on a

40 *People, place, language, and technology*

neat grid, providing an idyllic urban appearance with small streets, all divided into self-contained neighbourhoods, also known as Communities (d'Auria and De Meulder, 2010). Each Community had 'a fairly large market, a community centre, a health centre, a middle or secondary school, post office, police station, and branch library' (Alcock quoted in Jackson and Oppong, 2014: 479).

Tema's expatriate urban advisers drew sharp lines between village and city/traditional and modern forms of living in their architectural approach. Although people were expected to return to their village when retiring, their time as urbanites was destined to re-socialise them. The distinction between Tema Township as a symbol of development and Tema Manhean (the resettled fishermen village) as a 'preserved' rural community was meant to define the different demographics in terms of living arrangements, occupation, and identity (Jackson and Oppong, 2014). This dichotomy was partly expressed through the difference between modern housing units for the former and traditional compounds with shared toilet and cooking facilities for the latter (Chalfin, 2014).

However, certain traces of indigenous housing were retained in the new township as well, due to the durability and availability of local materials and their suitability in the tropical climate. According to d'Auria and De Meulder (2010: 119) this agenda also assumed that indigenous lifestyles can be copied and pasted into modern industrial life as an 'urban experiment' of development and 'changelessness.' For instance, the architects placed great importance on open and recreational spaces, backyards, and verandas. In his discussion on urban planning in the Gold Coast, for instance, Alcock, explains:

> One of the reasons why units of this size (3000 people) may be successful in recreating feelings of belonging is the West African custom, when people seek each other's company in the evening, of walking up and down the principal streets near their homes meeting, greeting and gossiping... The footpath and street system is therefore planned to focus on the few shops, the small trading area and the open-air meeting place, so that this natural social activity will be concentrated and will bring people into contact with each other and thereby, it is hoped, will recreate the social atmosphere of the village evenings.
>
> (quoted by d'Auria and Kootin Sanwu, 2010)

While trying to retain certain elements of familiarity and community in an otherwise alienated city life, Tema's middle-class houses were still designed as modern entities – places of leisure and nuclear family life, separated from the industrial workplace and the indigenous compound dwellings.[2] As stated in one of Tema's architectural plans: 'housing accommodation shall be non-traditional. The tribal compound has no place in Tema and is replaced by the private family dwelling' (quoted in Jackson and Oppong, 2014: 487). This paradoxical urban landscape means that Tema's residents and architecture were always engaged in tensions and hybridity, representing a new start alongside preserved customs in the spirit of Ghana's post-independence.

People, place, language, and technology 41

In its early years, state control in Tema was relatively firm and house design, maintenance, and renovations were uniform and regulated. However, after the 1966 military coup and the banishing of Kwame Nkrumah, life in the city was never the same. Debts, inflation, and mismanagement led to wide unemployment, population growth, and urban neglect in the entire Greater Accra Region (Pellow, 2008: 37). In those unstable years most of the factories around Tema closed down and sold their company-houses, many residents left the city, and new urbanites immigrated from neighbouring areas, dramatically changing the urban landscape once planned by expatriate architects.[3]

As Marshall-Fratani explains through the case of urban Nigeria,

> the anxiety created by the continued influx of dangerous strangers to urban centres as a result of increased rural urban migration… have introduced a kind of urban paranoia about 'evil doers' who are out to cheat, deceive, rob and kill.
>
> (1998: 284)

This 'urban paranoia,' of course, sets a fertile ground for Pentecostal messages on protection, healing, and the cutting of links with neighbours, friends, and family (especially those who remained in the village). Moreover, they dramatically influence the level of isolation, suspicion, and privacy-seeking needs among urbanites (Figures 3.1 and 3.2).

Figure 3.1 View of a pedestrian road, architectural plans of Tema, 1961, TDC (Tema Development Office).

42 People, place, language, and technology

Figure 3.2 The streets of Tema. Photo by the author.

3.2 Villages, cities: ruptures and continuities

The architectural and political history of Tema has an immense impact on how privacy is materially and socially constructed and how physical and symbolic boundaries are drawn. The tensions of urban life and modernity are often expressed as a semiotic opposition to the village. While often referring to villages as 'backwards' or 'dangerous,' most urbanites still keep financial and social ties with family members in the villages, which means urban practices are never fully detached from rural ones (Weiss, 2004; Ferguson, 2006; Bruijn, Nyamnjoh and Brinkman, 2009). Often using a nostalgic tone, residents of Tema also contrast their unstable and uncertain city life with the safety and familiarity of the village.

According to Asomani-Boateng (2011), the reliance on Western urban development models caused all sorts of problems in African cities such as unemployment, overcrowding, and inadequate infrastructure, which call to 'revisit Africa's urban past and examine her indigenous urban forms' (242). While the writer calls for more official policy, this process of revisiting, continuing, and reviving rural and pre-colonial memories happens informally (see Section 5.3). Moreover, these practices help urbanites gain a sense of control in a rapidly changing modern city. As van Binsbergen (2004: 138) explains concerning the introduction of ICT (information and communication technologies) to Africa:

> In modern Africa, one has always needed to compensate the insecurities of the modern, urban, state-based aspects of social life by maintaining (as far as possible) old systems of kin-based and

People, place, language, and technology 43

ethnic solidarity — orientated toward the village with its centuries-old practices and systems of representation encompassing many domains of life, and with its concomitant, endlessly proliferating and branching networks of social relations.

Some urbanites drew links between cultural trades and conventions that people 'brought' from the village to privacy-related urban etiquettes. For instance, in many villages, if a stranger is asking for the address of a particular person, people pretend not to know him or his whereabouts, to avoid exposing their neighbours to unwanted or harmful visitors. In contemporary urban houses, accordingly, door signs with surnames are hardly used, and residential addresses are kept informal, so strangers cannot identify the tenants.[4]

Village-oriented urban practices, such as domesticating streets, keeping addresses discrete, scarcity of night lights, outdoor cooking, and indoor privacy, imply that the discreteness of Ghanaians dates back to compound living. In these structures, each *Abusua* protected itself from intruders and enemies, while living a sustainable collective life. While these practices naturally express continuity and hybridity between cities and villages, middle-class urbanites (especially Pentecostals) simultaneously operate to sever financial, spiritual, and collective ties with the village. This dialectic process of rupture and continuation is a crucial feature of urban life (Robbins, 2003; Daswani, 2013).

Severing ties with the village goes beyond the dichotomy enforced by European urban architects in the 1960s to the theological climate of the city. The Pentecostal concept of rupture, for instance, take a firm stand against rural and traditional life. According to Wendl (2007: 5), Pentecostal discourse marks the village as a horrific past that may come back and 'haunt' urbanites. The 'horror of tradition sub-genre,' he explains, is 'rather negative about tradition, cultural heritage and village life' (Wendl, 2007: 4). Many Ghanaian and Nigerian films are in fact horror stories about urbanites visiting relatives in the village and being trapped in horrific pagan worship or human sacrifice.

By isolating the nuclear family from its extended ties (*Abusua*), detaching relations with rural life, and demonising pagan religions, the Pentecostal church plays a significant part in the transformation of the urban landscape and its domestic culture. This role helps the church cater to the upwardly mobile urban middle class that yearns for such liberation. However, detaching one's self from a rural past to an urban present is not an easy task; it requires clever manipulation between front and back, public and private, local and international spaces.

With the aim of completing their 'break with the past,' urbanites rely on Pentecostal practices of de-localisation and transcendence, embracing an international cosmopolitan Christian identity (Corten and Marshall-Fratani, 2001; Daswani, 2010).[5] In a similar manner, when urbanites meet new people, they are reluctant to enclose personal information

44 *People, place, language, and technology*

that reveals their local, ancestral, or ethnic identity. Many urbanites keep their ethnic and geographical origin private by interchanging between their Christian (international) name, Ghanaian (local) name, and sometimes an entirely fictional name (mostly online). Informants have told me that using fake names on Facebook, for instance, is often a way of preventing rural relatives and strangers from adding them, asking for remittances and mobile money transfers or 'snooping around' about their triumphs and failures.

Enclosing someone's full birth name may provide strangers with too much information and raise the danger of witchcraft. It can tell an observer which ethnic group a person comes from, what language he/she speaks, if he/she is a first-born or second-born, and on what day was he/she born (Odotei, 1989; Agyekum, 2006). Christian names, alternatively, are considered de-localised, generic, and therefore safe.[6] For example, if someone's Christian name is John and 'local' Ghanaian name is Kofi, it is more dangerous if an alleged witch (often a relative living in the village) knows the latter over the former. This is an interesting masking of private and public spheres; apart from revealing deep ongoing connections between urbanites and their home villages, it shows the contextual and semiotic constructions of identity as privatised and discrete – key characteristics of Ghana's emerging middle class.

3.3 Africa's rising middle class

I have described the people in this ethnography as 'middle-class urban Ghanaians.' However, I argue that this demographic is characterised by the mere inability to define it too rigidly: floating between new financial opportunities and old insecurities, cosmopolitan aspirations and local traditions, publicity and secrecy. Although the term 'middle class' is increasingly heard in Africanist, economical, and sociological literature, it is often incompatible with the rich, diverse, and dynamic character of the continent. This incompatibility may reside in two main reasons: first, 'middle class' is a term with history, origin, and development strongly tied to the West and the industrial revolution (Liechty, 2003; Besnier, 2009). Second, the term often fails to address issues like informal income, collective assets, and culturally constructed expressions of wealth.

There is no agreement among scholars regarding the correct definition of middle class in the 'developing world' (Lopes, 2016; Norman et al., 2016). Many scholars include in their definition anyone above the poverty line, which is about $2 per day per person (Banerjee and Duflo 2008; Ncube et al., 2011). This definition relies on a conceptual differentiation between the 'Western world's middle class' and the 'developing world's middle class'; the latter is seen as 'unique' and inherently more vulnerable (Ravalion, 2009)[7]. Others suggest a higher threshold in their statistical definition, about $10 per day per person (Banerjee and Duflo, 2008; Birdsall, 2010; Kharas, 2010), or use completely different parameters such as education, occupation, house ownership, and consumption.

People, place, language, and technology 45

The discourse about Africa's middle class follows this line of inconsistency. Many banks, NGOs, and research firms publish reports about the middle class in Africa, often addressing their potential as a consuming market group. While some of these reports claim Africa's middle class reaches over 34% of the population (Ncube, Lufumpa and Vencatachellum, 2011), others use a more cautious definition and state that only 6% of Africans can qualify as middle class (Kochhar, 2015).[8] Other reports pay less attention to income per capita and focus on spending habits, describing Africa's middle class as predominantly young, educated, technologically oriented, and consumerist (e.g., *The Rising Middle Class of Africa*, 2013). What are the reasons for such inconsistencies?

Generally, statistical attempts to define Africa's middle class are inconsistent because they measure the entire continent, or even the entire 'developing world,' as one analytical unit. As a result, they pay less attention to the particularities of each state and region. This tendency is a major downside to such reports, mainly due to the great diversity within Africa. Measuring and defining a middle class in the growing urban centres of Nairobi, Accra, or Addis Ababa has very little to do with war-torn areas such as Sudan or the Central African Republic. Also, while these reports rely on published research in finance, social policy, or statistics, they pay less attention to the contribution of ethnography, which has a unique way of including self-definitions and perceptions.

As a holistic, qualitative methodology, ethnography offers a rich, intimate, and nuanced description of daily middle-class lives and experiences. Ethnographers of the middle class explored diverse topics such as consumption and lifestyle (Miller, 1998; Liechty, 2003; Clarke, 2007; van Leeuwen, 2011), gender and social mobility (Freeman, 2000; de Koning, 2009; Earl, 2014; Spronk, 2014), immigration and the expatriate's life abroad (e.g., Walsh, 2005; Lauring and Selmer, 2010; Trundle, 2014), and the local perspective of neighbourhoods, gentrification, and suburbs (Mesch and Levanon, 2003; Brown-Saracino, 2010; Pattillo, 2013; Bott and Spillius, 2014).

The exploration of non-European, or more accurately non-White middle-class demographics, is particularly useful when viewed through an ethnographic lens, as it addresses the idea that the 'middle-class' (very much like 'the internet') cannot be defined universally. Moreover, certain minorities and ethnicities have radically different experiences of economic mobility and cultural habitus (Lacy, 2007; Vallejo, 2012; Pattillo, 2013). The middle class in Africa, for instance, is almost always synonymous with urban life while its American counterpart is usually associated with suburbia. These differences require a detailed investigation into the daily lives of different middle-class households in different cultural and geographical contexts. Notwithstanding all said above, it is still crucial to explore the main characteristics of the middle class in a Ghanaian context:

First, until Ghana's return to democracy in 1992 and the economic reformations it entailed, the middle class was virtually non-existent. The tight

46 *People, place, language, and technology*

control of changing military regimes and the severe economic challenges at the time downgraded the elites of colonial civil service and prevented the mobility of new urban groups. In fact, Jerry Rawlings targeted middle-class households as prime enemies of his populist socialist vision, expressing 'nothing but contempt for the bankers, academics, doctors, lawyers, journalists, wealthy farmers and large entrepreneurs' (Gifford, 1998: 70). The women of Makola Market, for instance, were beaten, arrested, and harassed regularly by Rawlings' soldiers due to their visible role as traders of 'the chief wholesale and retail market in Accra' (Robertson, 1983: 470).

As a result of this fraught history, many informants in this study talked about the challenge in defining a local middle class quantitatively, as if the mere term was still under negotiation. Still, I chose to differentiate them from their wider surroundings, as people who do not live in poverty but are also not regarded as financially secured elites. These 'inbetweeners' tend to generate multiple incomes by operating in both the formal economic sector and the informal cash-based sector (Hart, 1973; Ninsin, 1991; Yaw, 2007; Obeng-Odoom, 2011; Osei-Boateng and Ampratwum, 2011). Importing cars, selling second-hand goods via social media, investing in small businesses, cooking for events, and weaving hair extensions are just some of the secondary incomes middle-class informants managed.[9]

In our conversations about earnings, people often distinguished between 'salary' and 'income': 'salary' is the official pay check one earns every month while 'income' is a more informal and holistic category. For instance, many civil service employees sell local and imported products in their spare time, explaining that their official salary is simply not enough to get by. Corruption is another common practice of informal income. Although it is considered illegitimate and immoral, it is still widely practised in governmental office and state authorities such as the police or post office (Norman et al., 2016). While the literature about the informal economy is mostly associated with poverty, slum dwelling, and precariousness (Hart, 1973; Obeng-Odoom, 2011), it is of high relevance to all social classes in Africa.[10] Furthermore, According to this 'public secret' of informality, most surveys on Ghana's middle class are inaccurate because they cannot take into account unreported earnings.

Another feature of Ghana's middle class is the importance of discreteness in many aspects of their social and financial life. Ghanaians tend to 'hide' their income and often differentiate themselves from Nigerians, who are stereotypically notorious for flashing and exhibiting their wealth. While some middle-class members may express their wealth outwards even if they struggle to pay their bills, others may prosper financially but 'downplay' it to avoid jealousy, gossip, or exposure to robbers. The need to hide one's earnings is especially strong when family and the economy come together, due to the fear of jealousy and the high demands for stipends by close and distant relatives. This problem is often highlighted in Pentecostal churches, where spiritual assistance is given to 'liberate' the conjugal unit from the economic and spiritual pressures of extended family (van Dijk, 2003b; Sabar, 2010).

People, place, language, and technology 47

Overall, different political, social, and spiritual forces may condemn or praise someone's wealth and property. Even gifts in the form of money or objects may require spiritual 'cleansing' by a pastor to avoid the transfer of evil energy to the recipient (van Dijk, 2003b). The connection between wealth and spirituality, and between success and jealousy, alongside the unique financial challenges that Ghana poses, means middle-class households must strategically hide and show elements of their lives as they continue mobilising upwards. As this book shows, this strategic balancing between visibility and invisibility occurs in various urban spaces: nightly gathering spots, private houses, and social media platforms.

3.4 Mobile phones: Ghana's main digital technology

One of the main ways that lower- and middle-class Africans 'leapfrog' inadequate, poorly maintained, or non-existent urban infrastructures, as well as mobilise themselves financially and socially, is through mobile phone consumption (Slater and Kwami, 2005; Bruijn, Nyamnjoh and Brinkman, 2009; Aker and Mbiti, 2010; Powell, 2012; Mothobi and Grzybowski, 2017; Okae, 2018). In fact, the vast majority of digital practices described in this study occur via mobile phones, marking it a key material object for identity formation, social ties, mobility, and culture (Horst and Miller, 2006; Sey, 2011; Horst and Taylor, 2014).

Between the years 2000 and 2017 mobile phone subscriptions in Ghana dramatically rose from 0.13 to 36.75 million (Statista, 2017). Browsing the internet via mobile phones is significantly more common than fixed-wired broadband with over 80% subscribers in the former and only 0.3% subscribers in the latter (International Telecommunication Union, 2018). Generally, over 8 million Ghanaians use the internet, whether through laptops, tablets, or mobile phones.[11] In the last five years or so, more and more Ghanaians upgraded their handsets to smartphones, which offer an improved all-in-one experience, including touchscreen functionality, 3G and 4G internet, social media access, and high-quality cameras.[12] As a result, many Ghanaian urbanites own several mobile phone handsets and SIM cards, which they switch and alternate, in order to navigate between different charges, tariffs, reception zones, and other perks.

For instance, a banker living in Tema may use his Vodafone SIM card to call his office, communicate with his pastor via WhatsApp,[13] and switch to his Tigo SIM card when calling his mother, who uses the same network. Usually the older and less-frequently used mobile phone is jokingly called 'yam phone,' referring to its bulky and unstylish shape. People use their 'yam phones' when their newer one runs out of calling credit, has an empty battery (often during power cuts), or simply breaks down.[14]

Most Ghanaians use pre-paid top-up cards for both their calling credit and internet data, which means their mobile phone use is always quantified and limited to their budget and credit.[15] As a result, Ghanaians tend

48 *People, place, language, and technology*

to avoid streaming heavy multimedia (for instance, through YouTube) and prefer sending each other texts, images, and videos via WhatsApp. Buying each other top-up cards is a highly common expression of love and care and might happen as a romantic courtesy or an expression of respect to a parent or older family member.

In addition, Ghanaians use mobile banking and micro-financing services on a daily basis, turning their mobile phones into personal bank accounts, portable cash-points, and remote money-transfer services. Mobile banking and E-wallets influence middle-class lifestyles in terms of the management of small businesses, family obligations, and rural-urban economic relations. Furthermore, they offer access to banking services, in a region where most people lack bank accounts.[16] Such versatile, multi-purpose, and widespread use of mobile phones has profound influences in terms of wider access to financial, educational, agricultural, and health services (Mothobi and Grzybowski, 2017: 7). Furthermore, mobile phones play a crucial role in familial surveillance methods and practices of privacy.

3.5 Language and indirection

One day, I was at a restaurant typing up field notes on my laptop and the waitress, who knew me well by then, wanted to read what I was writing. When I said I'd prefer it if she didn't take a look (because she knew all the individuals mentioned in my fieldnotes), she replied: 'You are bad!' I was taken aback by her negative and unusual reaction, but I also knew it wasn't because I had refused to let her read through my notebook – it was because I'd been too direct about it, which embarrassed her. It would've been better to think of a lie, even if it wasn't a very good or convincing one. It would have shown respect. My closest informants and hosts often instructed me not to be too direct with locals but to use 'softer' expressions of what I wished to say; 'turn it into a lullaby,' someone suggested. For instance, if someone tried to sell me a product that I didn't want to buy I should never reply with: 'I don't want it.' A better response would be: 'Maybe I'll come back tomorrow.'

This tension between the truth and the lie, disclosing and withholding was a central theme in my conversations with informants. As described in Chapter 2, 'aesthetics of indirection' are a vital feature in Ghanaian personhood and communication. Scholarly work based in Ghana often deals with lying, spreading rumours, and indirect speech. Obeng (2003) links this phenomenon to the cultural importance of proverbs and the local grammar of indirection. As he writes in his book about indirect Akan communication:

> Implicitness, indirectness, vagueness, prolixity, ambiguity and even avoidance are even more cherished and preferred, especially when the subject matter of what is being communicated is difficult or face threatening.

People, place, language, and technology 49

This use of lingual strategies of indirection or 'the cultural authority of proverbial indirect speech' (Shipley, 2009: 600) has proven useful in political commentaries of Ghanaian rappers and the anonymous expression of political critique through graffiti and street art (Obeng, 2009). Politicians in Ghana are known for using 'evasion, circumlocution, innuendoes, and metaphors' to avoid dangerous or impolite public statements (Obeng, 1997). Indirect speech can also occur during domestic conflicts such as arguments between co-wives in a polygamous relationship (Obeng, 2003: 153) or to conceal same-sex relations between two married women in the presence of their families (Dankwa, 2009).

Overall, proverbs are used as a 'third party' in a conversation, representing a neutral moral authority (Yankah, 1989). In his article about nightlife in urban Mali, Chappatte (2014: 534) explains that people often depart from social gatherings by stating 'I go and I come,' 'I go on an errand,' or 'I go to sleep' when they actually just went away and 'unobtrusively tended to their own business.' Chappatte argues that these are 'empty idioms' and not malicious lies, borrowing the term 'modes of deception' from Barnes (1994) to stress that a language can be a tool for discretion. Ghanaians often use phrases such as *Merekoo aba* ('I am going and then coming back' in Twi) to end any interaction politely.

Obeng (1994) links this indirect character of Akan linguistics to Goffman's concept of 'face-work.' He argues that public image and social visibility are so central in Ghanaian society that people operate within linguistic patterns that prevent them from 'losing face' or shaming others. Accordingly, language is one of many ways to remain indirect and keep certain information confidential (Sarfo, 2011; Nyamekye Adjei and Bosiwah, 2015). Indirect speech, therefore, is a lingual manifestation of privacy and its social virtues: it protects one's reputation, relieves collective tensions, and prevents confrontation or shame. Indirect speech camouflages and conceals speakers true intentions in terms of their opinions, goals and attitudes (Mashiri, 2002).

In an increasingly digital age, indirection allows spreading rumours and stories that mediate the gap between 'direct experience' and desired outcomes. According to Burrell (2011: 156), producing rumours about successful internet scams among disadvantaged youth in Accra challenges the assumption that 'direct experience will offer the primary, inarguable evidence of a technology's utility.' A similar process occurs in Pentecostal philosophy, which uses stories (real and imagined) to reinforce the prosperity gospel as a viable cause (Maxwell, 1998). The cultural normativity of indirection, therefore, influences how technology and religion are used and perceived.

Many West African groups rely on lingual diversions, stories, and proverbs when asking for money, announcing someone's death, or presenting oneself in public. Most local languages in Ghana (e.g., Twi, Ewe, Ga) have no direct translation for the word privacy. The reason may be the strong link with Western citizenship and philosophy on the concept of privacy (see Section 1.1), the collective structures many Africans live in, or the cultural

50 *People, place, language, and technology*

importance of using metaphors to describe social terms. The following are a few words and terms in Twi that relate to privacy indirectly[17]:

Asisɛm: Translates as 'secret' but directly translates as 'hidden information.' The term relates to any occurrence or information that should not be disclosed publicly. For instance, if a hunter accidentally killed a man outside the village, he and his wife may decide to keep that hidden, and therefore the event becomes *Asisɛm*. The word is often related to death or other extreme events but can also relate to personal details like someone's Facebook password.

Aborome: This verb relates to the act of retrieving private or hidden information. It particularly relates to things that are mostly hidden but still slightly exposed, and to the action of finding out their source. For instance, digging in the ground around a yam that popped out, following a smoke cloud to locate a fire, or seeing the tip of a men's beard from outside his room. This verb insinuates that things can be told indirectly, using hints or partial information. 'Digging around' for these hints must be done delicately.

Ahintasem: This term strongly relates to privacy or discreteness as a social expectation. It merely means 'keep what you want to say in your mind; do not let it out by speaking.' Disclosing a person's real age, home address, full name, pregnancy status, or domestic income may be defined as *Ahintasem* and it is culturally acceptable to hide (and even lie about) these details.

Kokoame: This term connects privacy and space. It describes any place/site/space that is hidden, secret, or private. It could be the entire house, its kitchen, the toilet cells within public toilets, or a bank account where someone keeps secret savings. Thus, *Kokoame* spaces in traditional language connect to private places with limited access.

As seen in these translations, there are lingual roots to the politics of indirectness and discreteness within Ghana. Even if informants did not use these terms in the conversations we conducted, they are part of the lingual and cultural history of many ethnic groups within the city. Moreover, according to Dankwa (2009: 202), it is the absence of specific vocabularies or 'specialist language' that allows secrecy and privacy, more than its manifestation in language. The terms, therefore, do not refer directly to privacy but to the hidden information itself, the spaces that conceal it, the act of retrieving this information, and the expectation to keep it personal.

Studying social media in Brazil, Spyer, (2018: 42) uses the term 'speech encryption' to demonstrate how people apply indirect language in digital spaces. 'Speech encryption,' he argues, is a way of disguising the subject in a sentence by writing or speaking using codes. This strategy is required when privacy is not possible and more people are listening in or watching the conversation, as often occurs in Facebook. 'Speech encryption' also relates to Lange's (2007) idea of being 'privately public' online through coded content and strategic tagging.

Going back to Ghana and its particular spiritual climate, many of these indirections relate to indigenous philosophies that make explicit links

People, place, language, and technology   51

between people's minds, thoughts, and words to actual life events. In other words, they assign great importance to the power of speech and mind. Africans tend to attribute this power to issues of safety, dignity, and spiritual wellbeing. Furthermore, they aim to maintain this power by controlling how information is distributed and exhibited, to whom it is disclosed, and in what context.

References

Adams, S. (2011) 'Privatization and National Development: A Case Study of Ghana', *Public Organization Review*, 11(3), pp. 237–253. doi: 10.1007/s11115-010-0119-2.

Agyekum, K. (2006) 'The Sociolinguistic of Akan Personal Names', *Nordic Journal of African Studies*, 15(2), pp. 206–235.

Aker, J. C. and Mbiti, I. M. (2010) 'Mobile Phones and Economic Development in Africa', *Journal of Economic Perspectives*, 24(3), pp. 207–232. doi: 10.1257/jep.24.3.207.

Arthur, G. F. K. (2017) *Cloth as Metaphor: (Re)reading the Adinkra Cloth Symbols of the Akan of Ghana*. Second Edition. Bloomington: iUniverse.

Asomani-Boateng, R. (2011) 'Borrowing from the Past to Sustain the Present and the Future: Indigenous African Urban Forms, Architecture, and Sustainable Urban Development in Contemporary Africa', *Journal of Urbanism: International Research on Placemaking and Urban Sustainability*, 4(3), pp. 239–262. doi: 10.1080/17549175.2011.634573.

Azindow, Y. M. (1999) *Philosophical Reflections of Adinkra Symbols*. Bloomington: Y.M. Azindow.

Banerjee, A. V. and Duflo, E. (2008) 'What Is Middle Class about the Middle Classes Around the World?', *The Journal of Economic Perspectives*, 22(2), pp. 3–41A.

Barnes, J. A. (1994) *A Pack of Lies: Towards a Sociology of Lying*. Cambridge: Cambridge University Press.

Bennell, P. (1997) 'Privatization in Sub-Saharan Africa: Progress and Prospects during the 1990s', *World Development*, 25(11), pp. 1785–1803. doi: 10.1016/S0305-750X(97)00068-5.

Besnier, N. (2009) 'Modernity, Cosmopolitanism, and the Emergence of Middle Classes in Tonga', *The Contemporary Pacific*, 21(2), pp. 215–262.

Birdsall, N. (2010) 'The (Indispensable) Middle Class in Developing Countries', in Kanbur, R. and Spence, M. (eds) *Equity and Growth in a Globalizing World*. Washington, D.C.: The International Bank for Reconstruction and Development/ The World Bank, pp. 157–187.

Bott, E. and Spillius, E. B. (2014) *Family and Social Network: Roles, Norms and External Relationships in Ordinary Urban Families*. London and New York: Routledge.

Brown-Saracino, J. (2010) *A Neighborhood That Never Changes: Gentrification, Social Preservation, and the Search for Authenticity*. Chicago, IL: University of Chicago Press.

Bruijn, M. de, Nyamnjoh, F. and Brinkman, I. (eds) (2009) *Mobile Phones: The New Talking Drums of Everyday Africa*. Bamenda, Cameroon: Langaa RPCIG.

Burrell, J. (2009) 'Could Connectivity Replace Mobility? An Analysis of Internet Cafe Use Patterns in Accra, Ghana', in Bruijn, M. de, Nyamnjoh, F., and

52 *People, place, language, and technology*

Brinkman, I. (eds) *Mobile Phones: The New Talking Drums of Everyday Africa.* Bamenda, Cameroon: Langaa RPCIG, pp. 151–169.

Burrell, J. (2011) 'User Agency in the Middle Range: Rumors and the Reinvention of the Internet in Accra, Ghana', *Science, Technology & Human Values*, 36(2), pp. 139–159. doi: 10.1177/0162243910366148.

Burrell, J. (2012) *Invisible Users: Youth in the Internet Cafés of Urban Ghana.* Cambridge, MA: MIT Press.

Chalfin, B. (2014) 'Public Things, Excremental Politics, and the Infrastructure of Bare Life in Ghana's city of Tema', *American Ethnologist*, 41(1), pp. 92–109. doi: 10.1111/amet.12062.

Chappatte, A. (2014) 'Night Life in Southern Urban Mali: Being a Muslim Maquisard in Bougouni', *Journal of the Royal Anthropological Institute*, 20(3), pp. 526–544. doi: 10.1111/1467–9655.12121.

Cherlin, A. (1983) 'Changing Family and Household: Contemporary Lessons from Historical Research', *Annual Review of Sociology*, 9(1), pp. 51–66. doi: 10.1146/annurev.so.09.080183.000411.

Christaller, J. G. (1881) *A Dictionary of the Asante and Fante Language Called Tshi (Chwee, Twi): With a Grammatical Introduction and Appendices on the Geography of the Gold Coast and Other Subjects.* London: Evangelical Missionary Society.

Clarke, A. (2007) 'Making Sameness: Mothering Commerce and the Culture of Children's Birthday Parties', in Casey, E. and Martens, L. (eds) *Gender and Consumption: Domestic Cultures and the Commercialisation of Everyday Life.* Farnham: Ashgate Publishing, Ltd., pp. 79–95.

Corten, A. and Marshall-Fratani, R. R. (eds) (2001) *Between Babel and Pentecost: Transnational Pentecostalism in Africa and Latin America.* Bloomington: Indiana University Press.

d'Auria, V. and De Meulder, B. (2010) 'Unsettling Landscapes: New Settlements for the Volta River Project between Tradition and Transition (1951–1970)', *Oase: Tijdschrift voor Architectuur*, 82, pp. 115–138.

d'Auria, V. and Kootin Sanwu, V. (2010) 'Between Development and Experiment: The Volta River Project's (Un)settling Communities', in. *Urban Knowledge: Its Production, Use and Dissemination in Cities of the South*, LaCambreHorta-ULB - ASRO-KULeuven., pp. 93–110. Available at: https://lirias.kuleuven.be/handle/123456789/301550 (Accessed: 4 April 2018).

Dankwa, S. O. (2009) '"It's a Silent Trade": Female Same-Sex Intimacies in Post-Colonial Ghana', *NORA - Nordic Journal of Feminist and Gender Research*, 17(3), pp. 192–205. doi: 10.1080/08038740903117208.

Daswani, G. (2010) 'Transformation and migration among members of a Pentecostal Church in Ghana and London', *Journal of Religion in Africa*, 40(4), pp. 442–474. doi: 10.1163/157006610X541590.

Daswani, G. (2013) 'On Christianity and Ethics: Rupture as Ethical Practice in Ghanaian Pentecostalism', *American Ethnologist*, 40(3), pp. 467–479. doi: 10.1111/amet.12033.

de Koning, A. (2009) *Global Dreams: Class, Gender, and Public Space in Cosmopolitan Cairo.* Cairo: American University in Cairo Press.

De Witte, M. and Meyer, B. (2012) 'African Heritage Design: Entertainment Media and Visual Aesthetics in Ghana', *Civilisations*, 61(1), pp. 43–64.

Earl, C. (2014) *Vietnam's New Middle Classes: Gender, Career, City.* Copenhagen: NIAS Press, Nordic Institute of Asian Studies.

People, place, language, and technology 53

Feld, S. (2012) *Jazz Cosmopolitanism in Accra: Five Musical Years in Ghana*. Durham, NC: Duke University Press Books.

Ferguson, J. (2006) *Global Shadows: Africa in the Neoliberal World Order*. Durham, NC: Duke University Press.

Freeman, C. (2000) *High Tech and High Heels in the Global Economy: Women, Work, and Pink-Collar Identities in the Caribbean*. Durham, NC: Duke University Press.

Gifford, P. (1998) *African Christianity: Its Public Role*. London: C. Hurst & Co. Publishers.

Halle, D. (1991) 'Displaying the Dream: The Visual Presentation of Family and Self in the Modern American Household', *Journal of Comparative Family Studies*, 22(2), pp. 217–229.

Hansen, E. and Collins, P. (1980) 'The Army, the State, and the "Rawlings Revolution" in Ghana', *African Affairs*, 79(314), pp. 3–23.

Hart, K. (1973) 'Informal Income Opportunities and Urban Employment in Ghana', *The Journal of Modern African Studies*, 11(1), pp. 61–89. doi: 10.1017/S0022278X00008089.

Hart, K. (1985) 'The Informal Economy', *Cambridge Anthropology*, 10(2), pp. 54–58. doi: 10.2307/23816368.

Heath, C. W. (1997) 'Children's Television in Ghana: A Discourse about Modernity', *African Affairs*, 96(383), pp. 261–275.

Home, R. K. (2013) *Of Planting and Planning: The Making of British Colonial Cities*. London: Routledge.

Horst, H. A. and Taylor, E. B. (2014) 'The Role of Mobile Phones in the Mediation of Border Crossings: A Study of Haiti and the Dominican Republic', *The Australian Journal of Anthropology*, 25(2), pp. 155–170. doi: 10.1111/taja.12086.

Horst, H. and Miller, D. (2006) *The Cell Phone: An Anthropology of Communication*. New York: Berg.

International Telecommunication Union (2018) *Ghana Profile (Latest data available: 2018)*. Country Profile. Switzerland: ITU (International Telecommunication Union).

Jackson, I. and Oppong, R. A. (2014) 'The Planning of Late Colonial Village Housing in the Tropics: Tema Manhean, Ghana', *Planning Perspectives*, 29(4), pp. 475–499. doi: 10.1080/02665433.2013.829753.

Kharas, H. (2010) *The Emerging Middle Class in Developing Countries*. Paris: OECD Development Centre, pp. 1–61. Available at: http://www.oecd.org/dev/wp.

Kochhar, R. (2015) *A Global Middle Class Is More Promise than Reality: From 2001 to 2011, Nearly 700 Million Step Out of Poverty, but Most Only Barely*. Washington, D.C.: Pew Research Center.

Lacy, K. (2007) *Blue-Chip Black: Race, Class, and Status in the New Black Middle Class*. Berkeley: University of California Press.

Lange, P. G. (2007) 'Publicly private and privately public: Social networking on YouTube', *Journal of Computer-Mediated Communication*, 13(1), pp. 361–380. doi: 10.1111/j.1083-6101.2007.00400.x.

Lauring, J. and Selmer, J. (2010) 'The Supportive Expatriate Spouse: An Ethnographic Study of Spouse Involvement in Expatriate Careers', *International Business Review*, 19(1), pp. 59–69. doi: 10.1016/j.ibusrev.2009.09.006.

Liechty, M. (2003) *Suitably Modern: Making Middle-Class Culture in a New Consumer Society*. Princeton, NJ: Princeton University Press.

54 *People, place, language, and technology*

Lopes, C. (2016) *Emerging Africa, Its Middle Class and New Development Challenges.* Lecture. Netherlands: International Institute of Social Studies in The Hague Part of Erasmus University Rotterdam, p. 8. Available at: https://www.iss.nl/fileadmin/ASSETS/iss/Documents/Conference_presentations/lecture_carlos_lopes.pdf (Accessed: 4 September 2017).

Marshall-Fratani, R. (1998) 'Mediating the Global and Local in Nigerian Pentecostalism', *Journal of Religion in Africa*, 28(3), pp. 278–315. doi: 10.2307/1581572.

Mashiri, P. (2002) 'Saying "No" Without Saying "No": Indirectness and Politeness in Shona Refusals', *Zambezia*, 29(2), pp. 2–33.

Maxwell, D. (1998) '"Delivered from the Spirit of Poverty?": Pentecostalism, Prosperity and Modernity in Zimbabwe', *Journal of Religion in Africa*, 28(3), pp. 350–373. doi: 10.2307/1581574.

Meagher, K. (1995) 'Crisis, Informalization and the Urban Informal Sector in Sub-Saharan Africa', *Development and Change*, 26(2), pp. 259–284. doi: 10.1111/j.1467–7660.1995.tb00552.x.

Mesch, G. S. and Levanon, Y. (2003) 'Community Networking and Locally-Based Social Ties in Two Suburban Localities', *City & Community*, 2(4), pp. 335–351. doi: 10.1046/j.1535–6841.2003.00059.x.

Miller, D. (1998) *Shopping, Place, and Identity*. London: Psychology Press.

Mothobi, O. and Grzybowski, L. (2017) 'Infrastructure Deficiencies and Adoption of Mobile Money in Sub-Saharan Africa', *Information Economics and Policy*, 40, pp. 71–79. doi: 10.1016/j.infoecopol.2017.05.003.

Ncube, M., Lufumpa, C. L. and Vencatachellum, D. (2011) 'The Middle of the Pyramid: Dynamics of the Middle Class in Africa', *African Development Bank Market Brief*. Available at: https://www.afdb.org/sites/default/files/documents/publications/the_middle_of_the_pyramid_the_middle_of_the_pyramid.pdf.

Ninsin, K. A. (1991) *The Informal Sector in Ghana's Political Economy*. London: Freedom Publications.

Nippert-Eng, C. (1996) *Home and Work: Negotiating Boundaries Through Everyday Life*. Chicago: University Of Chicago Press.

Nkrumah, K. (1968) *Dark Days in Ghana*. First Edition. London: Zed Books.

Norman, I. D et al. (2016) 'The Middle Class Is Synonymous with Corruption in Sub-Sahara Africa', *Advances in Applied Sociology*, 6, pp. 179–198.

Nyamekye Adjei, L. and Bosiwah, L. (2015) 'The Use of Indirect Strategies among University Students in Ghana: A Case Study of University of Cape Coast.', *International Journal of Language and Linguistics*, 3(2), pp. 90–101.

Obeng, S. G. (1994). 'Verbal Indirection in Akan Informal Discourse', *Journal of Pragmatics*, 21(1), 37–65. doi: 10.1016/0378-2166(94)90046-9.

Obeng, S. G. (1997) 'Language and Politics: Indirectness in Political Discourse', *Discourse & Society*, 8(1), pp. 49–83. doi: 10.1177/0957926597008001004.

Obeng, S. G. (2003) *Language in African Social Interaction: Indirectness in Akan Communication*. New York: Nova Science Publishers.

Obeng, S. G. (2009) 'Doing Politics on Walls and Doors: A Sociolinguistic Analysis of Graffiti in Legon (Ghana)', *Multilingua - Journal of Cross-Cultural and Interlanguage Communication*, 19(4), pp. 337–366. doi: 10.1515/mult.2000.19.4.337.

Obeng-Odoom, F. (2011) 'The Informal Sector in Ghana under Siege', *Journal of Developing Societies*, 27(3–4), pp. 355–392.

Odotei, I. (1989) 'What Is in a Name? The Social and Historical Significance of Ga names', *Research Review*, 5(2), pp. 34–51.

People, place, language, and technology 55

Okae, P. (2018) 'A Qualitative Study of Smartphone Usage Patterns: The Case of Ghana', *Science World Journal*, 13(2), pp. 58–63–63.

Osei-Boateng, C. and Ampratwum, E. (2011) *The Informal Sector in Ghana*. Ghana: Friedrich Ebert Stiftung, pp. 1–40. Available at: http://library.fes.de/pdf-files/bueros/ghana/10496.pdf (Accessed: 9 July 2017).

Pattillo, M. (2013) *Black Picket Fences, Second Edition: Privilege and Peril among the Black Middle Class*. Chicago, IL: University of Chicago Press.

Pellow, D. (2008) *Landlords and Lodgers: Socio-Spatial Organization in an Accra Community*. Chicago, IL: University of Chicago Press.

Pieterse, E. (2009) 'Exploratory Notes on African Urbanism', *African Centre for Cities University of Cape Town*, (June), pp. 17–37.

Powell, A. C. (2012) *Bigger Cities, Smaller Screens: Urbanization, Mobile Phones, and Digital Media Trends in Africa*. Washington, D.C.: Center for International Media Assistance, National Endowment for Democracy. pp. 1–36.

Ravalion, M. (2009) *The Developing World's Bulging (But Vulnerable) 'Middle Class'*. Policy Research working paper: World Bank License: CC BY 3.0 IGO. World Bank. Available at: https://openknowledge.worldbank.org/handle/10986/4013.

Robbins, J. (2003) 'On the Paradoxes of Global Pentecostalism and the Perils of Continuity Thinking', *Religion*, 33(3), pp. 221–231. doi: 10.1016/S0048-721X(03)00055-1.

Robertson, C. (1983) 'The Death of Makola and Other Tragedies', *Canadian Journal of African Studies/Revue Canadienne des Études Africaines*, 17(3), pp. 469–495. doi: 10.2307/484928.

Sabar, G. (2010) 'Witchcraft and Concepts of Evil amongst African Migrant Workers in Israel', *Canadian Journal of African Studies/Revue canadienne des études africaines*, 44(1), pp. 110–141. doi: 10.1080/00083968.2010.9707561.

Sarfo, E. (2011) 'Variations in Ways of Refusing Requests in English among Members of a College Community in Ghana', *African Nebula*, 3, pp. 1–15.

Sey, A. (2011) '"We Use It Different, Different": Making Sense of Trends in Mobile Phone Use in Ghana', *New Media & Society*, 13(3), pp. 375–390. doi: 10.1177/1461444810393907.

Sherwood, M. (1993) 'Kwame Nkrumah: The London years, 1945–47', *Immigrants & Minorities*, 12(3), pp. 164–194. doi: 10.1080/02619288.1993.9974824.

Shipley, J. W. (2009) 'Aesthetic of the Entrepreneur: Afro-Cosmopolitan Rap and Moral Circulation in Accra, Ghana', *Anthropological Quarterly*, 82(3), pp. 631–668. doi: 10.2307/20638655.

Slater, D. and Kwami, J. (2005) 'Embeddedness and Escape: Internet and Mobile Use as Poverty Reduction Strategies in Ghana', *Information Society Research Group (ISRG) Report*. Available at: http://www.researchgate.net/profile/Janet_Kwami/publication/228635823_Embeddedness_and_escape_Internet_and_mobile_use_as_poverty_reduction_strategies_in_Ghana/links/00b7d530253d3b70b1000000.pdf (Accessed: 6 July 2015).

Spronk, R. (2014) 'Exploring the Middle Classes in Nairobi: From Modes of Production to Modes of Sophistication', *African Studies Review*, 57(1), pp. 93–114. doi: 10.1017/asr.2014.7.

Statista, I. (2017) *Number of Mobile Cellular Subscriptions in Ghana from 2000 to 2017 (in millions)*. Statistic. Available at: https://www.statista.com/statistics/498203/number-of-mobile-cellular- subscriptions-in-ghana/ (Accessed: 27 November 2018).

56 *People, place, language, and technology*

The Rising Middle Class of Africa (2013) *Johannesburg: Grail Research.* Available at: http://www .integreon.com/pdf/Blog/Grail-Research-The-Rising-Middle-Class-Africa_225.pdf.

Trundle, C. (2014) *Americans in Tuscany: Charity, Compassion, and Belonging.* New York: Berghahn Books.

Tsamenyi, M., Onumah, J. and Tetteh-Kumah, E. (2010) 'Post-privatization Performance and Organizational Changes: Case Studies from Ghana', *Critical Perspectives on Accounting*, 21(5), pp. 428–442. doi: 10.1016/j.cpa.2008.01.002.

Vallejo, J. (2012) *Barrios to Burbs: The Making of the Mexican American Middle Class.* Redwood City: Stanford University Press.

van Binsbergen, W. M. J. (2004) 'Can ICT belong in Africa, or Is It Owned by the North Atlantic Region?', in Binsbergen, W. M. J. van, and Dijk, R. A. van. (eds) *Situating Globality: African Agency in the Appropriation of Global Culture.* Leiden: Brill. pp. 107–146. Retrieved from https://hdl.handle.net/1887/13017.

van Dijk, R. (2003b) 'Religion, Reciprocity and Restructuring Family Responsibility in the Ghanaian Pentecostal Diaspora', in Bryceson, D. F. and Vuorela, U. (eds) *The Transnational Family: New European Frontiers and Global Networks.* First Edition. New York: Berg, pp. 173–196.

van Leeuwen, L. (2011) *Lost in Mall: An Ethnography of Middle-class Jakarta in the 1990s.* Leiden: KITLV Press.

Wajcman, J. et al. (2010) 'Enacting Virtual Connections between Work and Home', *Journal of Sociology*, 46(3), pp. 257–275. doi: 10.1177/1440783310365583.

Walsh, K. J. (2005) *British Expatriate Belonging in Dubai : Foreignness, Domesticity, Intimacy.* Ph.D. Royal Holloway, University of London. Available at: http://ethos.bl.uk/OrderDetails.do?uin=uk.bl.ethos.417134 (Accessed: 3 October 2017).

Weil, D. N., Mbiti, I. and Mwega, F. (2016) 'Mobile Banking: The Impact of M-Pesa in Kenya', in Edwards, S., Johnson, S., and Weil, D. N. (eds) *African Successes, Volume III: Modernization and Development.* Chicago, IL: University of Chicago Press (National Bureau of Economic Research), pp. 247–293.

Weiss, B. (2004) *Producing African Futures: Ritual and Reproduction in a Neoliberal Age.* Leiden: Brill.

Wendl, T. M. (2007) 'Wicked Villagers and the Mysteries of Reproduction: An Exploration of Horror Videos from Ghana and Nigeria', *Postcolonial Text*, 3(2). Available at: http://postcolonial.org/index.php/pct/article/view/529 (Accessed: 26 July 2018).

Wilk, R. R. and Netting, R. M. (1984) 'Households: Changing Forms and Functions', in Netting, Robert McC, Wilk, R. R., and Arnould, E. J. (eds) *Households: Comparative and Historical Studies of the Domestic Group.* Berkeley: University of California Press, pp. 1–28. Available at: https://www.google.com/books?hl=en&lr=&id=p_7nOGvDceAC&oi=fnd&pg=PA1&dq=H ouseholds:+Changing+Forms+and+Functions/+Richard+R.+Wilk&ots=1aRdfHu0nU&sig=NxvoReHAPeKPR uB0CTbsCheJ_ok (Accessed: 6 July 2015).

Williams, J. (2015) 'The "Rawlings Revolution" and Rediscovery of the African Diaspora in Ghana (1983–2015)', *African Studies*, 74(3), pp. 366–387. doi: 10.1080/00020184.2015.1015313.

Yankah, K. (1989) 'Proverbs: The Aesthetics of Traditional Communication', *Research in African Literatures*, 20(3), pp. 325–346.

Yaw A. D. (2007) 'Promoting the Informal Sector as a Source of Gainful Employment in Developing Countries: Insights from Ghana', *The International Journal of Human Resource Management*, 18(6), pp. 1063–1084. doi: 10.1080/09585190701321716.

People, place, language, and technology 57

Notes

1 Adinkra are visual signs and symbols made mostly by the Akan/Ashanti group to communicate ancestral phrases, proverbs, and social messages. These signs became strongly identified with Ghana's aesthetics and visual culture due to their presence on buildings, wood carvings, decorated cloth, and (most recently) digital imagery. See more in Arthur (2017) and Azindow (1999).

2 For more on the European division of labour between home and workplace after the industrial revolution and how the modern home became a place of leisure and rest see Cherlin (1983), Halle (1991), Nippert-Eng (1996), Wajcman et al. (2010), and Wilk and Netting (1984).

3 When discussing the issue with Tema's older residents they often brought up this painful history and stated: 'it wasn't always like this,' as if remembering the broken promise of Nkrumah. According to their memories, Tema was once a clean city with no mosquitos, no water or electricity breaks, and lots of greenery and flowers. Beyond their nostalgic tone, these memories challenge the linear assumptions of development and portray a slippery path full of contradictions, tensions, and ruptures. These tensions are at the heart of urban privacy-seeking practices.

4 In 2010 the Ministry of Local Government and Rural Development launched a 'street naming and property numbering project' to improve navigation in the city using digital mapping tools, but most properties in the area are still unmarked and informal. According to Okae)2018: 59), 'the lack of an effective addressing system has always compelled Ghanaians to develop a culture of relying on directions from people… In cases where emergencies occur such as accidents, giving directions to emergency personnel is really difficult.'

5 Burrell (2009, 2012) emphasised that internet cafés in Ghana become additional spaces of non-physical de-localisation and transcendence for Ghanaian youth. It may not be a coincidence that this young crowd is the main demographic of Pentecostal churches as well.

6 This resembles the practice of masking names and locations in ethnography using pseudonyms. In this research, I knew that I must mask names and personal details, to protect privacy, and despite some critical voices against masking names in anthropology. When converting the names, I used alternative names from the same ethnic group each informant belonged to. If he or she presented themselves with their Christian international name, I also tried to use similar biblically inspired names. Ironically, while these names are seen as English or American, it was me who often explained their original Hebrew meaning.

7 According to (Ravalion, 2009: 17) the need to re-define middle class, especially for developing countries, comes from the fact that between 1990 and 2005 only 80 million people in the entire developing world qualified as middle class by Western parameters.

8 Regarding Ghana, the latter meant that while the population grew from 19.3 to 24.8 million between 2001 and 2011, the middle class only climbed from 1.9% to 3.3% of the population.

9 The term 'informal economy' is a widely discussed term in social policy, anthropology, and sociology; it was first coined by British Anthropologist Keith Hart (1973) in his paper about urban employment in Ghana; thus, the link between the informal economy and Ghana is impossible to ignore. Hart was counter-arguing many economic theories by explaining that a substantial part of the economy in cities around the world is 'secret,' 'underground,' and 'black' (Hart, 1985).

10 According to a study by the OECD, in 2009, in Sub-Saharan Africa 'at least 80 percent' of all non- agricultural workers operate in the undocumented sector, grey economy, or black market (quoted in Powell, 2012: 9).

11 For the official statistics see http://www.internetlivestats.com/internet-users/ghana.

58 *People, place, language, and technology*

12 In his qualitative analysis of smartphones in Ghana Okae (2018: 58) writes: 'what is a smartphone? The simple answer is that it is still the same old mobile phone we have always known since its invention on 3rd April, 1973 by Motorola senior engineer Martin Cooper, except that these ones have more advanced computing power, more sophisticated add-ons such as a USB port that facilitates connectivity to other external devices such as a printer, a computer and are almost always very flashy.'

13 WhatsApp is a free private messaging and group-interaction mobile phone application (owned by Facebook). It requires a mobile phone number and an internet connection, allowing users to send text and voice messages, images, videos, and documents. WhatsApp also offers free voice and video calls, revolutionising the telecommunication habits of transnational families, migrants, and teenagers around the world.

14 The expected ratio of mobile phone lines per person in Ghana for the near future is 2:1, meaning two lines for each person (Okae, 2018: 59).

15 The introduction of pre-paid communication services revolutionised mobile phone usage across Africa. According to Mothobi and Grzybowski (2017), before this reform 'most individuals, and especially those living in remote areas, did not have access to any telecommunications services at all.'

16 According to a recent report by the World Bank, over 7 million Ghanaians have no bank accounts (*Gains in Financial Inclusion, Gains for a Sustainable World*, no date). Generally, 54% of the population in lower-income countries have bank accounts, while 94% are banked in high-income countries (quoted in Mothobi and Grzybowski, 2017). To read more about mobile banking and financial inclusion through digital finance see Weil, Mbiti and Mwega (2016) and Mothobi and Grzybowski (2017).

17 I collected the terms from the dictionary of the Asante and Fante language (Christaller, 1881), conversations with informants, and an interview with Prof. Edward Apenteng-Sackey, a linguistics specialist in the University of Ghana.

4 Treasures of darkness
Nightlife & surveillance

Louisa and Violet, two sisters who grew up in Tema, are both married and have lived in their own houses since their mid-20s. From a very young age, they both shared ambitions to study in a boarding school, despite its incredibly strict routine, after which they wished to be married as soon as possible. I was surprised that teenagers aspired to attend boarding schools, as I associated it with isolation and detachment from home, but according to Violet and Louisa, 'Everyone in Ghana loves going to boarding school.' The truth is they both desired liberation from familial and communal surveillance. Boarding schools and marriages are institutions that loosen the grip of families over their youngsters. Moving in with friends or living alone is highly frowned upon and so getting married becomes most people's 'only ticket out' as they phrase it.

Ghanaians strictly follow a set of gerontocratic rules that praise obedience, hard work, and respect. As Burrell (2009: 160) phrases it: 'young people were not expected to argue with, question or talk back to their elders and supervision and the enforcement of good behaviour was not limited to home and school but could also be witnessed on the streets.' Furthermore, it is completely normal for older urbanites to discipline children and youth, whether they know them or not. Having to navigate between state, school, church, and familial surveillance is not an easy task for young people, as these institutions strive to monitor anything from verbal and facial expressions, to 'how they spent their time and in whose company' (Burrell, 2012: 75).

When Louisa walks around her neighbourhood (also known as the 'community'), she is obliged to greet neighbours and cope with their judgemental gaze. Has she put on weight? Are her clothes all right? Did she attend evening prayers this week? Tema residents often state that there is a feeling that 'everyone knows everyone.' Louisa uses secret alleys and side streets when she is in a hurry, to avoid the constant interaction with neighbours. This skilful detouring requires knowledge of urban space and the social networks in it – who knows me? where are they? when are they there? where can I walk unnoticed? Violet, on the other hand, takes a more accepting

DOI: 10.4324/9781003187424-4

60 Nightlife & surveillance

approach to the matter and says European time can never be imposed on Ghanaians – it requires punctuality while Ghanaians are always late:

> It is very rude here to walk past someone you know without greeting them or talking to them, so on your way you are always held back. Everyone knows that setting a time here isn't set in stone.

Only when night falls can one walk around the neighbourhood more freely, and people do not recognise each other nor approach each other as frequently. Night allows urbanites to move freely from one place to another, like floating silhouettes, while daytime demands small talk and greetings with various strangers and acquaintances. Darkness, therefore, is an opportunity for anonymity in public space (Figure 4.1).

State authorities in Euro-American cities often use surveillance cameras and image recognition software to monitor crime and public behaviour; in London, for instance, a pedestrian strolling the town with public transport is likely to have his picture taken about 300 times per day (Coaffee, 2004). The individualisation of Western Europe meant most people became anonymous in public space, which meant street crime had to be stopped by using digital surveillance, facial recognition technologies, and local police forces or 'the neighbourhood watch' (Sasson and Nelson, 1996; Goold, 2003; DeNicola, 2011).

Figure 4.1 Hidden alleys in Tema. Photo by the author.

Nightlife & surveillance 61

According to Miller (2016: 90), while Euro-American journalism expresses increasing anxieties about the loss of privacy to digital companies and state authorities, people in other parts of the world tend to be more concerned about the surveillance made by those they actually know. National and technological surveillance could be seen as a 'replacement' for community surveillance, which is still practised in many parts of the world. In Ghana people battle crime, theft, and robbery not just by relying on police forces but mainly within tightly knit communities, which means both the criminal and the victim will be quickly identified in public space.

A beauty salon owner once told me with pride that if a person shoots someone in the street someone else was guaranteed to identify him, and they would not hesitate to reveal him to the police. 'In American TV people who witness a crime hide in their houses because they are scared to tell the police what they saw,' she explained. 'In Ghana, the streets are very safe all night because everyone knows everyone.'

By becoming part of the urban security chain, which relied on community surveillance by Tema's residents, I felt very safe in public spaces. Once I became known in the neighbourhood my whereabouts and the people I engage with were publicly known. Attending events that were integral to the local community such as weddings or soccer games marked me as an 'insider.' After watching a soccer game with dozens of other men from the neighbourhood, my host Yaw told me: 'now you can feel very safe. No one will touch you. You can walk around here all night if anyone tries to mess with you someone will see him and shout: Hey! He is from here!' Yaw's promise was another aspect of community surveillance, an alternative method of keeping law and order where police forces are perceived as corrupt and unreliable. In the words of Wishnitzer, who studied the nocturnal life of Istanbul in the 18th century,

> by intruding and exerting group pressure, neighbourhoods collectively policed the behaviour of their residents. The neighbourhood was thus an important, if informal, link in the network of urban order.
>
> (2014a: 516)

This protective surveillance can also become suffocating. Although I was acknowledged as an adult, my single status and position as a guest in a house with older people created a metaphorical parent-child relation.[1] Wherever I went and whomever I talked to was somehow reported to my hosts. When I went to meet new people across town, my hosts called their contacts to find out if the person I was meeting was reliable and 'correct' before I was allowed to leave. The more I got involved in the community, the more I participated in how order is kept through control and monitoring. I also refrained from drinking and smoking in the city because it was made clear to me that it will have a negative social impact. That is until I learned the game of darkness and indirectness.

62 *Nightlife & surveillance*

In recent years, there are increasing debates in Euro-America about 'light pollution' and health risks related to regular exposure to light after darkness due to an overload of technology, digital screens, and street lights (Bennie et al., 2014; Wishnitzer, 2014b). According to Davoudian (2019), 'research into the effects of urban lighting on behaviour, environmental psychology and social interaction is developing at a rapid rate.' Examining the sociological and historical literature about urban nightlife shows that these different states of illumination go beyond infrastructural or economic constraints. Boston, for instance, is highly illuminated at night but has a minimal and fairly sleepy nocturnal life (Beamish, 2015); Istanbul's evolution of light is strongly connected to lighting candles in mosques during Ramadan (Tureli, 2015); and Mumbai's intense night lights are a symbol of progress and prosperity in what the British empire called 'India's first city' (Woods, 2015).

Although there is a rich sociological literature about urban nightlife, there is a tendency in sociology to homogenise it as 'a singular cultural form' (Anderson, 2009: 918). This literature, very much like dominant writings in internet studies, tends to portray nightlife either as an idyllic and protective 'third space' of leisure, economy, and sociality (Gans, 1962; Oldenburg, 1989; Jacobs, 1992) or as a scary, violent, and oppressive urban time frame (Graham and Wells, 2003; Hall and Winlow, 2005; Grazian, 2007, 2009). Grazian (2009), for instance, argues that urban nightlife encourages race and class divisions, gender inequalities, and 'exclusivity rather than inclusiveness' (Anderson, 2009: 918). How can researchers avoid such generalisations?

This chapter shifts the focal lens from analysis of night-time economies (NTE) to a material culture approach. Reflecting on their applied ethnographic project about urban night-time design in Colombia, Slater and Entwistle (2018) turn our attention to the material properties of light with the aim of better understanding its sociological agency. They define light as 'a messy material that spills, bleeds and interchanges promiscuously with adjacent materials and spaces.' Light, they argue, is a 'relational material' experienced through different shadows and surfaces; it is fluid, uncontrollable, temporal, and a 'by-product' of social practices. Interpreting light and darkness as materials not only links this chapter to the following descriptions of houses and social media but also contributes to their role as enhancers of urban privacy due to their ability to reveal and conceal.

Residents of Tema strongly associate darkness with privacy, which is highly valued and desired. Katherine stays home alone for many weeks when her husband goes out of town as part of his job. She dislikes her house because it is a shared compound house, with a yard at the centre. When Katherine wishes to sit outside in the fresh air, she must socialise with her neighbours. If she sits there and doesn't engage in conversations, people will brand her as *Wo kyerε wo hu* (someone who 'thinks of herself as big,' or a snob). Katherine actually prefers staying indoors with the lights turned off, so that no one will know if she is there or not. Even if there is a power break and everyone sits outside because the fans are not operating, she uses

Nightlife & surveillance   63

a rechargeable fan and stays inside. Her desire to escape from the gaze of the community is not uncommon. Furthermore, her use of darkness as a material mask that creates privacy is integral to Tema's nightlife.

Darkness is perceived in Ghana as an entity that conceals individuals and their bodies, and by doing so protects sinners from exposing their sins or wrong ways. One can take advantage of the supposedly unfortunate circumstances of darkness to select his/her level of privacy, type of company, and kind of interaction. Being in the dark means stepping out of the watchful eyes of the church, schools, parents, bosses, and neighbours. Many Ghanaians draw a link between their preferences to socialise in the dark and their occasional need to avoid social surveillance. Moving away from the light into the dark is often considered as a symbolic transition from a social realm of truth and enlightenment into a world of lies, sins, and evil doings, but also of pleasure.

4.1 Dumsur and the politics of darkness

> The night affords an outlet – an insulating function – it reduces surveillance and prevents unwanted encounters.
>
> (Melbin, 1978: 9)

Tema's nightlife is a fascinating tale, but it is also a hidden one. Uncovering it required strolling the streets at night, spending many hours at pubs and bars, observing the hidden corners of the city, and conversing with inhabitants about their perception of night and darkness. Positioned just a few degrees north of the equator, Ghana's days and nights have a constant schedule throughout the year. Sunrise begins just before 6 AM and sunset ends shortly after 6 PM. This means a significant portion of the day is spent in the dark. Ghanaians tend to wake up as early as 6 AM, so most of their nightly activities happen in the early part of it. Public activities at night occur between 6 and 10 PM, when most bars and shops close.

The urbanisation and electrification of Ghana also affects the way night is perceived and consumed. After nightfall, when the intense tropical sun surrenders to a cool breeze and soft moonlight, many Ghanaians express a sense of liberation and relaxation, especially if electricity was not operating throughout the day and resumed after 6 PM. The tardy streets become lively and busy as night markets offer grilled kebabs (*Chichingas*), fresh fruits, and stir-fried noodles (*Indomie*), bars and nightclubs offer alcoholic drinks, gathering spots, and residential streets are filled with families sitting outside on plastic chairs. Unlike the cold nights of Western Europe, where each household remains closed behind the comfort of wireless internet, flowing electricity, and flickering television sets, the warm nights of Ghana bring the community together in public space. Many women, for instance, go to restaurants to watch the latest telenovela episode, instead of viewing it alone at home.

64 *Nightlife & surveillance*

The interplay between light and darkness has become even more significant in recent years through the issue of *Dumsor* – a Ghanaian slang word referring to irregular electric supply and constant power outages. *Dumsor* translates from Twi as 'to turn off or quench' (dum) and 'to turn on or to make light' (sor). The ECG (Electricity Company of Ghana) and the Minister of Energy started using load shedding with blackouts as a result of the power crisis – a shortage of about 600 megawatts in Ghana. This energy crisis started in 2001 but it was only after 2012 that it became a regular large-scale burden. In January 2016, towards the end of my fieldwork, the government announced that *Dumsor* had 'ended,' but Ghanaian urbanites know that (in varying degrees) it will always be a part of city life and nightlife.

There are various causes for *Dumsor*, each expressed by a different institute or individual. Some Ghanaians, for instance, argue that *Dumsor* is the inevitable result of environmental damages, causing a water shortage in the Akosombo and Bui Dams (Ghana's main hydro-electric sources). Other Ghanaians see *Dumsor* as the result of a large governmental debt (over $1.6 billion as of 2015) to ECG and as a result of the Volta River Authority (VRA) and the government of Nigeria. Inadequate maintenance of power facilities and deterioration of machinery is also stated as a significant reason for power shortages. TICO unit No. 1, for instance, is an electrical facility currently under renovations and enhancements that will add 100 megawatts to Ghana's grid. As a result of *Dumsor*, electricity in Ghana is experienced as a material resource that needs to be collected and stored. It is pre-paid and loaded into internal power switches, inverters, and 'power banks' – portable drivers used for charging mobile phones.

A 2015 report from the Institute of Statistical, Social and Economic Research (ISSER) stated that Ghana lost about 1 million dollars in 2014 as a result of *Dumsor*. Long hours without electricity are damaging to companies, trade, government offices, and public institutes. *Dumsor* also influences health and safety issues as domestic appliances get an irregular power supply, food isn't properly stored, rural vaccines aren't preserved, and hospitals have unstable energy. In Tema, each Community is usually divided into two sections, and the electric supply alternates between them more or less equally: if section A had no electricity during the day, section B would have no electricity during the night. Each power cut lasts about 12 hours, depending on the national energy supply, the weather conditions, and the number of community events such as holidays, weddings, and funerals.

Tema was a leading city in the introduction of electricity to post-independence Ghana because of its close proximity to the Akosombo dam, Ghana's central hydropower resource. This artificial dam was launched in 1967 as part of the Volta River Development Project and radically changed the national access to electricity (Ankomah and Attuquaye, 2007). However, whether in times of *Dumsor* or not, electricity and artificial lights in Ghanaian cities were never as widespread, stable, and dominant as in other big cities around the world.[2] The view of Ghana's skyline at night is that of a very dark country, with

Nightlife & surveillance   65

small florescent lights above each house door. Its urban landscape at night is far from the idealised images of New York, San Francisco, London, or Paris where 'the night skyline has become the signature image of the metropolis, a defining landscape of modernity' (Nye, 2013: 13).

To be clear, Accra, Kumasi, and Tema are not less lively or active at night. On the contrary, there is a vibrant nocturnal scene in Tema, but people seem to be more comfortable with darkness as part of its urban features. I would often stroll through Tema at night, having to ask the locals if the electrical grid is on or off at the moment. In fact, I claim that from a domestic perspective the lack of light is a minor discomfort brought with *Dumsor*; it is the limitations on charging phones, ironing clothes, storing food, fanning the rooms, playing music, and watching TV that harshly disturbs domestic life. The impact of nightly power cuts is not so much about how dark things get, but about the technological and domestic limitations that it entails.

For instance, due to the inability to charge phones during *Dumsor*, batteries are strictly saved, screen brightness is reduced to a minimum, and people generally avoid using their phones. Those with power banks and generators, however, use their phones as multimedia torches that help 'pass the time.' Groups of friends often sit around a single mobile phone and watch church services, gospel music videos, funny sketches, and movie scenes. Nenema, for instance, is a seamstress living in Tema, who has her own shop in front of her private house. When she knows of a blackout in her section of the neighbourhood that evening, she uses the day's electric supply to sew her clients' clothes as fast as possible. Customers, friends, and neighbours come in and out of her courtyard between the shop and the house collecting and delivering cloth, ordering school uniforms for their kids, and commissioning bridesmaids' dresses for an upcoming wedding. When the lights go off at 6 PM (dum) the house, yard, and shop become pitch black, and that announces the end of a day's work.

During power cuts, Nenema cannot operate her sewing machines, iron her clothes, or count money, so she is forced to take a break, relax, and enjoy an evening with friends and neighbours. No one seems anxious or worried; they keep on chatting and laughing, the baby isn't crying, and Ruth, the assistant, fetches a rechargeable lamp from the house. The lamp does not make much difference, but Nenema, Ruth, and the baby keep sitting there, talking, eating, enjoying the fresh air, and watching gospel music videos on Nenema's tablet, as if it were a digital bonfire. Papa Jo, the next-door neighbour, comes by as well carrying a cold drink that he made called *Sobolo* (made of Hibiscus leaves and ginger). He grabs a plastic chair and points at the moon:

> Only when the lights are off, we can see such a bright moon! God is keeping it full, so we can see each other.

Alongside the inconvenience of *Dumsor*, there is a unique, intimate atmosphere created by sharing the experience of darkness and its particular types

66   *Nightlife & surveillance*

of interaction amongst Ghana's urbanites. This feeling of ambivalence can be compared to a rainy day in London when it's cold, wet, and difficult to navigate, perhaps even dangerous, but there is also cosiness, rest, intimacy, and togetherness. As Nye phrased it in his historiographical account of blackouts in the early days of American electricity, blackouts bring darkness and darkness encourages candlelight – this light is simple and faint, but it also suggests 'a slower-paced world in which friendship, conversation, and intimacy had time to unfold' (Nye, 2013: 224). In this case, 'candlelight' was usually the soft light of rechargeable lamps, mobile phone screens, and tablets, illuminating the room like magical objects.

Dumsor particularly, and darkness at large, has a surprising social effect. It pushes family members out of the house in the evening, which means that it takes part in shaping memories and experiences of home. Electricity breathes life into the house and gathers its dwellers together around the television, kitchen, or air-conditioner; the absence of electricity, accordingly, disturbs a particular social order and manifests new yet somewhat nostalgic ones. The alternative social laws made possible at night, and especially during power cuts, have direct links to privacy and how the city makes itself available for private encounters. I heard residents claim that *Dumsor* increases the population as couples have the perfect conditions for sexual encounters, but I also heard about fathers sleeping in the office and children staying away from home to complete their homework in places with operating lights.

Overall, my ethnographic exploration showed a clear link between having electricity and staying home. As most businesses keep generators and most homes do not, the house becomes the main battleground during blackouts – it has no lights, no televisions, and no air fans. In other words, blackouts seemed to push people outside their homes and strengthen neighbourhood and community bonds. Residents were 'liberated' from the strict surveillance of the house into the wild darkness of city life. This socio-technical mechanism influenced family relations, domestic life, and the togetherness of urban neighbourhoods. When lights fail, as Nye argues about blackouts in the US, Americans are 'forcibly reminded that they are not isolated individuals, but a community that now needs electrical wires and signals to bring itself together' (2013: 4).

Ghanaians usually share their portable hard drives, solar lamps, and generators. Moreover, they share the time spent waiting for electricity to resume. Although power cuts damage businesses and households and violate 'the right to the city' (Lefebvre, 1968) and although most Ghanaians pray and sometimes protest for the end of it, there is an ambivalent feeling when it actually occurs. As a group of primary school teachers told me in an informal chat, *Dumsor* is both loved and hated; it stops the busy lifestyle and gives spare time for being together, but it is also tricky and hazardous.

More importantly, *Dumsor* enhances the pre-existing binary between day and night, as a significant framework of urban life. During the day power is

Nightlife & surveillance   67

exercised by showing the middle-class lifestyle – cars, clothes, technological gadgets, and Christian coherence. However during the night, power gives way to invisibility and the public surrenders to a more chaotic and dynamic social existence. Of course, the possibilities offered by night usually depend on the political and social order, which is always subject to change. As discussed earlier, Ghana was not always a democracy, and therefore its nightlife has historical, political, and theological baggage that may explain its contemporary meaning.

After the out-taking of Kwame Nkrumah in 1966, and especially during Rawlings' military regimes, various laws and regulations aimed to repress NTE and urban movements. Between 1982 and 1984, urban Ghanaians lived under a strict night curfew that prevented them from leaving the house between dusk and dawn, let alone having the freedom to operate nightly businesses. Leaving the house after dark could lead to arrests, beatings, and other sanctions, causing people to either stay indoors or pretend to be homeless if they were seen outside. According to Collins (2005: 18), 'night curfews drastically curtailed the activities of commercial nightclubs and local "pop," Highlife, and concert party bands.' Auntie Evelina, who was running her liquor shop and pub at the time, remembers having to work in extreme darkness so that Rawlings' soldiers would not identify the law-breaking pub goers. This repression of nocturnal liberties had profound influences on the collective memory of night-time, domesticity, and security.

4.2 Dark spots: how pub goers protect their privacy

Tema's urbanites handle the dark nights created by _Dumsor_ in various creative ways: Yevette, a 75-year-old African-American migrant from the US, likes gathering some of the neighbourhood kids in her yard and telling them ghost stories; Odame, an 18-year-old musician, pulls out a generator, an old television, large speakers, and some dusty sofas to the side of the road and watches thriller films with his friends; Henry, a 47-year-old _IT specialist,_ likes sitting by the kebab stand with other men in a circle, having beers and talking about politics; Nenema and Ruth like going to Action Chapel, praying, singing and learning until bedtime. As Gupta (2015) describes in his essay about the anthropology of electricity in the Global South, regarding a village in India:

> The darkness, paradoxically, enabled a sense of community to be built in the village. The contrast with larger villages that did have electricity was striking: there, people retreated to their own homes and were entertained by (centrally controlled) television and radio.

Some of those nightly communities and meet-ups express another highly crucial social element of urban nights: private socialising. Men, women, and teenagers make use of the darkness to engage in frowned-upon activities

68 *Nightlife & surveillance*

such as drinking, smoking, and associating with 'illegitimate' partners. Nightclubs, bars, and pubs mostly own generators, which means people can always escape the restrictions of home to a consumerist fantasy, where it is possible to watch the latest football game, listen to music, and charge phones, even when electricity is not available. These small bars tend to be very dark, casual, and minimal, filled with boxes of alcoholic bottles, beer cans, and plastic chairs. The staff is usually female (managers, waiters, and bartenders) who engage in flirting, dancing, and joking with the male customers.

It is frowned upon in Ghana for women to be seen drinking and smoking in pubs. Therefore, the majority of nightly pub goers are men and the staff usually comprises women. Issues of gender relations and labour should be further explored in this context but this particular study debates privacy practices of both men and women through a variety of mixed examples.[3] Nevertheless, darkness and night-time have connotations of privacy among both genders. For instance, Dankwa (2009) mentions that young women in boarding schools place a cloth on their mosquito bed nets at night to cover 'secret activities.' One night, as I was drinking beer with pub goers in a dark pub one of the men asked me:

> 'Did you get used to all the cultural differences in Ghana yet?' 'Which differences do you mean?' I asked back. 'As for us Ghanaians we hate the truth,' he stated. 'We see a person who tells the truth as evil. If I drank two beers, tonight everyone prefers if I say I drank only one. If my mother asks you what I drank, and you say two no one will like that.'

The man in the bar was connecting nightlife, darkness, and collective discretion. He explained that no one should say the exact number of beers they had and what people do in pubs and bars should not be publicly exhibited but be kept as private as possible. The community is thus expected to cooperate with this privacy. Unlike typical British office-talk about 'how much one had to drink last night' or 'how drunk you got on the weekend,' many Ghanaians would prefer their colleagues not even know they visited the pub.

In his book about nightlife in Philadelphia, Grazian (2008) describes taverns, nightclubs, and cocktail lounges as public spaces that contain private 'clusters' of friends and lovers who 'coexist alongside one another but never actually intermingle.' These strangers, he argues, cherish the ability of those spaces to establish 'moments of camaraderie' (Grazian, 2008: 13). While the American clusters he describes are usually well illuminated, relying mostly on urban anonymity and mutual trust, in Tema this would not be sufficient – and this is where darkness plays an important role. Most pubs, restaurants, night markets, and neighbourhood gatherings in Tema all occur in minimal lighting or even complete darkness.

Small pubs, where people drink, smoke, and listen to music, are spread across town, often known as 'spots' or 'joints.' These pubs are very dark;

Nightlife & surveillance 69

waitresses and managers are often instructed by clients to turn off what little light they had. The owners tend to know all of their clients personally, and the clients must trust their discreteness, or they will not return. At 'Auntie Evelina's Wholesale Liquor Shop and Pub,' for instance, the men always shift their chairs away from the streetlights or lamps into a dark circle on the sidewalk. The waitress thinks they prefer sitting where their faces are not easily recognisable: 'If someone from their family or workplace passes by, they won't notice them or make a comment the next day about their behaviour. They order a drink and stay in dark corners for hours' (Figure 4.2).

Indeed, these hidden outdoor pubs usually try to provide an ambience that conceals people's presence, fading them using plenty of darkness, especially in the seating areas, with minimal lights in the bar itself for functionality and very loud Afro-pop and Highlife music to overtake private conversations. The darkness covers the visual senses – the body – and the noise covers the oral senses – the speech. George, a 32-year-old financial consultant, always sits in the dark parts of the bar: 'For me when I sit in the dark, it's like, I can see you, but you can't see me.' Thus, George likes to maintain a position of power in public space, where he can choose who he wishes to interact with.

As an outsider I initially struggled to join these 'sacred circles' of men drinking and socialising in the dark; approaching a group of strangers sitting in complete darkness is not an easy task, in fact, it often feels intrusive and unsafe. One method I used to overcome this was by joining these groups when the sun was still up and chatting with them until darkness fell. However, it was only after a few months, when I got to know more people,

Figure 4.2 Sitting away from the light. Photo by the author.

70 *Nightlife & surveillance*

that I was asked to join these circles and I felt as though I was penetrating a very intimate encounter by getting a rare inside view. Often these circles of men who sat on plastic chairs felt more intimate here than when visiting private houses.

Those dark pubs and circles, or 'pockets of wakeful activity' to quote Ekirch (2006), are seen across town in various shapes and sizes. There were several pubs right outside the private houses of their owners who had converted their front yards into a liquor bar. Although it is a public business, the bar had an intimate semi-private feeling to it, and the bartenders tend to be members of the family, who live just behind the wall. Another pub was set up every night in the middle of an empty plot of land used for the neighbourhood's football games, funerals, and fire drills. This bar had very fresh air, as buildings did not cover it, and although it was in the heart of the neighbourhood, it felt secluded and secret. The more common bars are covered with curtains made of beads or bamboo fences, set like hideouts. I saw how men in those pubs smoke, drink, talk politics, do business, and even meet women outside of their marriages.

Efiyas bar is located right outside her house, facing the main street. She serves local and imported drinks to the neighbourhood's men who arrive every evening to drink and relax without the burden of driving home afterwards. They usually drink *Alomo Bitters* while sitting on plastic chairs by the sidewalk right outside the bar. Since they get drunk right in the heart of their community, the need for darkness as a type of veil is even stronger. One night, while I was enjoying a drink with these men, I started talking to Andrew, a Canadian Ghanaian who was visiting his family for three months. Andrew defined darkness as a beautiful feature of Ghanaian taverns that he often misses when living abroad:

> You wouldn't believe how comfortable people are in the dark. After a while, you stop thinking of it at all, and you develop eyes for it. There are so many things happening when it's dark, everything is possible.

In his ethnography of urban Mali, Chappatte (2014) discovered a remarkably similar phenomenon in the form of *maquis* – small and dark pubs located off the tarred roads of marginal residential streets. In those pubs, he argues, Muslims can consume alcohol using 'strategies of display and discretion' (Chappatte, 2014: 540). Very much like my experience, Chappatte testifies that he could not recognise individuals in these bars as he only saw human silhouettes. Most importantly, he explains that the *maquis* did not wish to 'domesticate the night; on the contrary, darkness constitutes the main feature of its ambience' (Chappatte, 2014: 532). Thus, through its opposition to light, darkness becomes indexical to social activities (and not the other way around as expected).

In Tema's dark pubs I also witnessed the practice of drinking marijuana cocktails, made from a mixture of weed, bitter herbs, and fruit juices. In

Accra, I was secretly told about such a drink, known as *Atemuda (Judgement Day)*, but in other pubs, these drinks were known as *Shockers, Two Fingers,* and *Amens.*[4] The widespread habit of cannabis drinks is another result of the social approach to truth and privacy. The drinks encourage consumption of marijuana without displaying the act of smoking or producing a distinctive scent. The innocent-looking cocktail glass camouflages an illegal and illegitimate substance but is publicly and institutionally tolerated thanks to its discrete form of consumption. This demonstrates Gal's (2002) notion of recursive public/private distinctions: the house and street are public in relation to the pub, just as the pub is public regarding the 'clusters' and consumption habits within it.

The convergence of marijuana with fruit cocktails also links with the use of proverbs and indirect talk, which increases the preference for discreteness and the avoidance of explicitness. Some of those hidden marijuana bars were operating right under my nose in various residential areas, but I only became aware of them when the people I met decided to take me there. One of these bars is actually a small and hidden room placed behind a restaurant, and meant for bringing secret girlfriends, known in Ghanaian slang and social media as 'side chicks.' The pub's DJ plays music videos on a plasma screen and, because it is in a hidden space with no windows, it has flashing and moving red lights, meant to create an erotic atmosphere. Couples come to this pub secretly after dark to have marijuana ice cream and then continue to a hotel or a 'movie house.'

Movie houses are another fascinating example of Ghana's secret nightlife. It is where couples go to watch a movie only as a public protocol that conceals their actual intent to have sex. These private houses offer bedrooms for hourly rent, but the service is sold like tickets to a movie. The sofa or bed is always in front of a television playing an African, Nigerian, or American film. Kwame, a 32-year-old blogger and programmer living in Accra, told me more about the taboo on public displays of romance and the importance of movie houses:

> Ghanaians have issues with women who dated too many people before marriage. She will be seen as a slut. This can be by her family or by her future boyfriend and his family. So this created a situation where you prefer people not knowing that you are dating until it is very very serious. Keeping your love life secret is important. Movie houses started as cinemas, but quickly people used them for sex and dating. If a girl tells her mother she is going out with her boyfriend the mother will not be happy and not allow it but going to the movies is fine. So the cinema is the perfect cover story, but it is really for dates because no one can bring the other one home... No one goes to a movie house to watch movies...

However, in recent years, the stigma around movie houses became too well known, and people started looking for new hideouts. In June 2016, a local

72 Nightlife & surveillance

news website published a short editor's tip with the title: 'Movie Houses... Be Aware They Are not a Place to Watch Films.' The article included a photo of a movie house from the inside and explained that although the idea of a 'local movie house, which offers VIP viewing for the latest movies,' is great in theory, their readers reported a different reality. These houses are actually 'brothels disguised as VIP movie venues. The only movies they provide are adult ones with a scantily clad lady waiting for you in a badly lit room to keep you company' (View Ghana, 2016).

Beyond the gendered injustices that might occur in these nightly hide-outs, such negative stigmas about certain urban spaces relate to Burrell's descriptions of internet cafés in Accra as enclaves dominated by young people who become 'partners in crime' as they escape from community surveillance. The mischievous behaviour of internet café users included scamming, spreading rumours, chatting with strangers, and watching porn. The latter is known as *Obonsam cartoons* (Twi for Satan's cartoons) and serves as an indirect codeword (Burrell 2012: 166).

Once again, employing indirectness, hints, and 'collective secrets' in urban pubs, movie houses, and internet cafés makes the interplay between private and public a semiotic issue. Whenever the hint becomes too direct, it disturbs the 'aesthetics of indirection' (Coe, 2008) and posts a risk of improper behaviour. To quote Simmel's idea of secret societies:

> The sociological significance of the secret is external, namely, the relationship between the one who has the secret and another who does not. But, as soon as a whole group uses secrecy as its form of existence, the significance becomes internal: the secret determines the reciprocal relations among those who share it in common.
>
> (Simmel, 1950: 345)

'Lover's Lane,' for instance, is a strip of land between 'Titanic Beach' and the Highway leading to Sakumono, a neighbourhood just outside Tema. This beach is commonly (yet secretly) known as a spot for 'naughty relationships.' This spot is interesting because it is not secluded in the apparent sense of the word; many people pass by there with their cars, and a major clubbing area is situated nearby. However, it is very dark, and the element of privacy is drawn from that darkness, not geographical distance or limited access. Secret lovers can park their cars by the cliff overlooking the sea; they play some music, chat, and socialise intimately. Dark drinking spots are very much the same, in the sense that they are at the heart of communal life like gas stations, residential streets, and trade centres, the only difference is they are entirely covered in darkness.

Many of the night's pleasures, therefore, are connected to 'secret love affairs' made possible after dark. In his article about life after dark in a Ghanaian village, van der Geest admits that he began his ethnography of night-time because of his own nightly affair with one of the villagers (2008: 23). He also

Nightlife & surveillance 73

describes an incident where four men attacked one of his informants after he was spotted talking to a married woman at night. In the Ghanaian context, he claims, such a nightly encounter can only mean one thing. However, speaking to the same woman during the day could have been even worse. van der Geest (2008: 29) quotes his research assistant who explains that visiting your secret lover at night indicates your respect and decency:

> If someone does see you, the person understands that you acted respectfully and he or she should in return respect you by not revealing what he saw. Flaunting your love and relationship in the daylight, however, would be a provocation. It implies that you do not care about what others think; that is where the disrespect lies.

Unlike Slater and Entwistle's (2018) interpretation of darkness and lights as 'messy materials,' van der Geest suggests that the night's cover is mostly symbolic: it sets a 'division of labour' between moral and immoral activities. Following the semantics of darkness is often more important than actually hiding your actions. In other words, it is about showing respect to the community by acknowledging that certain activities are inappropriate and should not be made visible.

Figure 4.3 Community surveillance at night meme. Author recreation.

74 *Nightlife & surveillance*

Proudly performing taboos is not seen as 'honest' or 'authentic' as it would be in more liberal societies. Being direct about one's sinful ways is seen as arrogant, impolite, and selfish. In a discussion about 'modes of silence' in African sexuality, Arnfred (2005: 74) gives the example of future wives instructed to keep their 'decent wifely behaviour' by keeping their love affairs secret, and of children instructed not to inform their father if they witnessed their mother in the act of infidelity. Once again, gender relations, darkness, and discreteness are intertwined in a complex system of ecological and cultural forces (Figure 4.3).

Daytime, as a semiotic and material opposition of night-time, is when everyone is obliged to follow the rules and obey their parents, teachers, pastors, and neighbours. People wait for night-time to release their hidden desires. The taboo around public displays of affection (PDA) is much debated in an African context.[5] In a journalistic article titled 'Talking to Strangers: Holiday in Ghana,' Tam (2012) asked Ghanaians 'deeply personal questions' which raised issues of privacy, darkness, and indirectness. Kape, a 28-year-old teacher, mentioned the link between darkness (or night-time) and the taboo on sexuality as he explained (Figure 4.4):

> Sometimes when I've talked to guys about sex ed[ucation], and they find out I'm selling condoms, they're like, 'Oh, what?' Meanwhile, they actually need a condom, and some will come and buy them at night. They feel shy, so they come by late.

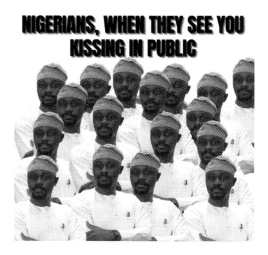

Figure 4.4 Nigerian man disapproving a public display of affection meme. Author recreation.

4.3 Spirits and symbols of darkness

One of my very first visits to a Sunday church service was in a newly established Pentecostal/Charismatic church, humbly located in a school classroom in a relatively distant residential area. The small room had about 12 people sitting on plastic chairs, all carefully listening to the young and enthusiastic Pastor Joseph. The service was an intense experience that included people speaking in tongues and demanding that our physical and spiritual enemies 'burn in a great fire.' These enemies are usually described as those kin members or friends who feel envious of our success and who wish us harm, whether consciously or not.

When the service was over Pastor Joseph, who had already heard about the 'special guest from Israel,' invited me to his office, where he wished to welcome me to the congregation. Due to my Jewish identity, he was incredibly excited to discuss theological, cultural, and political matters (like many other Ghanaians). During our conversation, I asked him about the theological meaning of darkness. He described the relationship between Ghanaians and darkness as a complex interaction with many 'layers':

> First, it's psychological. Ghanaians are very reserved people, very polite. We are not outgoing. So the dark often suits us better. Second is historical. Not too long ago, in the days of the military coup, many things were forbidden, and many people were hiding, so nightclubs and bars were very dark. It remained like that. Third is spiritual. In Ghana, the traditional belief is that the day cycle doesn't begin in the morning but once the sun has set on the previous night. So the peak of the energy is at night. At night is when the spiritual energy is at its strongest.

Pastor Joseph's interpretation of the Ghanaian bond to darkness is something that resonated with me throughout my fieldwork, and I could see how the discrete and reserved approach of many urbanites was often expressed concerning nightlife. A significant portion of this discourse about the night was connected to spirituality, Christianity, and prayer.

Pastor David, who lives in central Tema and works as a high school teacher, also discusses the issue of darkness in Ghana from a Christian perspective. He quoted the prophet Isaiah, who spoke about the spiritual and moral darkness that fell on the people of Israel. The prophecy includes the term 'treasures of darkness' (Isaiah, 45:3), which relates to the wealth and seduction entangled in pagan worship. Darkness can entice people to sin because they are hidden; therefore, it protects and threatens at the same time. For Pastor David, like other Christian guides in the community, night-time is a time to overcome our physical yearnings and engage in prayer.

Auntie Charity, who often visits Nenema's tailoring shop, stated, 'All human beings prefer the darkness and even Jesus said so. Because we love

76 *Nightlife & surveillance*

to sin, we love the dark. Light exposes us and no one wants to be exposed.'
Auntie Charity was actually referencing a verse from the New Testament
often quoted in Pentecostal churches: 'And this is the verdict: the light has
come into the world, but men loved darkness more than light because their
deeds were evil' (John, 3:19). This essential Christian, theological thought
assumes all men are sinners by nature and so they always wish to hide their
sinful ways. According to Meyer, this line of thought also relates to the
Pentecostal narrative of being 'born again' and making a 'radical rupture'
from one's personal sinful past and social environment (Meyer, 2004: 457).

Dumsor sets a 'fertile' ground for the use of darkness to conceal forbidden
activities. On one hot, dark night, Patience, a 65-year-old retired teacher,
was sitting on a plastic chair outside her house. We talked about the way
some Ghanaians prefer socialising in the dark. The preference is so evident,
she commented, that some urbanites actually 'enjoy' *Dumsor*:

> Our people need to know there is nothing good about *Dumsor*. As for us
> Christians, darkness is connected to the devil and lightness to Jesus. We
> used to live just like the enlightened world, most of my life, never had a
> power cut. Now darkness has come and with it the devil's ways.

That night I left Patience and retired to my room to write down her thoughts
and my impressions. After I fell asleep, and Patience had returned home, she
discovered that her husband died in his sleep. It was just as she had feared,
it was during darkness that she became a widow and it was the night that
took away her husband. As I lived nearby, I was woken up the next morning
by the sound of wailing women at dawn, shouting and mourning outside the
house and around the street: 'Papa is dead!'

Patience's view of the night as evil links to a strong Christian tradition in
West Africa that dichotomised white and black, light and dark, goodness
and evil. According to Meyer, such views go back to colonial missionaries
who disempowered traditional religions by incorporating them into Christianity as symbols of darkness (2012: 90). In his book *At Day's Close: Night in
Times Past*, Ekirch provides a historical account of the night and its perception across cultures. Regarding Christian Europe he writes:

> The Twenty-third Psalm speaks famously of the 'valley of the shadow
> of death.' Christianity, from its birth, revered God as the source of
> eternal light. His first act of creation, the gift of light, rescued the
> world from the domain of chaos. 'And the light shineth in the dark-
> ness,' declares the Book of John, 'and the darkness comprehended
> it not.' The Bible recounts a succession of sinister deeds – 'works of
> darkness' – perpetrated in the dead of night, including the betrayal of
> Christ in the Garden of Gethsemane. Following his crucifixion, 'there
> was darkness over all the land.'

(2006: 4)

Nightlife & surveillance 77

Ekirch (2006: 4) proposes that in many West African cultures 'like the Yoruba and Ibo peoples of Nigeria and the Ewe of Dahomey and Togoland, spirits assumed the form of witches at night, sowing misfortune and death in their wake.' Placed between such indigenous perceptions of darkness and such strong Christian symbolism around light and dark, many Ghanaians share the feeling that darkness is sinful and dangerous. Night-time is when witch-craft thrives, as witches are believed to elevate their souls while sleeping and invade their victim's slumber, leaving them with negative energies and wicked thoughts. Many people in Ghana, including the informants in this study, set an alarm clock to wake up just before dawn, when they are most vulnerable to witchcraft, so they can stay in control and pray for protection over them-selves and their dear ones. According to Meyer, 'born-again Christians are advised to play sermons and Christian music on cassettes during the night when demons are especially active' (Meyer, 1998: 341).

As Geschiere (1997) showed through his research in Southern Cameroon, African witchcraft is not a dying practice in the modern age but a response to it. In its modernised version, the fear of witchcraft is often interchange-able with that of crime, sin, political corruption, and improper behaviour (see Chapter 6 about digital witchcraft). Peter, a 28-year-old social media manager, living in Tema, for instance, does not like roaming around at night because it is when everyone's secret lives are manifested. Peter mentioned homosexuals and lesbians 'who come out only at night like vampires' and how people see them as spiritually dangerous due to their link with dark-ness. He said that he wouldn't be surprised if people in Ghana would begin to worship the devil soon because they adopt 'a Western behaviour,' often keeping it hidden.

Potently, Peter contrasted 'Western behaviour' with 'Christian behav-iour,' linking secular and liberal lifestyles to homosexuality and Satan. As a Pentecostal Christian who manages the church's weekly youth meetings, he feels strongly about abandoning the paths of his ancestors but not for the sake of being 'Western.' For Peter, following the path of God is about being modern, enlightened, and moral. The night, therefore, is not only a time of protection by limited visibility but also a time of danger and spiritual vulnerability.

Being hidden has a dialectic meaning of both liberation and fear, but per-ceptions about darkness go beyond a purely spiritual perception or a purely practical one. They often entail a modernist African approach to city life: the link Patience makes between night lights and 'the enlightened world' relates to a modernised and urbanised belief that 'outdoor illumination was now an "objective", almost scientific index of the "level of civilisation" of a given country' (Wishnitzer, 2014b: 79).

Kwabena, a returnee from London and a father of two children living in Tema, drew the same link between darkness and danger. He talked about his experience whilst visiting family in his hometown/village last summer. He had to go there because there was the funeral of a relative, who had been

78 *Nightlife & surveillance*

beheaded and murdered at night. No one knows exactly why, but the person who killed him was found holding his head, which was covered in blood. Kwabena hates going to his hometown and associates it with backwardness and nightmares – a way of life he cannot relate to and has nothing to do with. 'I cannot even spend one night there. I must drive to the nearest city and stay in a hotel.' 'Why?' I asked.

> It is too dark there! Yes, Tema is not like London, there are not many city lights, but I don't mind it. The village darkness is different. You might as well keep your eyes shut because you can't see anything. You see the lanterns floating around between the houses, only the light of lanterns. The people there love it this way. They don't mind it at all. Oh, When I go to Europe how I love the lights.

Kwabena attends a Pentecostal church, and it is evident that his self-definition as a modern, cosmopolitan, and morally lifted individual requires severing ties with his rural past and extended family. His hometown and its residents are associated with physical and spiritual darkness that he contrasts with his urban habitus and lifestyle. Therefore, the assumed parallels between light, order, morality, and truth on the one hand and darkness, chaos, sin, and lies on the other is often expressed by tagging certain areas, villages, or cities as dangerous and sinful. A well-known example is Ashaiman – a working-class town near Tema. Ashaiman is a relatively poor town, crowded and neglected, populated mostly by the Muslim community.[6] A drive through the town at night reveals vibrant, nocturnal activity in the form of clubs, pubs, markets, and informal street gatherings. The smell of dirty gutters and open sewers come up as beggars and drug sellers make their way amongst the cleaners, hawkers, and construction workers, who go from Ashaiman to Tema every day on foot. Kerosene lamps provide minimal light to allow for the correct transactions of money on each stall, but overall the streets remain very dark.

Tema residents mostly refer to Ashaiman town as a place of darkness, crime, and danger. Even though they appreciate the bargain finds and vibrant nightlife of this neighbouring town, they perceive Ashaiman as a hub for drugs, prostitution, and armed robbery. 'If you want to see real darkness,' I was told, 'go to Ashaiman.' Middle-class Tema men had stories about the dangers of night-time and how the youth of Ashaiman may attack, steal, and rob from anyone who wasn't careful. During Tema's Christmas festival, for instance, many of the locals chose to stay at home as 'Ashaiman boys get drunk and may rob you.'

As Ashaiman's residents are less likely to afford the luxury of generators or topped-up electricity, the impact of *Dumsor* is even more dramatic there. People in Tema draw implicit links between the town's darkness and the immoral and disobedient behaviour of its residents. Moreover, many Christian residents of Tema associate the alleged 'backwardness'

Nightlife & surveillance 79

of Ashaiman's population with their Islamic religion. This is a common practice of middle-class Pentecostals who often draw sharp lines between themselves (the 'saved' ones) and 'the Other' ('dead Christians,' Pagans, or Muslims). While Ghana's multiple religious groups live peacefully side by side, religious tensions surely exist. Ethnic divisions, public debates, church sermons, electronic and digital media (also known as televangelism) often reflect these tensions.

According to Hackett (1998), the enthusiastic use of media by Pentecostals is often seen as a threat by Muslim Imams in Ghana and Nigeria, who worry that their fellow Muslims will consume this captivating content in their private domestic settings. However, some Muslims look down at the evangelist culture of urban Pentecostals as overly exhibitionist, materialistic, and commercial (Hackett, 1998: 271). The core point is that boundary work between middle-class Pentecostals and surrounding groups is expressed through urban geography, theology, class, and nightlife cultures.

If night-time is considered so dangerous and chaotic, it is not a coincidence that many Pentecostal churches operate at night. After the hustle and bustle of daily life, many devoted Christians attend evening prayers or 'all nights,' accompanied by loud and bright audio-visual technologies that aim to penetrate both public and private urban spheres (van Dijk and Studiecentrum, 2001). Praying, singing, and listening to Charismatic pastors all night is a way of colonising the darkness and channelling its spiritual power to all that is divine and pure. The role of churches at night becomes even stronger during *Dumsor* when the generator-equipped churches offer nightly services with music, air fans, and lights. This advantage attracts many middle-class residents during the hot nights of lights-out, where the sight of youth and adults heading to church as a leisurely activity is very common.

Multimedia is an essential part of nocturnal worshipping in Ghanaian Pentecostal churches: plasma screens, speakers, lights, and microphones are an inseparable part of what defines an excellent service (Meyer, 2006). During night-time, technology becomes a spectacle of light and modernism. As Hackett (1998: 258) phrased it, 'the "modern" media are deemed an acceptable weapon for God's army in the battle against Satan.' During the military regime's night curfews, many Highlife musicians and bands 'migrated' to churches and 'gospelised' their secular music while mixing them with international genres such as Black American gospel, Rap, and Reggae (van Dijk and Studiecentrum, 2001). The international style of this music relates to the ban on traditional African music and instruments, which symbolise a continuation with the ancestral past and block the path to prosperity and fulfilment.

Some congregations operate more informally at night by gathering a relatively small audience in various recreational spaces and football courts, without any artificial lights. People gather and pray under the night sky, where only God, nature, and the congregation are present. This type of church service may feature prophets and spiritual rituals such as demon

80 *Nightlife & surveillance*

possession, singing, and wailing. These 'all nights' happen in complete darkness and include men, women, and children who pray together, over each other, and share their visions, nightmares, and hardships (Gifford, 2015: 157). The gatherings are relatively small and express a strong sense of intimacy, commitment, and privacy that allows a particular mode of liberation and release.

Darkness does not only elevate the spiritual awareness of the churchgoers but it also conceals them in a way that the highly visible and public Sunday church services can never do. On a typical Sunday church service, people come to see and be seen, carefully managing their reputation and external appearance while wearing their 'Sunday Best.' In Ghana, this usually means tailor-made dresses and suits made of colourful wax-cloth often called 'African cloth.'[7] Neatly ironed and hand-washed, these clothes, accompanied by 'technological jewellery' such as smartphones and tablets, are essential agents in the presentation of families and individuals as ideal members of the community – Christian, African, wealthy, and stylish.

Pentecostalism, with its shiny audio-visual effects and lavish decorations, created a commercial urban sphere that often 'distracts from the genuine religious experience' (Meyer, 2006: 299). As anthropologists showed, nocturnal activities are often guided by the dangers of limited visibility leading to the full exploitation of other senses such as touch and hearing (Galinier et al., 2010: 827). During nightly prayers like these, people can focus on spiritual worship and rituals without the additional layer of collective visibility and the inevitable judgements and surveillance it entails. In other words, night restores prayer to its private state.

Although they often brand themselves as Pentecostal, these special nightly services are more associated with the AIC (African Independent churches) movement that aimed to establish 'authentic' African worship detached from colonial influences (Meyer, 2004; Engelke, 2010). Only lower middle-class informants and working-class acquaintances took me to these churches, and the experience was radically different. The sharp differences between the audio-visual extravaganza of Pentecostal nightly services and the intimate natural darkness of AIC reflect the ongoing boundary work between these competing types of worship and the symbolic connection between economy, spirituality, and darkness.

We can place the practice of worship and prayer, therefore, on a spectrum that moves between a private or isolated prayer at home, or on a mobile phone, to public collective prayer. This spectrum also runs between prayer at night, which limits vision and heightens spiritual focus, to prayer at day, which gains its impact by seeing and being seen and by presenting oneself as the 'correct' middle-class church goer based on visual cues. These parallels echo the scholarly distinctions between privacy as the space between visibility and invisibility versus its role as a barrier between individuality and collectivity (Weintraub, 1997). Such a complex network of churchgoers, technological infrastructures, and environmental conditions is the foundation of many privacy practices and how people keep certain aspects of themselves hidden.

To sum, the ethnographic exploration of night-time in Tema during *Dumsor* shows a constant tension between the different approaches to night-time: should we fight the darkness with artificial lights, or should we give in to it? Should we see what possibilities it offers, or should we tame it? Are we losing valuable labour time or are we pausing the 'prosperity gospel' and merely enjoying the moonlight?

Darkness is embraced and resisted; it symbolises danger, witchcraft, sin, and demons but also liberation, intimacy, and leisure; it poses risks such as crime and supernatural attacks, but it also allows unique forms of interaction and spiritual worship. As Slater and Entwistle (2018) noted regarding light, darkness is also a 'relational material.' By departing from the sociological readings of night-time as a form of economy and addressing darkness as a material entity, I was able to explore its essential role in facilitating urban privacy.

Crucial to the next chapters is how darkness in urban Ghana relates to privacy and secrecy in symbolic and material ways. The line between night and day is often a metaphorical line between private and public. This line is needed for the social order as urbanites use it to fulfil their 'forbidden' desires, but this line is also crossed and challenged in various ways. The recursive divisions of night-time into public Pentecostal church services versus private pubs and bars is yet another example of the semiotic and dynamic nature of urban privacy in Ghana.

References

Anderson, T. L. (2009) 'Better to Complicate, Rather than Homogenize, Urban Nightlife: A Response to Grazian', *Sociological Forum*, 24(4), pp. 918–925. doi: 10.1111/j.1573-7861.2009.01144.x.

Ankomah, F. and Attuquaye, E. (2007) 'Ghana's Electricity Industry', *ESI-Africa. com*. Available at: https://www.esi-africa.com/news/ghana-s-electricity-industry/ (Accessed: 6 February 2017).

Arnfred, S. (2005) '"African Sexuality"/Sexuality in Africa: Tales and Silences', in Arnfred, S. (ed.) *Re-thinking Sexualities in Africa*. Second edition. Sweden: Nordic Africa Institute, pp. 59–76.

Beamish, A. (2015) 'Boston', in Isenstadt, S., Malie Petty, M., and Neumann, D. (eds) *Cities of Light: Two Centuries of Urban Illumination*. New York and London: Routledge, pp. 10–19.

Bennie, J. et al. (2014) 'Contrasting Trends in Light Pollution Across Europe Based on Satellite Observed Night Time Lights', *Scientific Reports*, 4. doi: 10.1038/srep03789.

Burrell, J. (2009) 'Could Connectivity Replace Mobility? An Analysis of Internet Cafe Use Patterns in Accra, Ghana', in Bruijn, M. de, Nyamnjoh, F., and Brinkman, I. (eds) *Mobile Phones: The New Talking Drums of Everyday Africa*. Bamenda, Cameroon: Langaa RPCIG, pp. 151–169.

82 *Nightlife & surveillance*

Burrell, J. (2012) *Producing the Internet and Development: An Ethnography of Internet Café Use in Accra, Ghana*. Ph. D. The London School of Economics and Political Science (LSE).

Chappatte, A. (2014) 'Night Life in Southern Urban Mali: Being a Muslim Maquisard in Bougouni', *Journal of the Royal Anthropological Institute*, 20(3), pp. 526–544. doi: 10.1111/1467–9655.12121.

Coaffee, J. (2004) 'Rings of Steel, Rings of Concrete and Rings of Confidence: Designing out Terrorism in Central London pre and post September 11th', *International Journal of Urban and Regional Research*, 28(1), pp. 201–211. doi: 10.1111/j.0309–1317.2004.00511.x.

Coe, C. (2008) 'The Structuring of Feeling in Ghanaian Transnational Families', *City & Society*, 20(2), pp. 222–250. doi: 10.1111/j.1548-744X.2008.00018.x.

Cole, C. M., Manuh, T. and Miescher, S. (2007) *Africa After Gender?* Bloomington: Indiana University Press.

Collins, J. (2005) 'A Social History of Ghanaian Popular Entertainment since Independence', *Transactions of the Historical Society of Ghana*, 9, pp. 17–40.

Dankwa, S. O. (2009) '"It's a Silent Trade": Female Same-Sex Intimacies in Post-Colonial Ghana', *NORA – Nordic Journal of Feminist and Gender Research*, 17(3), pp. 192–205. doi: 10.1080/08038740903117208.

Davoudian, N. (2019) *Urban Lighting for People: Evidence-Based Lighting Design for the Built Environment*. London: RIBA Publishing.

DeNicola, L. (2011) 'The Digital as Para-World: Design, Anthropology and Information Technologies', in Clarke, A. (ed.) *Design Anthropology: Object Culture in the 21st century*. New York: Springer, pp. 202–211.

Ekirch, A. R. (2006) *At Day's Close: Night in Times Past*. New York; London: W. W. Norton & Company.

Engelke, M. (2010) 'Past Pentecostalism: Notes on Rupture, Realignment, and Everyday Life in Pentecostal and African Independent Churches', *Africa*, 80(2), pp. 177–199. doi: 10.3366/afr.2010.0201.

Gal, S. (2002) 'A Semiotics of the Public/Private Distinction', *Differences: A Journal of Feminist Cultural Studies*, 13(1), pp. 77–95.

Galinier, J. et al. (2010) 'Anthropology of the Night: Cross-Disciplinary Investigations', *Current Anthropology*, 51(6), pp. 819–847. doi: 10.1086/653691.

Gans, H. J. (1962) *The Urban Villagers: Group and Class in the Life of Italians-Americans*. New York: Free Press of Glencoe.

Geschiere, P. (1997) *The Modernity of Witchcraft: Politics and the Occult in Postcolonial Africa*. Charlottesville: University of Virginia Press.

Gifford, P. (2015) *Christianity, Development and Modernity in Africa*. London: Hurst.

Goold, B. J. (2003) *Public Area Surveillance and Police Work: The Impact of CCTV on Police Behaviour and Autonomy*. SSRN Scholarly Paper ID 1585513. Rochester, NY: Social Science Research Network. Available at: http://papers.ssrn.com/abstract=1585513 (Accessed: 17 August 2016).

Graham, K. and Wells, S. (2003) '"Somebody's Gonna Get Their Head Kicked in Tonight!" Aggression Among Young Males in Bars—A Question of Values?', *The British Journal of Criminology*, 43(3), pp. 546–566. doi: 10.1093/bjc/43.3.546.

Grazian, D. (2007) 'The Girl Hunt: Urban Nightlife and the Performance of Masculinity as Collective Activity', *Symbolic Interaction*, 30(2), pp. 221–243. doi: 10.1525/si.2007.30.2.221.

Nightlife & surveillance 83

Grazian, D. (2008) *On the Make: The Hustle of Urban Nightlife*. Chicago: University of Chicago Press.

Grazian, D. (2009) 'Urban Nightlife, Social Capital, and the Public Life of Cities1', *Sociological Forum*, 24(4), pp. 908–917. doi: 10.1111/j.1573-7861.2009.01143.x.

Gupta, A. (2015) 'An Anthropology of Electricity from the Global South', *Cultural Anthropology*, 30(4), pp. 555–568. doi: 10.14506/ca30.4.04.

Hackett, R. I. J. (1998) 'Charismatic/Pentecostal Appropriation of Media Technologies in Nigeria and Ghana', *Journal of Religion in Africa*, 28(3), pp. 258–277. doi: 10.2307/1581571.

Hall, S. and Winlow, S. (2005) 'Night-Time Leisure and Violence in the Breakdown of the Pseudo-pacification Process', *Probation Journal*, 52(4), pp. 376–389. doi: 10.1177/0264550505058943.

Jacobs, J. (1992) *The Death and Life of Great American Cities*. Reissue edition. New York: Vintage.

Lefebvre, H. (1968) *Le droit à la ville*. Paris: Anthropos.

Melbin, M. (1978) 'Night As Frontier', *American Sociological Review*, 43(1), pp. 3–22. doi: 10.2307/2094758.

Meyer, B. (1998) '"Make a Complete Break with the Past." Memory and Post-Colonial Modernity in Ghanaian Pentecostalist Discourse', *Journal of Religion in Africa*, 28(3), pp. 316–349. doi: 10.2307/1581573.

Meyer, B. (2004) 'Christianity in Africa: From African Independent to Pentecostal-Charismatic Churches', *Annual Review of Anthropology*, 33(1), pp. 447–474. doi: 10.1146/annurev.anthro.33.070203.143835.

Meyer, B. (2006) 'Impossible Representations. Pentecostalism, Vision, and Video Technology in Ghana', in Meyer, B. and Moors, A. (eds) *Religion, Media, and the Public Sphere*. Bloomington: Indiana University Press, pp. 290–312. Available at: http://dare.uva.nl/record/1/261248 (Accessed: 19 July 2016).

Meyer, B. (2012) 'Religious and Secular, "Spiritual" and "Physical" in Ghana', in Bender, C. and Taves, A. (eds) *What Matters? Ethnographies of Value in a (not so) Secular Age*. New York: Columbia University Press (SSRC), pp. 86–118.

Miller, D. (2016) *Social Media in an English Village*. London: UCL Press. doi: 10.14324/111.9781910634431.

Nye, D. E. (2013) *When the Lights Went Out: A History of Blackouts in America*. Cambridge, MA: The MIT Press.

Oldenburg, R. (1989) *The Great Good Place: Café, Coffee Shops, Community Centers, Beauty Parlors, General Stores, Bars, Hangouts, and How They Get You Through the Day*. St. Paul: Paragon House Publishers.

Oyuke, A., Halley Penar, P. and Howard, B. (2016) *Off-Grid or 'Off-On': Lack of Access, Unreliable Electricity Supply Still Plague Majority of Africans*. Dispatch: Round VI 75. Africa: Afro Barometer, p. 26.

Sackeyfio, N. (2017) *Energy Politics and Rural Development in Sub-Saharan Africa: The Case of Ghana*. New York: Springer.

Sasson, T. and Nelson, M. K. (1996) 'Danger, Community, and the Meaning of Crime Watch an Analysis of the Discourses of African American and White Participants', *Journal of Contemporary Ethnography*, 25(2), pp. 171–200. doi: 10.1177/089124196025002001.

Schildkrout, E. (1973) 'The Fostering of Children in Urban Ghana: Problems of Ethnographic Analysis in a Multi-Cultural Context', *Urban Anthropology*, 2(1), pp. 048–073.

84 *Nightlife & surveillance*

Simmel, G. (1950) 'Sociologie: Inquiries into the Construction of Social Forms', in Wolff, K. H. (ed.) *The Sociology of Georg Simmel*. Glencoe: Free Press, pp. 307–375.

Slater, D. and Entwistle, J. (2018) 'Light as Material/Lighting as Practice: Urban Lighting and Energy', *Science Museum Group Journal*, 9(9). doi: 10.15180/180906.

Tam, R. (2012) *Talking to Strangers: Holiday in Ghana, Nerve*. Available at: http://www.nerve.com/love-sex/talking-to-strangers/talking-to-strangers-holiday-in-ghana (Accessed: 6 July 2017).

Tureli, I. (2015) 'Istanbul', in Isenstadt, S., Malie Petty, M., and Neumann, D. (eds) *Cities of Light: Two Centuries of Urban Illumination*. New York: London: Routledge, pp. 1–9.

van der Geest, S. (2008) 'Life After Dark in Kwahu Tafo, Ghana', *Etnofoor*, 20.

van Dijk, R. A. and Studiecentrum, A. (2001) 'Contesting Silence: The Ban on Drumming and the Musical Politics of Pentecostalism in Ghana', *Ghana Studies*, 4, pp. 31–64.

View Ghana (2016) 'Movie Houses, Be Aware They Are Not for Watching Films', *View Ghana: Putting Ghana online*, 2 June. Available at: http://www.viewghana.com/movie-houses-be-aware/ (Accessed: 29 June 2017).

Weintraub, J. (1997) 'The Theory and Politics of the Public/Private Distinction', in Kumar, K. (ed.) *Public and Private in Thought and Practice: Perspectives on a Grand Dichotomy*. Chicago, IL: University of Chicago Press, pp. 1–39.

Wishnitzer, A. (2014a) 'Into the Dark: Power, Light, and Noctorunal Life in 18th Century Istanbul', *International Journal of Middle East Studies*, 46(3), pp. 513–531. doi: 10.1017/S0020743814000579.

Wishnitzer, A. (2014b) 'Shedding New Light: Outdoor Illumination in Late Ottoman Istanbul', in Meier, J. et al. (eds) *Urban Lighting, Light Pollution and Society*. First Edition. New York: Routledge, pp. 66–84.

Woods, M. N. (2015) 'Mumbai', in Isenstadt, S., Malie Petty, M., and Neumann, D. (eds) *Cities of Light: Two Centuries of Urban Illumination*. New York: London: Routledge, pp. 37–44.

Notes

1 According to Schildkrout (1973), it is highly prevalent in Ghanaian cities to establish 'fictive kin,' 'parental transactions,' and 'child fostering' due to the diluting of family support systems as people move from villages to cities. People in Tema often refer to each other as mother, father, brother, and sister, creating a familial atmosphere in an unfamiliar urban melting pot.

2 In 2007 only 45%–47% of Ghanaians, including 15%–17% of the rural population, had access to regular grid electricity (Ankomah and Attuquaye, 2007). By 2014/2015 although over 80% of Ghana's population was connected to a grid, only 37% reported constant connection (Oyuke, Halley Penar and Howard, 2016). Therefore, there is a difference in official access to 'actual connectivity, quantity and supply' (Sackeyfio, 2017: 60).

3 To read more about the unique experience of gender in Africa see Oyewumi (2005), Cole, Manuh, and Miescher (2007).

4 Cocktails infused with marijuana tend to have spiritual and religious names, relating their powerful psychic effects to divine revelations. They are often sold as sex-enhancing beverages (*'Atemuda' Is Laced with Indian Hemp - GSA | General News 2012-03-28*, 2012).

Nightlife & surveillance 85

5 An interesting project about this issue is by the Nigerian filmmaker Zina Saro Wiwa who created a documentary project titled 'Eaten by the heart' with a chapter called "How do Africans kiss?" The video features various young Africans confronting this supposedly simple question and describing the public affection of love and kissing as essentially 'un-African.' Most interviewees in the video stated that they have never seen Africans kissing, some referred to kissing as a European invention, and others pointed out the secret and hidden manner of African kissing.

6 Muslims constitute about 20% of Ghana's religious sphere and are concentrated mainly in the Northern Region (*Adherent Statistics of World Religions by Country*, 2016). Ghana's Muslim communities are mostly indigenous groups (such as the Hausa and Wangara) who adopted Islam in the 15th century and have a language, cuisine, and tradition distinct from surroundings groups in Ghana but also from the Arab world.

7 A Dutch company called Vlisco most notably manufactures the cloth but once it enters the West African consumer markets its rich patterns and illustrations are assigned with proverbs and idioms from Ghana's rich oral culture. Thanks to competitors such as Hitarget and other Chinese manufacturers the imported cloth now caters to an urban middle-class consumer who gets to combine African aesthetics with international prestige.

5 Hidden and incomplete
Middle-Class houses

Urban life in Ghana is divided into highly public and highly private spheres according to a temporal structure of night and day. However, this division is incomplete without a detailed examination of its architectural structure, especially in the private domestic sphere.[1] Keeping in mind the contextual role of houses in a binary system between villages and cities (Chapter 3), this chapter gradually enters the home, starting from its exterior surroundings (infrastructure and front yards), into its indoor spaces (living rooms and bedrooms).

Two modernist ideologies, the architectural and the theological, operate in Tema and promote a conjugal (and often isolated) middle-class lifestyle. Urbanites draw physical and metaphorical boundaries around their geographical origins, local names, construction sites, gated houses, front yards, living rooms, and bedrooms according to these sets of values and oppositions. The digitisation of domestic and urban spaces is an additional force that challenges, enhances, and reflects these spaces. By adopting a material culture approach, I analysed privacy practices in middle-class households, whilst also addressing the growing presence of digital media and how they influenced such practices.

There is a rich body of anthropological literature about houses and domestic spaces as material embodiments of otherwise intangible social relations, values, and identities. Anthropologists examined the gendered divisions of domestic spaces (Bourdieu, 1970; Moore, 1986; Pink, 2004), the house's role in shaping identities and consumption habits (Halle, 1991; Miller, 2001; Marcus, 2006; Money, 2007; Horst, 2009), the symbolic parallels between vernacular architecture and the body (John, 1963; Blier, 1983; Carsten and Hugh-Jones, 1995; Joyce and Gillespie, 2000), and the profound relationship between houses, history, and memory (Bahloul, 1996; Marcoux, 2001; Drazin and Frohlich, 2007; Morton, 2007). A more contemporary wave of literature examines the domestication of digital and electronic technologies and how they influence relations within the home (Silverstone et al., 1989; Silverstone, 1992; Haddon, 2004).

It was probably Levi-Strauss (1988) who began this anthropological endeavour, through his account of 'house societies.' Houses, he argued, have

DOI: 10.4324/9781003187424-5

Hidden and incomplete 87

the ability to bridge between separate families, genders, and communities, by uniting them in time and space, and replacing 'an internal duality with an external unity' (Lévi-Strauss quoted in Buchli, 2013: 72). This move away from kinship as the main focal point of ethnography into domestic spaces is more suitable to many non-Western societies where household and biological families are not necessarily interchangeable (Yanagisako, 1979). However, Levi-Strauss paid minimal attention to the actual material properties of 'house societies' (Buchli, 2013: 6).

Through his pivotal analysis of the Berber Kabyle house, Bourdieu (1970) offered a distinctly material reading of the house itself as a social text that not only symbolises but embodies social practices and habitus. Bourdieu pointed at two separate spaces within the house as a set of binary oppositions between women and men, nature and culture, light and darkness, death and life, private and public, respectively (Bourdieu, 1970: 157). Furthermore, he suggested that these inner oppositions are re-enacted between the house as a whole and the rest of the world (Bourdieu, 1970: 160). This idea echoes Gal's concept of fractal recursions: the house marks an entirely private sphere when opposed as a whole to the public street, but this division is reproduced internally, between the living room and bedrooms (Gal, 2002: 82). Even the public living room, Gal argues, can be divided into private and public interactions through certain gestures, sounds, and (I would add) digital communications (2002: 82).

The case of urban Ghana further challenges these binary divisions, as the streets and yards around the house often become 'publicly private' – public platforms that people use for domestic interactions (Lange, 2007). Furthermore, the literature about women as bounded to the private sphere and men as essentially public entities (e.g., Bourdieu, 1970; Moore, 1986; Landes, 2003) seems inapplicable in the urban Ghanaian context, where women take a highly visible role in both private and public space, for instance, in markets and trade points. Divisions between strangers and insiders, adults and children, believers and sinners, characterise the spacework in urban Ghana more accurately than gendered divisions.

My experience of researching private households was quite challenging, as outsiders are not easily welcomed into the house. Many house-related ethnographic methods proved to be incompatible in this field.[2] For instance, while my original research plan included full 'video tours' inside the house (as suggested by Pink and Mackley, 2012), informants generally refused this request directly and indirectly.[3] In his introduction to the book *Home Possessions: Material Culture Behind Closed Doors*, Miller (2001: 15) states that 'anthropology that thinks that sensitivity about being too intrusive is demonstrated by remaining outside and respecting the distance of conventional social proxemics is a dead anthropology.'

This statement poses a threat to the data presented herein. However, in the Ghanaian context even close friends and family avoid intrusive or rude behaviour regarding the home. Pentecostal pastors often warn the

88 *Hidden and incomplete*

Figure 5.1 Sketch of a typical house in Tema. Sketch by the author.

community about guests poisoning their food or leaving harmful enchanted objects in the house. According to this discourse, although an envious or sinful relative is not a burglar in the legal sense, his/her intrusion to the private nuclear realm can be just as harmful. Churchgoers often engage in 'cleansing rituals' meant to disinfect their private homes after such visits. The fear of one's domestic privacy being invaded, therefore, is also a fear of losing control over one's spiritual and physical wellbeing.

As an alternative research method, I had to work according to the cultural codes communicated to me and respect the clear boundaries of inside and outside/ private and public. At one end of the scale were the families I lived with, where I got to see the entire house and its daily routine, but most people were on the other end of the scale, which means I mostly spent time in their yards and verandas. This challenge alone became an insight from which I drew knowledge about cultures of privacy and divisions of space. Whilst gently trying to push those boundaries, I was mostly interested in mapping them. This chapter's structure follows this spectrum, starting from outside the house and working its way inwards. Overall, I visited about 40 households throughout the course of my fieldwork. Figure 5.1 provides a rough outline of a typical house in Tema, based on the spatial divisions that this chapter explores.

5.1 God will make a way: the unfinished house

Action Chapel International is a Pentecostal church based in Tema and known for its young and urban middle-class congregation, Charismatic sermons, stylish and colourful fashion, and live gospel music. To show what the

Hidden and incomplete 89

church is doing with the regular tithes and donations given by its members, the bishop decided to hold this year's New Year's Eve prayers at the construction site of the new church. It may take a few years before the building is completed and the flock can attend church in this improved and magnificent structure but what could be better than talking about hopes and future aspirations for the upcoming year in a construction site of a church – the heart of communal, familial, and spiritual life in urban Ghana.

In tune with the Pentecostal promise to domesticate and brighten urban night-time, the service began just before 12 AM. Hundreds of guests wearing tailor-made white clothes with iPads and mobile phone cameras in hand gathered for praying. They sang and danced right into the New Year. They arrived as nuclear families in private cars, carrying an array of holiday gift packages such as decorated African cloth, rice bags, and tropical juice cartons. The vast and tall structure still lay bare, made of cement, stones, and wooden poles, with large architectural arches and many plastic chairs. There was neither a roof nor walls, neither doors nor windows but there was a material concept – a promise – 'this will be our church.'

Due to the lack of electric infrastructure at the site, large generators provided power for lights and music. It was loud and festive, and trumpets, drums, and keyboards played alongside the charismatic speeches, the singing, and chatter. Precisely at 12 AM fireworks filled the sky where a ceiling should have been. Ironically, at this point, the generators failed, causing complete darkness and silence. This didn't stop people from celebrating and worshipping in total darkness, without any music. After a few minutes, the generators resumed – 'The house of the lord' was almost flickering between spirit and matter, modernity and tradition, technology and prayer.

Over a year afterwards, the church was more or less still in the same bare state. Most of the funds were used to build an office building and a Sunday school behind the cathedral (the most expensive part of the building). However, by then the weekly Sunday prayers were still regularly held at the construction site, and the old church had been left behind. In that sense, the unfinished structure became a permanent one. The church was being used and occupied long before its completion. Moreover, the structure became a site to build memories, hopes, love, and relations since its very beginning, much like a mother to be celebrating her ultrasound scan during pregnancy.

The story of Action Chapel may seem very symbolic, but it also reflects a very ordinary economic reality in Ghana, whereby unfinished structures become dynamic living spaces. In his book *Home Possessions: Material Culture Behind Closed Doors* (2001), Miller calls to examine houses as processes rather than places, arguing that the house is never a fixed nor a completed material entity but a constantly evolving space. This point is illustrated vividly across Africa, where house constructions and renovations can last decades and families can often dwell in houses since the early stages of construction. This rudimentary housing culture remains, as houses are in an ongoing process of renovating, building, furnishing, and expanding.

90 *Hidden and incomplete*

Samuel (28) and his mother (55) were living in one of the first Communities in Tema, building their new family home in one of its 'new lands,' an up and coming, middle-class residential area. Although they planned to move to the new house at a later stage because it was still incomplete, their landlord at the time raised their rent so they decided to move out right away: 'the windows and doors are already there so we can move in. Then we can do the rest from there.' Together with his mother, sister, and brother-in-law, Samuel brought mattresses, clothes, and toiletries, connected the electricity and water, and moved into the house in the midst of the building process. After about a year, Samuel and his family painted the walls, tiled the floors, and purchased furniture, but only in certain parts of the house. Most of it was still under construction or unfinished.[4]

A European building engineer working in Accra once told me that when building houses in Ghana, gates, doors, and windows are not installed last as he commonly knew but instead they'd be fitted in the very early stages of construction. The aim is to initiate the structure as a place of living as soon as possible. Once people can sleep and store their belongings safely in the construction, it can be used as a 'house.' Usually, the first tenants to move in are villagers or working-class families, who are hired to guard the construction site and building materials. This informal renting period can take a few years.[5] At a later stage, after renting out the uncompleted house to fund additional building works, the home owners or their relatives settle in. Generally, families reside in houses with many bare or raw architectural elements such as cement floors, unplastered walls, and uncompleted interior instalments (e.g., doors and door frames; Figure 5.2).

Figure 5.2 Unfinished house. Photo by the author.

Hidden and incomplete 91

What are the reasons for this phenomenon? Enyonam, a young architect living in Tema, tells me most Ghanaians buy land and houses because renting is perceived as unstable or risky. This means the building process is slow and complicated and is not often backed up with the necessary funds. 'Ghana only has about 900 registered architects because Ghanaians can't really afford their service,' she explains. 'Sometimes clients come with an initial budget that cannot support their dream. A client can come with 300,000 cedis and describe a 2-million-cedi house.'[6] A common Ghanaian Christian phrase in this context is 'When I start God will make a way,'[7] which means once a person begins a project, even if it is beyond his or her initial means, things will fall into place. Such philosophy is critical in understanding middle-class life and the Pentecostal prosperity gospel – budget may not be on their side, but time, aspiration, and belief surely are.

Due to financial limitations or living abroad until retirement, many home owners save up their money in batches and invest it in different sections or elements of their houses, every few years.[8] During my fieldwork, I received photos via WhatsApp from informants who were constructing their houses; I saw the stages as they gradually added more layers and features. Furniture can be passed on to family members or friends but tiled floors, for instance, are an expensive luxury and many houses either choose to keep the raw cement floor or install temporary patterned linoleum flooring. Similarly, doors, even bathroom and toilet doors, are often missing inside the house and are replaced with curtains or beads. All these circumstances count towards the cultural perception of the house interior as a highly private space.

While the house interior is a hidden and rudimentary space, the house exterior is a public statement of wealth, power, and taste. van der Geest (2000) describes how in rural Ghana, right before a funeral, the houses of the deceased get a full 'facelift': the outside walls are freshly painted, yards are cemented, the roofs and electricity are repaired, and even the road leading to the house is improved. These are all preparations for visitors to see the mourning family in a respectful manner. The allocation of funds to the exterior, he argues, sometimes comes at the expense of actual care for the elderly still living. Thus, investing resources in what is exposed to public gaze often means neglecting what is hidden.

Sometimes waiting patiently for a specific element of the house exterior to be completed is a result of an ambitious taste and the desire to reference architecture 'from outside' (abroad). For instance, Robert, a hotel owner and businessman who also lives in an old part of Tema, is building his future home in an up and coming residential area 'new land.' He uses an American website called Houzz.com which offers 'a new way to design your home' by discovering design ideas, connecting with professionals, and looking at photographs. This digital platform allows him to 'import' architectural ideas and express a cosmopolitan and prestigious identity through tiled walls, colourful structures, high turrets, and European gazebos.

92 *Hidden and incomplete*

Robert also draws inspiration from his upper-class neighbours, such as the American-Ghanaian returnee who built his fancy house nearby. Robert likes to drive around his new neighbourhood and snap photos with his mobile phone. He later sends these photos to his designer (an informal architect) and together they decide on a plan. Robert then spends the next couple of months saving up for the materials and construction fees he needs. It will take a few years before his vision is complete.

The 'dream house' is thus built slowly but surely while staying in tune with financial abilities and social aspirations. As Horst phrased it in her ethnography of return migrants in Jamaica, 'the home is a rite of passage that embodies the crowning achievement of a lifelong dream' (Horst, 2011: 5). Robert explained it clearly: 'if I wanted a normal house, I would have finished it a long time ago.' As he goes on his routine visit to the construction site, he climbs up a cement stairway that provides a bird's-eye view of the structure. Up there he imagines his future house and even guides me through his fantasy. He describes the modern kitchen and 'traditional' outdoor kitchen, the house shop, and the ground floor bedroom for elderly relatives, and the tropical fruit trees along the wall. He then points at the 'summer hut' built for 'when guests come, but we don't want them to enter the house' and even the medieval-looking peephole in the gate, which allows the guard to see who seeks entrance. At this very moment, most of it was still cement, but he knew it would not take long before I'd revisit him to see his vision fulfilled. Meanwhile, he proceeded to take dozens of photographs on his mobile phone, and when I asked if he intended to share them on Facebook, he replied: 'No, no. When I finish, I will invite all my friends and family and show them how I worked hard when I was a young man.'

Robert's decision to keep the building process private is crucial in understanding privacy in Ghana. There is a clear division between what should be exhibited and performed versus what should be kept discrete. The incomplete should be kept hidden from public view because premature exposure puts the risk of jealousy and negative intentions of the community to 'jinx' it. This taboo applies during pregnancy, travelling abroad, planning a wedding, saving up to buy a mobile phone, and more (see Chapter 6). Social media threatens the same convention as people face a new dilemma – to share or not to share? In the words of Palen and Dourish (2003: 135), digitisation creates 'a set of tensions between competing needs.' The ritual of installing doors and windows, in this context, can be compared to setting up a password when opening a social media account, or making it un-searchable through privacy settings; it is about monitoring the crossings in and out of one's private sphere and maintaining control through material objects that regulate visibility, access, and privacy. Moreover, if uncompleted things are deemed as private and if the house is never truly completed, I argue that the house – in varying degrees – is forever private (Figure 5.3).

Figure 5.3 Envisioning the 'dream house.' Photo by the author.

5.2 The fortress: material culture of gates & walls

> To understand city walls and other settlement enclosures in tropical Africa, one should perhaps rid oneself of Eurocentric ideas of city walls, in which seemingly impregnable urban fortifications... are closely manned by valiant defenders, who rain death and destruction on the heads of massed, determined attackers...
>
> (Connah, 2000: 42)

In his historical study about African urbanism and 'contained communities,' Connah claims that although walls in pre-colonial African cities were meant to protect the communities within their boundaries, this protection was often more psychological than physical. The walls do not block vicious attackers but set the social demarcation of each group, play a role as status symbols, and help regulate and control movement. These 'contained communities' can nowadays be seen in the form of gated communities and houses. Gating entire neighbourhoods tend to be more orientated towards nuclear, upper-class, elite families with an exceptionally modernised lifestyle but gating individual houses or a few living units is standard all across Ghana, including its rural areas and especially in cities (Grant, 2009: 63).

The gate system in Tema (and to an extent all of Sub-Saharan Africa) is such an essential part of the urban landscape that it is nearly impossible to ignore its material properties and effects on everyday life. Tema urbanites install iron gates with padlocks, connected to walls made of stone that are often topped with electric fences or shards of glass for extra protection. While strolling through the streets of Tema, you will most likely see high

94 *Hidden and incomplete*

walls and colourful gates and rarely get a glimpse of the actual houses. The colourful iron gates regulate the movement of household members and guests, block the house from pedestrians' sight, protect the tenants from armed robberies and stray animals, and express middle-class lifestyle.

The proliferation of gated neighbourhoods and gated houses is part of a global middle-class consumer market whereby gates and walls reflect the need of particular circles to protect and enclose themselves from the uncertainties of city life (Caldeira, 2000; Low, 2001). Low (1997) named these gated spaces as 'fortresses of fear' and other scholars have shown how these walls materially produce 'new forms of disjointed, fragmented life and fragmented forms of citizenship' (Buchli, 2013: 102). According to Murray (2004: 9):

> The exponential expansion of such fortified enclaves as gated residential communities, enclosed shopping malls, cocooned shopping complexes, and luxury entertainment sites offers a globally tested mechanism for the propertied middle (and upper) classes to insulate themselves from the threats – real or imagined – to their physical security and sense of wellbeing... part and parcel of the *revanchist* (original emphasis) urbanism where the defence of lifestyle and privilege is governed by the spatial logic of exclusion and intolerance and insularity.
>
> (Quoted in Otiso and Owusu, 2008: 152)

The emergence of gated communities in Greater Accra was first taken on by non-resident Ghanaians and expatriates, but its luxurious aura quickly spread to the middle class and is becoming increasingly popular across the country (Grant, 2005). In his detailed study of gated communities in Accra, Grant (2005: 669) lists crime statistics in Ghana showing that it actually has a relatively low number of burglaries and robberies per year.[9] He explains the security discourse in Ghana as mostly media driven, often as a way of delegitimising emigration waves from Nigeria, Liberia, and Sierra Leone. Finally, he states that 'perceptions of crime' are far more critical than actual crime rates when it comes to the popularity of gated residential areas. Somewhat similar to Connah (2000), Grant is suggesting that these gates may be 'cognitive and mental walls for urban residents.' However, this choice of psychology over rationalism fails to see the multi-layered experiences of the wall-gate system and its overlapping meanings.

When discussing safety and security strategies in Ghana, one must keep in mind that in case of an emergency, calling the police or other authorities is not seen as a useful or reliable option. There is no emergency phone line and the police are seen as corrupt and slow; most people live with the knowledge that in case of an emergency they are on their own, especially if they live in big isolated houses where even the surveillance of neighbours is non-existent. These middle-class architectural practices are therefore not only the point where the 'informal city' shapes housing and land use (Hansen

Hidden and incomplete 95

and Vaa, 2004), but also the point where privacy protection, security, and social status overlap.

Walls, alarms, watchdogs, electric fences, and padlocks are all part of the boundary that exists between house residents and the city. George, a 33-year-old accountant, living in one of Tema's new neighbourhoods, has a 'ritual' of locking up the house every night after everyone's gotten in. He locks the doors and windows of the house with iron bars, and the main gate with two big padlocks. When the electricity is running he even turns on the electric fence. Such strict security measures are commonly seen in new development areas such as George's neighbourhood, where houses are far apart, lighting is scarce, and there is no communal surveillance on strangers and potential robbers.

Ironically, some urbanites claim that the walls damage domestic security because they keep the house too secluded, which means if someone breaks in, the neighbours won't be aware of it. The gaze of outsiders into the contemporary urban house in Ghana is incredibly compromised, and the walls may even fade out intrusion noises, screams, or any unusual activity. The police issued several warnings against high walls and architects were instructed to reduce the height of walls as they damage security and urban scenery. 'The walls brought isolation and neighbours don't know each other anymore,' Akyaa, a young architect living in Accra, told me. 'But people want to have them because they are fancy.'

Akyaa claims that the only rationale for setting up walls and gates is social status, inspired by Euro-American housing styles and led by upper-class households and returnees. However, city life poses security issues and raises the need to mark material boundaries between inside and outside. Moreover, Ghanaian urbanites who cannot afford such walls and gates do not see them as mere issues of fashion but as essential objects to their security and livelihood. Such families expressed genuine concerns over the safety of their home and felt exposed to the dangers of city life. The walls of their neighbours 'encode fear' (Low, 1997: 53) in their wall-less homes.

Violet, who recently returned to Ghana from the UK, lives with her husband and two children in a quiet residential neighbourhood in Tema. Living in a 'good neighbourhood,' she explains, is paradoxically more dangerous as it attracts more thieves and burglars. Almost every house in Violet's street is surrounded with walls and gates, except her own. Violet's landlord refused to invest money in a gated fence despite her persistent requests and she's felt unsafe ever since. As a compromise, the landlord allowed her husband, Kwabena, to build a wall round the back of the house at his own expense. If the front street cannot be blocked, at least the back entrance leading to a small and dark forest will be somewhat protected.

Every night, after she returns home from work, Violet locks her doors and windows with multiple padlocks and keeps her curtains closed. She hears about armed robberies and burglaries on the news and on social media. Whilst watching Nigerian and Ghanaian cinema she sees horrific scenes of robbers,

96 *Hidden and incomplete*

witches, and demons breaking into defenceless urban houses and spreading evil. This climate affects her perception of the house as a highly private space. For instance, when a young man knocks on the door and presents himself as a researcher conducting a survey, Violet does not invite him in but keeps the net used as a door locked and speaks through it. 'We must ask god for safety at all times,' she explains. 'I hope next year we will be able to build a proper wall.'

It is clear, therefore, that for Violet and Kwabena domestic security, spiritual wellbeing, and architectural aesthetics are all tied into one. One might ask whether Ghanaians invest their funds in house-surrounding walls and large iron gates to express wealth and prestige or to improve domestic security, but this question is too simplistic. 'Security' can carry multiple meanings such as the fear of envious, greedy, or sinful visitors. As Meyer states: 'The fear of powerful things, being hidden in private space and affecting unsuspecting people, runs as a red thread through popular Christianity in Ghana' (2010: 121). Pentecostal house cleansing rituals are additional reflections of the need to protect the house spiritually.

The walls and gates, therefore, express three dimensions of meaning by domesticating the boundaries between private and public spaces: the criminal fear of burglaries and intruders, the spiritual fear of jealousy or demons, and the social desire for symbols of wealth and aesthetics. Also, the walls are used to reinforce power relations between members of the household and to surveil the comings and goings of individuals in the house. This last dimension is often discussed in literature about privacy that comes from social psychology (Altman, 1975; Petronio, 2002). It asks how people coordinate a 'collective boundary' through agreement, synchronisation, and terms of permeability – how private it should and can be (Petronio, 2002: 99).

The gate system in Tema's houses manifests this 'collective boundary permeability' (Petronio, 2002) – It is not merely an 'open and close' matter. As most middle-class families cannot afford to hire a guard who will operate the gate at all times, there are particular habits around managing the gates between members of the household. Iron gates have padlocks and drop rods that are only lockable from one side at a time – outside or inside. This means if all the household members are out, they can lock the gate with a padlock. However, if one of the tenants is still in the house, he or she might be trapped. To avoid this situation, whoever stays indoors must escort the person who is leaving and lock the gate behind him/her.

This arrangement means whoever is inside has full control over the outsiders, unlike conventional doors where anyone holding a key has equal access to the house. Moreover, whoever wishes to leave must announce his/her departure so that another tenant may escort him/her. Because the gates are often distant from the actual house, people agree on various coordination methods. For instance, if someone leaves the house, he or she must make sure there is no one left before locking up with a padlock. Also, keys are not duplicated for each tenant but are collectively passed around to prevent people from being locked in and out.

Hidden and incomplete 97

During the day these rules work relatively well, but during the night things get more complicated: household members cannot go to sleep until everyone is indoors. Otherwise, they will have to wake up and open the gate. In worse cases, they may not hear the knocking, raddling, and shouting from outside or the mobile phone calls that follow.[10] When I lived with a local family, I too had to participate in the rules revolving around the gate – I had my own set of keys, but these mostly allowed me to leave the house last. However, if I wanted to enter the house last, my keys were useless. When I was in the house, I had to stay alert in case someone knocked and wanted to go in. I also had to be home by a certain hour so the gate could be locked in time.

One night, I was out exploring pubs and night markets in Tema's city centre; by the time I arrived home, it was about 10:15 PM and the gate was already closed. I walked around the house and knocked on a window above Maria's bed until she woke up and opened the gate.[11] Maria was a 19-year-old fostered child from a rural town, who was working at my hosts' shop. Her age and position made it easier for me to wake her up, which was in line with the age hierarchies of the house. I walked in, slightly embarrassed, locking the gate behind me.

In his ethnography of sleeping in rural Ghana, van der Geest (2006: 79) suggests that 'the gate provides secure protection against (non-existing?) thieves but not against (omnipresent) lovers.' Trying to enter the house after 'curfew,' sometimes with secret lovers, was a common experience shared by many Ghanaian youngsters, who often have schemes to overcome the gate system. These include climbing up the gate, sneaking in through a window, or texting their siblings via WhatsApp. Mobile phones, in that sense, challenge the monitoring of people in and out of the house and establish privacy within this monitored space.

The gate arrangement, therefore, expresses the cultural perception of the house as a private space with highly restricted access. Moreover, it reflects power relations between adults and children, wives and husbands, tenants and guests. The house comprises various individuals who may or may not be bound to a nuclear, biological unit so hierarchy and authority within it rely mostly on age (Schildkrout, 1973; Goody, 2007). Younger residents are expected to announce before leaving the house, so they do not lock anyone in accidentally. The gate, therefore, becomes a material tool for imposing domestic surveillance and gerontocratic family regulation.

In an article titled 'The Berlin Key or How To Do Words with Things,' Bruno Latour (2000) described a special key, symmetrical and two-sided, which determines if the door will be locked, or remain unlocked, by restricting the possibility to pull the key out after turning it. During the day, tenants cannot pull the keys out if they have locked the main entrance, but during the night they are obliged to. Latour (2000: 18) argued that these technological objects play a social role that sole verbal communication cannot. The keys, door, tenants, and concierge (who alternates the day and night bolts) are engaged in 'a bitter struggle for control and access' (Latour, 2000: 19).

Figure 5.4 Gates: status symbols or security measure? Photo by the author.

Like the Latourian Berlin Key, technology can be regarded here not only as a reflection or mediation of some pre-existing social reality, but as 'a social actor, an agent, an active being.' The gate system, accordingly, does not 'reflect' perceptions of privacy, nor does it 'mediate' between people and objects. The gate manifests and produces relations by doing what words, signs, and values cannot. Mobile digital platforms such as WhatsApp create new avenues for such material practice of privacy, like a virtual reincarnation of gates and walls (see Chapter 6; Figure 5.4).

5.3 The courtyard: memory and practice

> If we approach it [the compound] as anthropologists, we stress its semi-tribal or 'extended family' occupation, its communal hearth, its arrangement of small rooms around a courtyard, its self-sufficient, wall-enclosed unity. This, we say, is the expression of a way of life that must be respected.
>
> (Maxwell Fry quoted in Jackson and Oppong, 2014: 487)

This quote, by one of Tema's leading British architectural advisers, demonstrates his ideological interpretation of compound housing as something that should be preserved and respected. However, the architect is referring to the resettlement project of Tema's old fishing village. When it comes to the 'new town' in Tema, the hope was to abandon all traditional housing culture and take on a modern built environment (d'Auria and De Meulder, 2010). Adopting what he described as an anthropological point of view, the

Hidden and incomplete 99

architect reconfigures the binary divisions between city and village, modern and traditional, tribal and Western.[12]

Compounds and courtyard houses were the primary forms of architecture in West Africa for centuries, both in cities and in villages (Asomani-Boateng, 2011: 251). The compound usually includes several private rooms surrounding a central open yard enclosed by four walls and a gate, providing a strict division between open and closed/public and private spaces. Compound houses were developed in accordance with West Africa's climate, culture, gender roles, kinship structure, and economic life (Prussin, 1969; Agbontaen, Ogunje and Oladipupo, 1996; Connah, 2000; Figure 5.5).

The Akan *efihyia* (house), for instance, was the common architectural method in the city of Kumasi. According to Asomani-Boateng (2011: 251), the Akan compound demarcates between the *fie* (inside, private) and *abonten* (outside, public), and symbolises protection, security, and spirituality. Are these traditional architectural features expressed in the modern housing units of Tema or are they 'lost' in the history?

Whilst life in Tema mostly brought an end to the compound life in favour of modern neighbourhoods, some of its elements are preserved in backyards, verandas, and residential streets (see Figure 5.6). After the 1966 military coup, as governments began to neglect urban maintenance, families began to build walls around their front yards. By doing so, they regained privacy in an uncertain urban environment and continued compound-related practices. Tema's informal version of compound houses is a hybrid of modern living units with open courtyard areas. The central yard can accommodate one or two families who share the same secured complex while sharing electricity and water bills. Renting out units within the complex allows urban families to generate informal income if their relatives are dispersed around the city, country, or world.

Robert and Roberta live with their daughter Liza in such a compound. As described earlier, Robert is building his dream house in one of Tema's new neighbourhoods, but, meanwhile, he is renting out an extra living unit to another young couple, saving up the extra income for more building materials. The two families share a yard, which is mostly used for parking their cars and keeping their watchdog. A wall and gate with trees and plants in front of the house surround the yard, turning it into a compound. Robert and Roberta installed separate meters for measuring the water and electricity usage of each family, merging traditional and familial living arrangements with modern urban life.

The traditional compound yard is a space for consuming food, cooking, cleaning, resting, pounding yams, singing, dancing, and hosting neighbours. Tema's converted yards recreate many of those activities.[13] Mansa uses her yard for baking cakes and cookies by placing an oven and a large table outside. She bakes sugar-free health cakes for middle-class families in Tema, who come and collect the cakes from the yard, never entering the actual house. Mansa's house is located in a small residential street, so if she wishes

100 *Hidden and incomplete*

to invite people in, she leaves her gate partly open. However, if she's busy, or not in the mood for hosting, Mansa keeps it closed and watches the street through decorated carvings, known as 'design blocks.' These blocks allow her to 'see without being seen' (as George commented about dark pubs in Chapter 4) and are seen all over the city.[14]

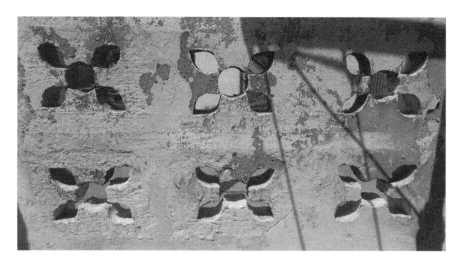

Figure 5.5 Design blocks: see without being seen. Photo by the author.

Figure 5.6 The modern compound. Photo by the author.

Hidden and incomplete   101

The yards, therefore, help monitor the division between public and private spaces in the house. When a relative visits Ghana from abroad, for instance, friends and family are often seen walking in and out of the yard collecting packages and various commodities such as clothes, technological gadgets, perfumes, or alcohol that were passed on to them by other relatives who live abroad. The courtyard turns into a docking station of the 'diasporic family social networks' (Burrell, 2012: 14) almost like a physical manifestation of a WhatsApp family group – not entirely private and not fully public.

Auntie Evelina's courtyard is at the heart of a very central neighbour-hood, where houses are in very close proximity to each other, and when her daughter's childhood friend got married, she held the engagement party (also known as the 'Traditional Wedding') in the street behind the house. Evelina's courtyard was declared as the docking station for this party and people were coming in and out of it throughout the day, as if stepping into the back scene of a theatre show (making Goffman's dramaturgical model of the front and backstage especially vivid).

The bride to be and her bridesmaids took over the yard early in the morning, arranging their hair and make-up and fine-tuning traditional cos-tumes. During this time, they chatted, told jokes, gossiped, and groomed themselves for the ceremony. Towards the afternoon auntie Evelina sent them a large pot of Okro stew. They sat around the bowl and ate together in the courtyard; they shared plates and spooned the warm food with their freshly cleaned hands.

At one point, one of the bridesmaids took out her mobile phone and asked to take photos of the bride, instructing her on how to pose and where to stand. Another woman grabbed a white bed sheet to cover the clutter and mess that overtook the yard and used it as a backdrop for the photograph. Throughout the entire day, none of the women walked into the indoor sec-tion of the house. Water was fetched to the yard, and the toilets were just not used. There was an unspoken understanding that indoors was off-limits and they had everything they needed in the enclosed yard. These moments revive the yard as the familial, social space that is traditional of rural compounds.

The yard, and in its absence on the street, can also be a space of mourning and funeral gatherings. When Patience's husband passed away that night (see Chapter 3) the elderly women who lived nearby walked back and forth in the street crying over the loss of her respected neighbour. I got up and ran to the gate of the house, opened it slightly, and saw the dramatic display of emo-tions in the street. By 6 AM, the street was full of neighbours comforting each other, mourning and passing on the news. After a few hours, a red and black tent was set up with a lot of plastic chairs so that elders, relatives, friends, and colleagues could visit and pray throughout the week without entering the house. Again, the tent and the yard assisted in monitoring, reducing, and controlling the presence of 'outsiders' in the sacred intimacy of the house.

I also welcomed visitors to my hosts' front yard, and it was clear that my guests did not expect me, nor did my hosts allow me, to invite people indoors.

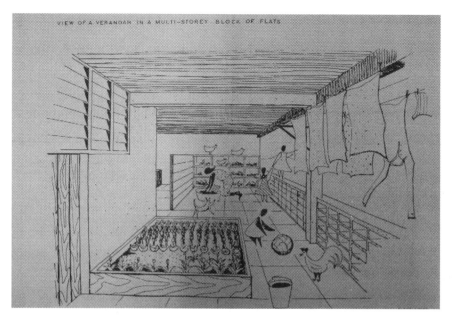

Figure 5.7 'View of a veranda in a multi-story block of flats,' Architectural plans, 1961, TDC (Tema Development Office).

The unspoken rule was to sit by the entrance and fetch cold drinks from inside. Access indoors often depends on intimacy, trust, and respect. I claim, therefore, that the building of walls to surround the houses and the use of yards in urban Tema reflect a collective memory of traditional compound houses. Moreover, they show how residents become agents of culture and history by shifting architecture away from the modernised universal vision of Tema into their pre-existing desires and values. In other words, the traditional compound is re-imagined and re-staged in a modern urban context (see Figure 5.7).

5.4 'Living-roomisation' of public spaces

> Akin to the home itself, front rooms and living rooms often act as the interface between the private and the public world.
>
> (Horst, 2011: 6)

Studies in Material Culture about domestic spaces often illustrate how these spaces (and the objects they contain) express certain aesthetics, taste, and identity formation from which we can learn about societies (Miller, 1988, 2001; Woodward, 2001; Money, 2007; Daniels, 2015). Material and visual analysis of living rooms in urban Ghana reinforces such claims, as it shows an unusually unified collective taste and structure, but a social study of

Hidden and incomplete   103

this space may remain rather slim. This incommensurability is because Ghanaians tend to invest efforts into the material properties of the living room but practise the social functions that are associated with it (especially in Western thinking) outside.

The 'typical' Ghanaian living room has multiple sofas and armchairs pushed against the walls, facing a central object – the television. The TV's size varies by income, but plasma and LCD screens are prevalent. The TV is often connected to a cable box, DVD player, and an old video player. In recent years, many houses added long-standing stereo speakers and placed them by each side of the television. Family photographs and Christian iconography are framed and hung on the upper part of the walls, very close to the ceiling.[15] Traditional African wooden ornaments and cloth are often incorporated for additional decoration. Unlike bathrooms, bedrooms, and kitchens that are reserved only for house residents, lots of effort is put into making the living room presentable for family ceremonies and guests, a semi-public residential space. However, this idyllic living room often remains more or less untouched. How come?

Araba who lived in the UK for 23 years has recently migrated back to Ghana. She now lives in her childhood home, amongst many of her parental memories and old objects. Araba's father was a 'typical Anglo-Fanti' (as she phrased it), meaning he was an elite member of the Fanti people, known for passionately adopting British culture. One of the expressions of this identity was socialising in an 'English-looking' lounge, and so Araba's father had a beautiful and elegant living room, equipped with brown and yellow armchairs, ornaments, and plenty of sunlight. As an Anglican priest, Araba's father used to host members of the church every Sunday. This was when they gathered in the living room and discussed community, finance, religion, and culture, 'like true gentlemen,' as Araba described.

Araba's memory is that of a highly privileged family involved in colonial civil service or missionary leadership. Furthermore, her memories portrayed Ghanaian living rooms as spaces reserved mostly for educated, Christian, urban men, which differs from its contemporary familial associations. According to Miescher's (2007) socio-historic account on Akan domesticity and masculinity, both the traditional and the colonial versions of living rooms in Ghana are strongly linked to elderly, elitist, and literate males. Miescher claims that the new middle and upper class of the 1940s expressed their modernity and prestige as *Akrakyefoo* (gentlemen) by redefining the living room and the compound.

As Ghanaian men abandoned the traditional chamber separation between men and their (often multiple) wives and moved into shared conjugal residence, the modern European living room was born in Ghana (Miescher, 2007: 137). This shift stood in line with broader theological, cultural, and familial transformations of the colonial era. It also aligns with Protestant notions of 'making a complete break with the past' (Meyer, 1998) by severing ties with extended family structures and focusing one's full attention

104 *Hidden and incomplete*

in the conjugal union and nuclear family (van Dijk, 2003). The previously gendered division of space and the absence of non-elderly women from living rooms gave way for a familial area that projects tranquillity, comfort, style, and modernity. This transformation was made possible through the consumption of electronic technologies (e.g., radio, television) and their placement in the living room. As Pertierra (2015: 416) states in her ethnography of middle-class houses in southeastern Mexico (Figure 5.8):

> Domestic comfort, it can be argued, has become one of the organising principles of modern life – and as a modern ideology, it relies heavily upon the incorporation of modern technologies to be upheld.

However, apart from spending some evenings and Sundays relaxing in the living room, or using it for ceremonial purposes, living rooms in Ghana mostly remain unoccupied.[16] Due to the tropical heat, limited electric supply, busy schedules, and the fact that many bedrooms have their own TVs and air-conditioners, living rooms are not used very often and are mostly occupied by children in their limited free time. However, the social virtues and interactions associated with living rooms seem to emerge at the outskirts of the house, in the yards and streets. This habit taught me about the concepts of privacy in urban space. How exactly is it expressed?

In the heart of the neighbourhood, between the restaurants and bars, stands a long and narrow open structure made of metal poles and colourful canvas,

Figure 5.8 'Typical' Ghanaian living room. Photo by the author.

Hidden and incomplete 105

flags of various states, and a large sign titled 'Soccer City.' Inside this semi-open space, there are four different plasma screens and plastic chairs laid out in rows. Members of the community, predominantly men, gather in 'Soccer City' to watch sports games every week for a small entrance fee of about 3 cedis. Before being seated, the usher points at the specific screen, according to the game each client comes in to watch, so they know where to look.

This communal gathering is not necessarily aimed at residents who have no television sets at home; dozens of men who have plasma screens in their bedrooms and living rooms still choose to come and watch the game while crowded on plastic chairs. Sometimes they'll even watch the games without audio because only one screen is connected to the speakers. During the commercial breaks, some stay in the structure and chat while others go outside for some fresh air and catch up on their mobile phones. Although it is set in a public space, men gather, bond, chat, drink, and eat in a familial and intimate atmosphere. As Botticello (2007: 9) found among Yoruba/Nigerian migrants in South London, and how they domesticate open spaces and street markets: 'Homemaking practices in themselves are not confined solely to the domestic arena but may occur in other places outside that space.'

'Soccer City' has a unique private/public position. Unlike the nightly pub gatherings, these meetings are completely legitimate, secure, and familial, but they are neither domestic nor institutional. It substitutes the invitation of fellow men into the private home to watch sports together by meeting in a 'neutral' zone, maintaining public personas and protecting private spaces.[17] During *Dumsor*, when people can't watch TV at home, 'Soccer City' is full of people who escape their homes and charge their mobile phones whilst watching a game or two (or even three). Neighbourhood 'sport bars' are common across the globe but in Tema they have become a technological necessity, fulfilling the need for televised entertainment when the home fails to provide it. The absence of domestic electricity, therefore, pushes people outside the house, weakening nuclear ties and strengthening neighbourhood ties (see Chapter 4).

An evening stroll in Tema's streets may reveal a father holding his baby with his wife and daughter sat beside him on plastic chairs, as they watch television outside. Or a man sat outside his house in an armchair with large speakers and a glass of Alomo Bitters (Ghanaian herb liquor), listening to Afro-beat or Highlife music whilst relaxing. On a Sunday morning, Tema's residents always find teacher Annan sitting on a cement block outside his house chatting with his friends and neighbours. Most people only meet outside their homes, in outdoorsy resting spots. I knew I could find them at these spots, even though it wasn't part of their house. Almost every grocery shop or hair salon has a television and business owners stay in their shops until night-time, nap on the floor, converse on WhatsApp, and hang out with clients and friends. This domestication of stores and businesses also constitutes feelings of home outside of it.

The street is experienced as an extension of the home regarding socialisation but also concerning urban duties and domestic responsibilities.

106 *Hidden and incomplete*

Cleaning gutters and sweeping floors are a daily chore for Ghanaian maids, housewives, and children. The very first sounds of the city at dawn are those of sweeping the leaves and dirt that falls during the night with a traditional palm leaf broom locally known as *Pray3*. Because city hall doesn't clean up regularly, burning rubbish is another expression of urbanites tending to their urban environment, beyond the boundaries of home. Household members are also in charge of renovating and maintaining the street, installing streetlights, fixing potholes, and even paving the sidewalk. Urban maintenance, in this sense, blurs with home maintenance and each household sees nearby public spaces as an integral part of home living.

The importance of Tema's residents 'hanging out' in the streets is in how the field and its ethnographic experience shifts initial assumptions; my aim was to study the middle-class urban home, but I quickly realised it could not be fully understood when disconnected from the street. By looking after the streets and using them as sites of dwelling, residents guard the house as a private space. This inclination is reflected in the presence of domestic technologies in these streets. Botticello (2007: 9) argued that these technologies, which are necessary for the constitution of middle-class tranquillity, their presence outdoors, and the audio-visual ambience they create, uniquely domesticate these spaces. These technologies sometimes gain full attention but often run in the background, establishing what Jo Tacchi (2012: 420) has described as the 'texture of a domestic space.'

As in the case of front yards, using the streets for informal familial gatherings could be a continuation of traditional compounds as part of Tema's modern planning. As Enyonam, the young architect based in Tema, suggested: 'the courtyard system is in the memories of all Ghanaians.' Either way it is clear that although European living rooms were imported as an architectural feature that embodies ideas about Westernisation and nuclear family life, their social semantics – resting on sofas and armchairs, watching television, napping, hosting guests, spending time with family, telling stories and jokes – are expressed outdoors, in these spontaneous gathering spots.

Although middle-class Ghanaians eagerly participate in the global consumption of domestic technologies that mark the living room as a place of leisure and style (Botticello, 2007), these idyllic spaces often remain unoccupied and merely symbolic, due to their highly private indoor atmosphere. The rapid consumption of mobile phones (especially smartphones) allows urbanites to listen to music, watch videos, and read while sitting outside and socialising with friends and neighbours. Much like 'Soccer City,' these devices assist in leaving the house extremely private and intimate by re-situating technologies and changing their 'zones of consumption' (Pertierra and Turner, 2012). This stands in contrast to the scholarly discourse about the decline of 'street culture' in the modern age (Low, 1997; Caldeira, 2000; Livingstone, 2007; Low and Smith, 2013; Pertierra, 2015; Sennett, 2017). The streets become not only spaces of mobility and transportation but also spaces of intimacy, stillness, and leisure (Figure 5.9).

Hidden and incomplete 107

Figure 5.9 The living-roomisation of streets. Photo by the author.

5.5 Bedroom culture: 'the holy of holies'

Ama was born and raised in London, but she visits her family in Tema every year. During her 2017 visit, she went to an art gallery called 'Gallery 1957,' set in the prestigious new Kempinski Hotel Gold Coast City, Accra. The upscale style of the hotel and gallery allowed for a very daring artistic tone, which may not have been tolerated in a more public space. The Ghanaian-Togolese multidisciplinary artist, Va-Bene Elikem Fiatsi (also known as 'crazinisT artist'), takes gallery-goers on an intimate tour into a staged African bedroom titled 'The Red Sanctuary,' where he performs his 'rituals of becoming' – his bodily preparations to the outside world. Upon entering this dark space with no windows, Ama becomes invisible because the artist ignores her (and my) presence entirely. In this virtual reality, he creates a space where we can penetrate the most private domestic space in Ghanaian culture – bedrooms.

'I feel like I've stepped into my mother's bedroom,' Ama stated in amazement. She was surprised that this intimate scenario was brought to life so freely. The artist took a slow bucket shower fully nude. We could smell the soap as he rubbed it on his skin. Then he applied cream all over his body, arranged his hair, and finally chose his clothes. He had slowly transformed himself from a 'raw entity' into cultural subject and – to make this contrast even stronger – he transformed his gender in the performance as well. By the end of the ritual, CrazinisT turned into a woman.

In the context of this ethnography, CrazinistT's 'Butlerian' transition from man to woman was symbolic of the extreme gaps between the private

108   *Hidden and incomplete*

and the public sphere in urban Ghana, particularly the difference between the seen and the unseen. Furthermore, it reflects the opposition between one's body and home: the former is carefully composed, stylised, and exhibited while the latter serves as a 'backstage,' hidden from the public gaze. According to the curator's notes 'the exhibition questions the assumed distinctions between real and virtual, gender identity, class privilege, political injustice, violence and the objectification of humans.'

These various performances – class, gender, online personas – therefore, can also symbolise Ghana's middle class, where people seem rich when they are actually poor or saints when they are actually sinners. The cultural codes in Ghana place rituals of 'becoming' as the 'proper' and 'correct' way to participate in social and religious life. People make themselves visible only when they fulfil specific codes of normativity. The young artist wished to challenge this convention by inviting us into what should never be seen in the 'aesthetics of indirection' (Coe, 2011) – bedrooms.

As depicted in the art exhibit, bedrooms in Ghana are often full of clutter, piles of clothes, old appliances, photo albums, papers and magazines, unused furniture, kitchen utensils, dried food, curtains, mosquito nets, and toiletries. Christian portraits (particularly images of Jesus) are hung on the walls alongside family portraits, and wardrobes are sometimes locked with small keys. Bedrooms often lack natural light or windows, especially if they were built as an extension. As Bourdieu (1970: 155) noted about the lower part of the Kabyle home, bedrooms are 'well-protected and sheltered from intrusions and the gaze of others.' Furthermore, they signify 'the place of the most intimate privacy within the very world of intimacy' (Bourdieu, 1970: 155).

Access to Ghanaian bedrooms is highly restricted and was least common in this study. In her analysis of Pentecostal iconography, Meyer (2010: 116) discloses that she was not able to verify claims about Ghanaian urbanites praying in front of Jesus pictures at night, since 'it takes place in the seclusion and intimacy of the bedroom.'[18] van der Geest (2006: 75) shares his challenges when studying the sleeping practices in Kwahu since people associate being observed or photographed in beds with death and funerals. Bedrooms in Ghana are hidden not only from the eyes of strangers or anthropologists but from all members of the community. Many urbanites told me they've never stepped into the bedrooms of their closest friends and relatives.

However, one must not confuse the privacy of bedrooms in Ghana with individuality. Privacy often has overlapping meanings: it can signify solitude versus collectivity or invisibility versus visibility (Weintraub, 1997). Bedrooms in Ghana usually fall into the second category. It is normative among urban Ghanaians to accommodate more tenants than rooms in their often-crowded houses. Due to their economically strategic residential location, and ongoing contacts with rural relatives, urban Ghanaians have a variety of kin and kit living in their households. The nuclear model of two

Hidden and incomplete 109

parents and two children was a European ideal adopted by elites but not by most middle- and lower-class members (Pellow, 2008: 35). The overcrowding in Tema led to the unauthorised building of house extensions and conversions of backyards and verandas into additional bedrooms (Pellow, 2008: 35). Academic claims that 'enforced conviviality being a thing of the past for all but the poor' (Livingstone, 2007) is far from true in Ghana's domestic landscape.

This point is made clear when considering co-sleeping practices, whereby parents and children share the same bedroom. van der Geest (2006: 78–79) describes these practices in detail, including the techniques adults use to have intimate relations when sharing their room with children (e.g., creating internal divisions with curtains or waiting for them to fall asleep). In urban Ghana, people often sleep on the streets, in shops, or at spaces for public gatherings, taking pride in their ability to doze off in noisy conditions. This also relates to the non-individual nature of bedrooms as familiar for Ghanaians since childhood.[19]

Another feature that undermines any assumption that bedrooms are individually private is the recent introduction of domestic air-conditioning. The clear preference to install these units in bedrooms (and not in living rooms) relates to the unpopular use of living rooms on the one hand, and the undeniable pleasure of having a good night's sleep in ideal temperatures on the other. This privilege is usually reserved for older tenants or any respectable guests but children often 'tag along' to enjoy the luxury as well.

The installation of air-conditioners, therefore, takes place in the master bedroom, attracting younger residents to sleep with their parents during hot nights. This process happens alongside the rapid introduction of small plasma screens in front of beds. Together, these technologies redefine the bedroom from a functional place of slumber, bodily preparations, and storage, to a space of leisure, tranquillity, and escapism. As Pertierra (2015: 424) explains, 'the ways in which these technologies work together seems to be the most compelling factor in the production of comfortable and desirable home environments.'

Alongside televisions and air-conditioners, the adaptation of mobile phones, tablets, and other internet-enabled devices connects the bedroom to the outside world, overcoming its strictly private function. Moreover, using the internet to interact with strangers and friends, or to consume frowned-upon content, bypasses the surveillance of the house and transcends its tenants beyond the yards, gates, and residential streets into previously unexplored terrains (see Chapter 6). As Burrell (2009: 152) argues, the internet offers a substitute to restricted or impossible physical mobility by providing 'opportunities for engaging fantasies about foreign lands and international travel.'

There is a growing body of literature about bedroom cultures in sociology and media studies, most commonly associating bedrooms with youth culture, identity formation, privacy, and individualism (Brown et al., 1994;

110   *Hidden and incomplete*

Bovill and Livingstone, 2001; Curran, Morley and Morley, 2007; Livingstone, 2007; Horst, 2009). The assumed parallel between bedrooms and individualism relates to European ideas about childhood (Zelizer, 1994), growing conceptions of public spaces as dangerous for teenagers (boyd, 2014), increasingly liberal parent-child relations, and the notion of privacy as an individual legal 'right.'

As Horst (2009) has shown in her ethnography of Silicon Valley households, young people view their social media pages and practices to be as private as their bedrooms. This parallel is made visually apparent as teenagers design their bedrooms and profiles in similar shapes and colours (Horst, 2009). The shift from communal television viewing in the living room to individual media consumption, and from 'kitchen table society' to 'desktop society,' is another factor in this Euro-American privatised sense of space.

> 'Bedroom culture' in this sense is very much a Western phenomenon, being dependent on a high degree of modernisation, individualisation and wealth.
>
> (Livingstone 2007: 9)

This almost natural attachment between bedrooms and individualism led certain scholars to conclude that 'the dominant principle no longer being that of 'front' and 'back' (Goffman, 1956) but rather that of communal space and personal spaces' (Livingstone, 2007: 5). As I have shown above, the case of urban Ghana challenges these findings by pushing us to distinguish between privacy as invisibility and privacy as solitude. Tenants move in and out of the house, room compositions change, storage needs shape aesthetics, and familial surveillance is stricter indoors than anywhere else. These spaces are far from being individualised but are by all means private and concealed.

If we follow Livingstone's definition of bedroom culture as 'a set of conventional meanings and practices closely associated with identity, privacy and the self' we may miss out issues of domestic surveillance and co-sleeping. Furthermore, it is essential to address the unique combination of air-conditioners, televisions, and mobile phones as technologies that resituate the bedroom as a space of leisure and tranquillity. Using digital media in the streets, and in bedrooms, shifts these 'zones of consumption' (Pertierra and Turner, 2012) from a centralised nuclear family living room into a more complex interplay of private and public urban living.

5.6   The extended home: thinking beyond domestication theory

The rapid consumption of domestic electronic and digital technologies during the 1990s brought with it an approach in media studies, sociology, and anthropology known as 'domestication theory' (Silverstone et al., 1989; Silverstone, 1992; Haddon, 2004; Hynes and Richardson, 2009). Scholars have explored how the introduction of new technologies, and their physical location in the house, influences everyday life in terms of familial relationships (Haddon, 2004; Tacchi, 2012), gender relations (Laurence Habib and Tony Cornford, 2002), parent-child struggles (Horst, 2012; boyd, 2014; McDonald, 2015), and links between work and home (Nippert-Eng, 1996; Broadbent, 2013).

According to Silverstone (1992: 21) there are four main stages to domestication: (1) the appropriation of technology from store-owned commodities into private household objects, (2) the objectification of these devices through spatial and symbolic positioning around the house, (3) incorporation with pre-existing objects, practices, routines, rituals, and technologies, (4) conversion from new and generic devices to personal and familiar communication tools, shaped by the unique experience of each household. Further adjustments to this theory stressed that the domestication process is never linear, nor does it have a pre-defined ending point (Hynes and Richardson, 2009; McDonald, 2015). Can this theory be applied in the urban Ghanaian context?

As this chapter demonstrated in detail, access to private sections of the house has social, spiritual, and symbolic significance. People can know each other for years without ever seeing each other's private spaces.[20] As a result, middle-class homes in Tema extend and expand themselves into streets, yards, and social media platforms with the aim of regulating privacy. Houses are in constant states of refurbishment and expansion, enclosing and upgrading concerning infrastructure and domestic technology. Due to their unique infrastructure and history, these houses strive to become increasingly connected but also increasingly sustainable and autonomous. As a result, they are more connected to the world around them than ever before.

Alongside the ongoing flow of internet data, electric voltages, piped water, and cellular reception, Tema's urbanites also face regular power cuts (*Dumsor*), water breaks, and infrastructural disruptions. During these times, which can vary from a few hours to a few days, the house becomes a lifeless dark shell. These circumstances push tenants outside their homes to charge their phones, relax in the outdoor breeze, and socialise in pubs or churches. These domestic 'pulses' regulate flows of substances and information in and out of the house, shaping the daily routine of Ghanaians, and their use of public and private space (Ben Elul, 2020). Mobile data is quantified through pre-paid top-up cards, electricity is stored in power banks, fuel is kept in generators, water is reserved in large Polytank containers,[21] and sunlight is preserved in solar lamps and panels.

As Gupta (2015) explained in his call for an 'Anthropology of Electricity from the Global South,' when infrastructures function, they 'tend to disappear into the background... They become visible only when they break down.' In her article 'Ethnography of Infrastructure,' Star (1999) also notes that 'the normally invisible quality of working infrastructure becomes visible when it breaks.' Acknowledging these local infrastructures

112   *Hidden and incomplete*

– telecommunications, urban maintenance, electricity, and water – and how they 'create the skeleton of urban life' (Larkin, 2008: 5, 21) forces us to question the 'universalist notion on technology' and the assumption that homes are holistic, bounded, and always connected units.

As described in Chapter 3 middle-class Ghanaians use mobile phones to overcome the challenges of inadequate or non-existing infrastructures. Social media, emails, photo-taking, and mobile banking are essential practices that transcend urbanites beyond their physical surrounding, even when they do not function. By comparing the intensity of night lights to mobile phone consumption habits, Mothobi and Grzybowski (2017: 2) discovered that people who live in areas with poor infrastructure (reflected through weak night lights) are 'more likely to use mobile phones for financial transactions than individuals living in areas with better infrastructure.' Therefore, it is of no coincidence that in Tema where streets are dark and *Dumsor* is a constant problem, the vast majority of people gain access to the internet not via fixed landlines, domestic computers, or internet cafés, but through mobile phones. These devices enhance the fragmented, portable, individualised, and multiplied lifestyle that middle-class Ghanaians lead, by allowing them to shift from private to public spheres online and offline.[22]

While occasionally pointing at new technological links between the home, the school, or the workplace, domestication theory tends to analyse the family home as a holistic, enclosed, and ever connected unit (Harper, 2011). It is often associated with nuclear families in Western middle-class households, where the house has become the primary site of dwelling, leisure, and familial life (Miller, 2001; Livingstone, 2007; Horst, 2012). This approach cannot be directly applied in the case described here. Although this project initially meant to explore digital technologies and privacy within the home, the ethnographic data required a broader, more contextual, and diachronic/historic observation (Joyce and Gillespie, 2000). By expanding dimensions of time and space to include architectural history and urban street culture, I was able to see the extended nature of the houses of the middle class.

Much of the literature in material culture discusses the process in which people extend their minds, emotions, memories, and social ties through material objects and spaces (Belk, 1988; Latour, 1993; Douglas and Isherwood, 1996; Gell, 1998; Mauss, 2002; Pinney, 2002; Miller, 2008). As Latour (2000) argues concerning the Berlin Key, looking for 'the social dimension of technology' or 'the material aspect of societies' is simply missing the point: that technologies, whether digital or architectural, produce experiences and relations in a constant process of mutual extension.

Horst (2010: 164) has described how children in Silicon Valley often extend the boundaries of the home by visiting friends and grandparents to avoid parental supervision over their use of new media and gaming. However, in Ghana, houses are not extended onto parallel houses but onto alternative spaces that become domesticated. Therefore, I argue that the home and its inhabitants engage in a dialectic process of privacy-making: people extend themselves onto spaces outside the home to find privacy through physical mobility or internet communication, and the home extends itself onto its urban and digital spaces by recreating some of its related practices outside and online. This mutual process of extension and multiplication, enhanced by mobile phones on the one hand, and inadequate infrastructure on the other, must be added to domestication theory before it can be used in this context. Furthermore, it demonstrates clearly how privacy, technology, and space-work operate together.

References

Agbontaen, K. A., Ogunje, A. A. and Oladipupo, A. O. (1996) 'The Impluvium-Courtyard (Oto-. Eghodo) in Indigenous Benin Architecture', *Nigerian Field*, 61(1–2), pp. 54–64.

Altman, I. (1975) *The Environment and Social Behavior: Privacy, Personal Space, Territory, and Crowding*. Monterey: Brooks/Cole Publishing.

Amarteifio, G. W., Butcher, D. A. P. and Whitman, D. (1966) *Tema Manhean: A Study of Resettlement*. Ghana Universities P. for the University of Science and Technology, Kumasi.

Asomani-Boateng, R. (2011) 'Borrowing from the Past to Sustain the Present and the Future: Indigenous African Urban Forms, Architecture, and Sustainable Urban Development in Contemporary Africa', *Journal of Urbanism: International Research on Placemaking and Urban Sustainability*, 4(3), pp. 239–262. doi: 10.1080/17549175.2011.634573.

Bahloul, J. (1996) *The Architecture of Memory: A Jewish-Muslim Household in Colonial Algeria, 1937–1962*. Cambridge: Cambridge University Press.

Belk, R. W. (1988) 'Possessions and the Extended Self', *Journal of Consumer Research*, 15(2), pp. 139–168. doi: 10.1086/209154.

Ben Elul, E. (2012) 'Memory Sticks: Domestic Archiving among Ghanaian Families Abroad in a Cross-Cultural Perspective'. University College London.

Ben Elul, E. (2020). 'Noisy Polymedia in Urban Ghana: Strategies for Choosing and Switching between Media under Unstable Infrastructures', *New Media & Society*, doi: 1461444820925047.

Blier, S. P. (1983) 'Houses Are Human: Architectural Self-Images of Africa's Tamberma', *Journal of the Society of Architectural Historians*, 42(4), pp. 371–382.

Botticello, J. (2007) 'Lagos in London: Finding the Space of Home', *Home Cultures*, 4(1), pp. 7–23. doi: 10.2752/174063107780129671.

Bourdieu, P. (1970) 'The Berber House or the World Reversed', *Information (International Social Science Council)*, 9(2), pp. 151–170.

Bovill, M. and Livingstone, S. (2001) 'Bedroom Culture and the Privatization of Media Use', in Livingstone, S. and Bovill, M. (eds) *Children and Their Changing Media Environment: A European Comparative Study*. Mahwah, NJ: Lawrence Erlbaum Associates, pp. 179–200.

boyd, D. (2014) *It's Complicated: The Social Lives of Networked Teens*. First Edition. New Haven, CT: Yale University Press.

Broadbent, S. (2013) 'Approaches to Personal Communication', in Horst, H. and Miller, D. (eds) *Digital Anthropology*. London; New York: Berg Publishers, pp. 127–142.

114 *Hidden and incomplete*

Brown, J. et al. (1994) 'Teenage Room Culture: Where Media and Identities Intersect', *Communication Research*, 21(6), pp. 813–827. doi: 10.1177/009365094021006008.

Buchli, V. (2013) *An Anthropology of Architecture.* London: A&C Black.

Burrell, J. (2009) 'Could Connectivity Replace Mobility? An Analysis of Internet Cafe Use Patterns in Accra, Ghana', in Bruijn, M. de, Nyamnjoh, F., and Brinkman, I. (eds) *Mobile Phones: The New Talking Drums of Everyday Africa.* Bamenda, Cameroon: Langaa RPCIG, pp. 151–169.

Burrell, J. (2012) *Producing the Internet and Development: An Ethnography of Internet Café Use in Accra, Ghana.* Ph. D. The London School of Economics and Political Science (LSE).

Caldeira, T. P. R. (2000) *City of Walls: Crime, Segregation, and Citizenship in São Paulo.* Berkeley: University of California Press.

Carsten, J. and Hugh-Jones, S. (eds) (1995) *About the House: Lévi-Strauss and beyond.* New York: Cambridge University Press.

Coe, C. (2011) 'What Is Love? The Materiality of Care in Ghanaian Transnational Families', *International Migration*, 49(6), pp. 7–24. doi: 10.1111/j.1468-2435.2011.00704.x.

Connah, G. (2000) 'Contained Communities in Tropical Africa', in Tracy, J. D. (ed.) *City Walls: The Urban Enceinte in Global Perspective.* Cambridge: Cambridge University Press, pp. 19–45.

Curran, J., Morley, D. and Morley, F. P. of T. C. H. D. (2007) *Media and Cultural Theory.* London: Routledge.

d'Auria, V. (2010) 'From Tropical Transitions to Ekistic Experimentation: Doxiadis Associates in Tema, Ghana', *Positions: On Modern Architecture and Urbanism/ Histories and Theories*, 1, pp. 40–63.

d'Auria, V. and De Meulder, B. (2010) 'Unsettling Landscapes: New Settlements for the Volta River Project between Tradition and Transition (1951–1970)', *Oase: Tijdschrift voor Architectuur*, 82, pp. 115–138.

d'Auria, V. and Kootin Sanwu, V. (2010) 'Between Development and Experiment: The Volta River Project's (Un)settling Communities', in. *Urban Knowledge: Its Production, Use and Dissemination in Cities of the South*, LaCambreHorta-ULB - ASRO-KULeuven., pp. 93–110. Available at: https://lirias.kuleuven.be/handle/123456789/301550 (Accessed: 4 April 2018).

Daniels, I. (2015) 'Feeling at Home in Contemporary Japan: Space, Atmosphere and Intimacy', *Emotion, Space and Society*, 15, pp. 47–55. doi: 10.1016/j.emospa.2014.11.003.

Douglas, M. and Isherwood, B. C. (1996) *The World of Goods: Towards an Anthropology of Consumption: With a New Introduction.* London: Routledge.

Drazin, A. and Frohlich, D. M. (2007) 'Good Intentions: Remembering through Framing Photographs in English Homes', *Ethnos*, 72(1), pp. 51–76.

Gal, S. (2002) 'A Semiotics of the Public/Private Distinction', *Differences: A Journal of Feminist Cultural Studies*, 13(1), pp. 77–95.

Gell, A. (1998) *Art and Agency: An Anthropological Theory.* Oxford: Clarendon Press.

Goffman, E. (1956) *The Presentation of Self in Everyday Life.* New York: Doubleday.

Goody, E. N. (2007) *Parenthood and Social Reproduction: Fostering and Occupational Roles in West Africa.* Cambridge: Cambridge University Press.

Grant, R. (2005) 'The Emergence of Gated Communities in a West African Context: Evidence From Greater Accra, Ghana', *Urban Geography*, 26(8), pp. 661–683. doi: 10.2747/0272-3638.26.8.661.

Grant, R. (2009) *Globalizing City: The Urban and Economic Transformation of Accra, Ghana*. New York: Syracuse University Press.

Gupta, A. (2015) 'An Anthropology of Electricity from the Global South', *Cultural Anthropology*, 30(4), pp. 555–568. doi: 10.14506/ca30.4.04.

Haddon, L. (2004) *Information and Communication Technologies in Everyday Life: A Concise Introduction and Research Guide*. London: Bloomsbury Academic.

Halle, D. (1991) 'Displaying the Dream: The Visual Presentation of Family and Self in the Modern American Household', *Journal of Comparative Family Studies*, 22(2), pp. 217–229.

Hansen, K. T. and Vaa, M. (2004) *Reconsidering Informality: Perspectives from Urban Africa*. Uppsala: Nordic Africa Institute.

Harper, R. (2011) *The Connected Home: The Future of Domestic Life*. New York: Springer.

Hirsch, M. (1997) *Family Frames: Photography, Narrative, and Postmemory*. Cambridge, MA: Harvard University Press.

Horst, H. (2009) 'Aesthetics of the Self: Digital Mediations', in Miller, D. (ed.) *Anthropology of the Individual: A Material Culture Perspective*. New York: Berg Publishers, pp. 99–113.

Horst, H. (2010) 'Families', in Ito, M., Baumer, S., Bittanti, M., Cody, R., Stephenson, B.H., Horst, H., Lange, P.G., Mahendran, D., Martínez, K.Z., Pascoe, C.J. and Perkel, D. (eds.) *Hanging Out, Messing around, and Geeking Out: Kids Living and Learning with New Media*. London: MIT Press, pp. 149–194.

Horst, H. A. (2011) 'Reclaiming Place: The Architecture of Home, Family and Migration', *Anthropologica*, 53(1), pp. 29–39.

Horst, H. (2012) 'New Media Technologies in Everyday Life', in Miller, D. and Horst, H. (eds) *Digital Anthropology*. Oxford: Berg.

Hynes, D. and Richardson, H. (2009) 'What Use Is Domestication Theory to Information Systems Research?', in Dwivedi Y., Lal B., Schneberger L. S., Wade M. (eds) *Handbook of Research on Contemporary Theoretical Models in Information Systems*. New York: Information Science Reference, pp. 482–494.

Jackson, I. and Oppong, R. A. (2014) 'The Planning of Late Colonial Village Housing in the Tropics: Tema Manhean, Ghana', *Planning Perspectives*, 29(4), pp. 475–499. doi: 10.1080/02665433.2013.829753.

John, J. L. (1963) 'Temne Space', *Anthropological Quarterly*, 36(1), pp. 1–17. doi: 10.2307/3316519.

Joyce, R. A. and Gillespie, S. D. (2000) *Beyond Kinship: Social and Material Reproduction in House Societies*. Philadelphia: University of Pennsylvania Press.

Kirk, D. and Sellen, A. (2010) 'On Human Remains: Values and Practice in the Home Archiving of Cherished Objects', *ACM Transactions on Computer-Human Interaction*, 17(3), pp. 1–43.

Landes, J. B. (2003) 'Further Thoughts on the Public/Private Distinction', *Journal of Women's History*, 15(2), pp. 28–39. doi: 10.1353/jowh.2003.0051.

Lange, P. G. (2007) 'Publicly Private and Privately Public: Social Networking on YouTube', *Journal of Computer-Mediated Communication*, 13(1), pp. 361–380. doi: 10.1111/j.1083-6101.2007.00400.x.

Latour, B. (1993) *We Have Never Been Modern*. Cambridge, MA: Harvard University Press.

Latour, B. (2000) 'The Berlin Key or how to do words with things', in Graves-Brown, P. (ed.) *Matter, Materiality, and Modern Culture*. London: Routledge, pp. 10–21.

116   *Hidden and incomplete*

Larkin, B. (2008) *Signal and Noise: Media, Infrastructure, and Urban Culture in Nigeria*. Durham: Duke University Press Books.

Laurence Habib and Tony Cornford (2002) 'Computers in the Home: Domestication and Gender', *Information Technology & People*, 15(2), pp. 159–174. doi: 10.1108/09593840210430589.

Levi-Strauss, C. (1988) *The Way of the Masks*. Reprint edition. Translated by S. Modelski. Seattle: University of Washington Press.

Livingstone, S. (2007) 'From Family Television to Bedroom Culture: Young People's Media at Home', in Devereux, E. (ed.) *Media Studies: Key Issues and Debates*. London: Sage Publications, pp. 302–321.

Low, S. and Smith, N. (2013) *The Politics of Public Space*. London: Routledge.

Low, S. M. (1997) 'Urban Fear: Building the Fortress City', *City & Society*, 9(1), pp. 53–71.

Low, S. M. (2001) 'The Edge and the Center: Gated Communities and the Discourse of Urban Fear', *American Anthropologist*, 103(1), pp. 45–58.

Marcoux, J.-S. (2001) 'The Refurbishment of Memory', in Miller, D. (ed.) *Home Possessions: Material Culture behind Closed Doors*. Oxford: Berg, pp. 69–85.

Marcus, C. C. (2006) *House as a Mirror of Self: Exploring the Deeper Meaning of Home*. Lake Worth, FL: Nicolas-Hays, Inc.

Mauss, M. (2002 [1950]) *The Gift: The Form and Reason for Exchange in Archaic Societies*. London: Routledge.

McDonald, T. (2015) 'Affecting Relations: Domesticating the Internet in a South-Western Chinese Town', *Information, Communication & Society*, 18(1), pp. 17–31. doi: 10.1080/1369118X.2014.924981.

Meyer, B. (1998) '"Make a Complete Break with the past." Memory and Post-Colonial Modernity in Ghanaian Pentecostalist Discourse', *Journal of Religion in Africa*, 28(3), pp. 316–349. doi: 10.2307/1581573.

Meyer, B. (2010) '"There Is a Spirit in that Image": Mass-Produced Jesus Pictures and Protestant-Pentecostal Animation in Ghana', *Comparative Studies in Society and History*, 52(1), pp. 100–130. doi: 10.1017/S001041750999034X.

Miescher, S. F. (2007) 'From Pato to Parlor: Domesticity, Masculinity, Religious Space, and Alternative Archives in 20th Century Ghana', *Comparativ: Zeitschrift für Globalgeschichte and vergleichende Geschichtsforschung*, 17(5/6), pp. 131–45.

Miller, D. (1988) 'Appropriating the State on the Council Estate', *Man*, 23(2), pp. 353–372. doi: 10.2307/2802810.

Miller, D. (ed.) (2001) *Home Possessions: Material Culture behind Closed Doors*. First edition. London: Berg Publishers.

Miller, D. (2008) *The Comfort of Things*. First Edition. London: Polity Press.

Miner, C. S., Chan, D. M. and Campbell, C. (2001) 'Digital Jewelry: Wearable Technology for Everyday Life', in *CHI '01 Extended Abstracts on Human Factors in Computing Systems*. New York: ACM (CHI EA '01), pp. 45–46. doi: 10.1145/634067.634098.

Money, A. (2007) 'Material Culture and the Living Room the Appropriation and Use of Goods in Everyday Life', *Journal of Consumer Culture*, 7(3), pp. 355–377. doi: 10.1177/1469540507081630.

Moore, H. L. (1986) *Space, Text and Gender: An Anthropological Study of the Marakwet of Kenya*. Cambridge: CUP Archive.

Morton, C. (2007) 'Remembering the House Memory and Materiality in Northern Botswana', *Journal of Material Culture*, 12(2), pp. 157–179. doi: 10.1177/1359183507078123.

Mothobi, O. and Grzybowski, L. (2017) 'Infrastructure Deficiencies and Adoption of Mobile Money in Sub-Saharan Africa', *Information Economics and Policy*, 40, pp. 71–79. doi: 10.1016/j.infoecopol.2017.05.003.

Nippert-Eng, C. (1996) *Home and Work: Negotiating Boundaries through Everyday Life*. Chicago, IL: University Of Chicago Press.

Otiso, K. M. and Owusu, G. (2008) 'Comparative Urbanization in Ghana and Kenya in Time and Space', *GeoJournal*, 71(2–3), pp. 143–157. doi: 10.1007/s10708-008-9152-x.

Palen, L. and Dourish, P. (2003) 'Unpacking "Privacy" for a Networked World', in *Proceedings of the SIGCHI Conference on Human Factors in Computing Systems*. New York: ACM (CHI '03), pp. 129–136. doi: 10.1145/642611.642635.

Pellow, D. (2008) *Landlords and Lodgers: Socio-Spatial Organization in an Accra Community*. Chicago, IL: University of Chicago Press.

Pertierra, A. C. (2015) 'Practicing Tranquilidad: Domestic Technologies and Comfortable Homes in Southeastern Mexico', *The Journal of Latin American and Caribbean Anthropology*, 20(3), pp. 415–432. doi: 10.1111/jlca.12186.

Pertierra, A. C. and Turner, G. (2012) *Locating Television: Zones of Consumption*. London: Routledge.

Petronio, S. (2002) *Boundaries of Privacy: Dialectics of Disclosure*. Albany: State University of New York Press.

Pink, S. (2004) *Home Truths: Gender, Domestic Objects and Everyday Life*. English ed. Oxford; New York: Berg.

Pink, S. and Mackley, K. L. (2012) 'Video and a Sense of the Invisible: Approaching Domestic Energy Consumption through the Sensory Home', *Sociological Research Online*, 17(1), pp. 1–19. doi: 10.5153/sro.2583.

Pinney, C. (2002) 'Photographic Portraiture in Central India in the 1980s and 1990s', in Buchli, V. (ed.) *The Material Culture Reader*. London: Berg, pp. 87–104.

Prussin, L. (1969) *Architecture in Northern Ghana*. Oakland: University of California Press.

Schildkrout, E. (1973) 'The Fostering of Children in Urban Ghana: Problems of Ethnographic Analysis in a Multi-Cultural Context', *Urban Anthropology*, 2(1), pp. 48–73.

Sennett, R. (2017) *The Fall of Public Man (40th Anniversary Edition)*. New York: W. W. Norton & Company.

Silverstone, R. (1992) *Consuming Technologies: Media and Information in Domestic Spaces*. London: Psychology Press.

Silverstone, R. et al. (1989) 'Families, Technologies and Consumption: The Household and Information and Communication Technologies', in *CRICT Discussion Paper*. Uxbridge: Centre for Research into Innovation, Culture & Technology. Available at: http://eprints.lse.ac.uk/46657/.

Star, S. L. (1999) 'The Ethnography of Infrastructure', *American Behavioral Scientist*, 43(3), pp. 377–391.

Tacchi, J. (2012) 'Radio in the (i)Home: Changing experiences of domestic audio technologies in Britain', in Bessire, L. (ed.) *Radio Fields: Anthropology and Wireless Sound in the 21st Century*. New York: New York University Press, pp. 233–249.

118 *Hidden and incomplete*

van der Geest, S. (1998) 'Yebisa Wo Fie: Growing Old and Building a House in the Akan Culture of Ghana', *Journal of Cross-Cultural Gerontology*, 13(4), pp. 333–359.

van der Geest, S. (2000) 'Funerals for the Living: Conversations with Elderly People in Kwahu, Ghana', *African Studies Review*, 43(3), pp. 103–129.

van der Geest, S. (2006) 'Sleeping in Kwahu, Ghana', *Medische Antropologie*, 18(1), pp. 73–86.

van Dijk, R. (2003) 'Religion, Reciprocity and Restructuring Family Responsibility in the Ghanaian Pentecostal Diaspora', in Bryceson, D. F. and Vuorela, U. (eds) *The Transnational Family: New European Frontiers and Global Networks*. First Edition. New York: Berg, pp. 173–196.

Weintraub, J. (1997) 'The Theory and Politics of the Public/Private Distinction', in Kumar, K. (ed.) *Public and Private in Thought and Practice: Perspectives on a Grand Dichotomy*. Chicago, IL: University of Chicago Press, pp. 1–39.

Woodward, I. (2001) 'Domestic Objects and the Taste Epiphany a Resource for Consumption Methodology', *Journal of Material Culture*, 6(2), pp. 115–136. doi: 10.1177/135918350100600201.

Yanagisako, S. J. (1979) 'Family and Household: The Analysis of Domestic Groups', *Annual Review of Anthropology*, 8, pp. 161–205.

Zelizer, V. A. R. (1994) *Pricing the Priceless Child: The Changing Social Value of Children*. Princeton, NJ: Princeton University Press.

Notes

1 The aim of naming the kind of houses I discuss here "middle class" is to avoid generalisation and flattening of the various architectural, geographical, and socio-economic housing types across Ghana. However, traditional compound houses, slums, mud huts, luxury buildings, and premium villas may all express similar practices of privacy preservation and boundary making. The commonality and diversity of the houses I visited during my fieldwork simply reflect my main informants – middle-class urban residents.

2 It may not be a coincidence that studies such as Kirk and Sellen's (2010) cataloguing and archiving of domestic objects, Pink and Mackley's (2012) video footage of houses, Hirsch's (1997) study on domestic photography and frames, and Miller's (2008) intimate portraits of material culture indoors are all based in Euro-American households. The methods taken in these previous works (e.g., a detailed registry of domestic objects) are seen as intrusive and even dangerous from the West African perspective.

3 This difference also resides in the context of the project and the relationships it facilitates: Pink and Mackley's applied project required one, or two, house visits, offering participants to review their videos. This project, however, required informal and potentially continual ethnographic engagement, and therefore was in tune with local norms.

4 Living in bare, uncompleted structures is not limited to private households but also shops and even hotels, such as the large un-plastered cemented business hotel in Ashaignman (a town near Tema). The hotel management completes each floor according to their budget and then offers the refurbished rooms for booking.

5 There are unfortunate cases where these temporary tenants try and take over the house by performing witchcraft to set an energetic barrier between the house owner and his land. This barrier appears as a sudden fear to enter the house,

Hidden and incomplete 119

which is deemed as dangerous or spiritually 'polluted.' In other instances, the witchcraft victim simply forgets the exact location of his/her property or even about the house's mere existence.

6 According to the latest exchange rate 1 euro is worth 6.23 cedis (https://www. euro-currency.eu/EUR_GHS, accessed: 11 March 2019).

7 It is based on the song God Will Make a Way (2003) by the American pastor and songwriter Don Moen, who was inspired by Proverbs 3:5-6 NIV: 'Trust in the Lord with all your heart and lean not on your own understanding; in all your ways submit to him and he will make your paths straight.' These songs are part of the gospel-life genre developed after the migration of Highlife music from nightclubs into churches (see Chapter 4).

8 van der Geest quotes a related story about a retired teacher who felt ashamed that he did not have any furniture in his room: 'whenever he got a visitor, he rushed to the door and met the person outside. Only after he had proper furniture, he invited people in' (Miescher quoted in van der Geest, 1998: 364).

9 Interpol (2004) crime statistics show 5.4 burglaries per 100,000 persons in Ghana, compared with 76.9 per 100,000 in Kenya, and Ghana ranks 19th of fewest burglary occurrences globally (Grant, 2005: 669).

10 The use of locked gates and walls is also common in public dwellings like hotels or schools. When travelling to Winneba, a town in the Central Region of southern Ghana, I once returned to a hotel and got locked outside the gate. The reception was closed, and it took a long time before my knocking and shouting got me back in. Eventually, I had to return to the hotel by 11 PM every night.

11 When Ghanaians knock on gates or doors it is customary to include a kind of 'verbal knocking' sound: 'Ko Ko Ko.' Using sounds while knocking transforms the generic knock by incorporating a vocal identification method – the person inside recognises the visitor by his or her verbal knock. Shouting 'Ko Ko Ko,' therefore, is not only about grabbing the attention of whoever is inside, but it is also about saying: 'It is me – you can open' (of course there is always the option of sending a WhatsApp message or calling as one approaches the house).

12 The dialectic aspect of this division is that Fry and Drew's 'traditional' compounds were re-worked as open spaces to improve health and hygiene while Tema's modern neighbourhoods included traces of compound life in recreational areas and backyards (d'Auria, 2010; d'Auria and De Meulder, 2010; d'Auria and Kootin Sanwu, 2010).

13 In their survey about the resettlement of villagers from Tema in Tema Manhean, Amarteifio, Butcher, and Whitman (1966: 63) found that women and men rejected the indoor kitchens in their new houses: 'Over one third of the sample households store, prepare and cook food in places other than the kitchens, usually the veranda or yard.'

14 'Design blocks' are perhaps the most recognisable architectural feature in Ghana. The blocks are a decorative shading and ventilating system that maintain privacy in the yard but still let air and light flow in. Also, they allow looking out to the street through the carved holes, often shaped according to traditional Adinkra symbols. 'Design blocks' come in various shapes and are used in private houses, churches, and schools. They are often sold by the side of the road and are valuable in thinking of how material objects express the need of individuals for privacy but not isolation or in other words: the need to see without being seen. This delicate balance was shown in the discussion about dark pubs as well.

15 A similar living room model is even reproduced amongst members of the Ghanaian diaspora as they construct their domestic spaces according to the Ghanaian interior design codes (Ben Elul, 2012).

120 *Hidden and incomplete*

16 Ceremonial uses of the living room include the traditional 'knocking ceremony,' in which the family of the groom arrives with gifts for the family of the bride in order to introduce themselves and request blessings for the union.

17 A parallel tradition occurs among the neighbourhood's women who gather every night and watch 'Telenovelas' (usually South American soap operas dubbed in English) and Nigerian cinema in restaurants and shops. During my early fieldwork the flickering images and loud sounds of 'La Gata' ('The Stray Cat'), a Mexican telenovela, were impossible to ignore.

18 As an alternative methodology, Meyer analysed Ghanaian films that depict bedrooms. Like my use of an art exhibition, she explains that films cannot replace participant observation, but they are by no means inferior to it, as they 'dramatize, condense, and offer a specific perspective' on cultural matters (Meyer, 2010: 117).

19 In their survey of the Tema Manhean resettlement project Amarteifio, Butcher, and Whitman (1966: 63) write that 'any room providing a reasonable standard of privacy and shelter is regarded as living space and used as a sleeping room, and that this attitude is not necessarily the result of overcrowding.' The main point is that 'bedroom culture' is not prevalent in Ghana.

20 The documentary film *Paa Joe & The Lion* (2016) tells the story of Jacob, a young artist specialising in carving artesian fantasy coffins in Greater Accra. After Jacob and his father gained international recognition and exhibited their artwork abroad Jacob told the director about his newly found respect in the village: I could remember there was a friend of mine, and I would visit her, but every time I would visit her, she would make sure we sat outside and had the conversation. But after my trip from the UK when I visited her, she said, "Come inside, come inside!" I said: "Wow! So, you were waiting for me to travel overseas before you allowed me to come inside" so that was the first time I entered her room. I said: "Oh! This is so funny in Ghana."

21 These large plastic containers, placed in the backyard, bathroom, and rooftop, are strictly measured and filled as a reserve water source during water breaks. The domestic scenery is also equipped with small yellow gallons used for filling and transferring water from central water points into the house. These boxes are informally known as 'Kufuor gallons,' named after president John Kufuor because during his presidency (2001–2009) water shortages was a common problem.

22 As the artistic exhibit of a Ghanaian bedroom portrayed, the body is another form of extending the house and its functions by way of opposition: while the house interiors are kept hidden, private, dark, and often messy, the body is strictly composed through 'rituals of becoming' that include hand-washed, neatly ironed, tailor-made clothes, strict shaving, hair-cutting, and hair-weaving routines, and the wearing of 'technological jewellery' (Miner, Chan and Campbell, 2001) such as smartphones. The body, thus, becomes a vehicle for the public exhibition of gender, class, and religion, keeping the house out of sight. This claim differs from literature in the anthropology of houses that drew analogies and metaphors between bodies and built forms (John, 1963; Bourdieu, 1970; Blier, 1983; Carsten and Hugh-Jones, 1995; Buchli, 2013).

6 In a relationship with God
The discretness of Social Media

In August 2015, Vodafone, one of Ghana's major telecommunication companies,[1] launched a commercial campaign promoting their new offer: for only 2 Ghana cedis, customers get 250 minutes of airtime, limited to two days only. The advert demonstrates how one can use such an opportunity – lots of minutes in a short time – by displaying a 'typical' Ghanaian mother-in-law declaring: 'I need two whole days to tell my son's wife how to keep him happy.' The mother constantly calls her daughter-in-law to supervise, check, and instruct her about cooking, religion, and domestic life. The wife, in turn, is forced to answer her phone day and night, obediently respecting the authority of her elder, as she repeatedly answers the phone with 'Yes, Ma' (short for mother).

The Vodafone advert became incredibly popular on Ghanaian social media, as it tapped into collective experience and a very local sense of humour. Moreover, the advert demonstrates the link between digital communication and familial surveillance in Ghana. Simply put, in a Ghanaian context the opportunity for unlimited communication is also the opportunity for unlimited surveillance. How do people use their digital devices to navigate between their familial or religious obligations and their own individual aspirations?

The information in this chapter is based on public and private posts of informants and their contacts, which are altered to maintain anonymity. In addition to status updates, videos, and images, I also used memes as a critical source of ethnographic data. According to Shifman (2013), an internet meme is 'a piece of digital content that spreads quickly around the web in various iterations and becomes a shared cultural experience.' In their comparative social media ethnographies, Miller et al. (2016) describe memes as the 'moral police' of the internet. According to Sinanan (2017: 206), who explored the case of Trinidad, 'the moral lessons that emerge through memes and the semiotics that appear in photos posted to social media are thus deeply reflective of the societies that produce them.'

In his study about social media in Brazil, Spyer (2018: 62) identified two domains of online interactions: 'lights on' refers to public and collective online domains with high levels of surveillance, while 'lights off' is used

DOI: 10.4324/9781003187424-6

122 *In a relationship with God*

for gossip, political incorrectness, and sexual content. Internet memes, as Spyer (2018: 62) argues, are distributed in the intermediate 'shadowed' space between 'lights on' and 'lights off,' because they carry public yet anonymous content ('publicly private' according to Lange 2007). This hybrid visual genre, he explains, is known in Brazil as 'Indirects' (*indiretas*) – images and verbal exchanges that 'make conflicts public without directly referring to the other person (the adversary) involved in the problem' (Spyer, 2018: 91).

Memes in Ghana provide spiritual, psychological, and social guidance, for example, about love life or parenting. They usually combine text and images using a friendly and motivational tone (catchphrases, poems, quotes, stories) and are spread across families, colleagues, and church groups. They can be duplicated or they can inspire response/follow-up memes, according to their impact and popularity. On Instagram (a popular social networking application across Ghana, used through mobile phones to share visual content), memes carry a predominantly humorous tone. These humorous memes

Figure 6.1 Vodafone Ghana advert links family and technology.

In a relationship with God 123

were especially useful for my digital ethnography[2] thanks to their ability to both express and challenge collective experiences and social norms.

Going back to my discussion on language and indirection (Chapter 3), memes are used as 'digital proverbs' in their African context. They serve as a 'third party' in private and public discussions online, representing a neutral moral authority (Yankah 1989). Furthermore, by continually distributing and reinforcing specific values and experiences (whether they are 'real' or not), memes bridge between direct lived experience and rumoured, indirect, or desired experience. Such mediation between actual and virtual experience was described by Burrell (2011) concerning scamming rumours in internet cafés and by Maxwell (1998) concerning the Pentecostal prosperity gospel, and its need to mediate between economic hardships and financial aspirations. It is no coincidence that so many memes bear a religious significance, whether through humour or through moral guidance (Figure 6.1).

6.1 'You came out of my privacy': family surveillance on social media

As discussed, middle-class urban households extend many of their functions onto external spaces such as streets and social media. As a result, familial presence online becomes an extension of domestic surveillance and co-inhabitation. Familial control begins within the home, by regulating movements and routines, as well as the use, access, and ownership of technology. This extended dwelling reaches beyond the house by gaining more knowledge about the whereabouts and actions of relatives through their social media posts. Familial presence online, therefore, is often what leads people in and out of applications and dictates the content they share or hide.

According to Coe's (2008) research on transnational parenting among Ghanaians, the goal of many middle-class urban Ghanaian parents is to raise a 'hard-working and obedient child who is respectful toward his or her elders.' Coe shows how migrating to Western, secular, and liberal countries often poses a challenge to this mission, as children are exposed to systems and ideas that contradict Ghana's educational values. Digital technologies in urban Ghana operate in similar ways – they expose people to an alternative set of values and public/private spaces. The child (or young adult) experiments with new cultures of sharing, seeing, and being seen online (Burrell, 2009, 2012; Marwick and boyd, 2014; Pertierra, 2015; Sinanan, 2017).

Meanwhile, adults feel it is up to them to 'correct' their child because his or her behaviour (online or offline) will reflect the parent's reputation and may cause long-term damages (Coe, 2008: 232). Sharing a minor's photograph online or allowing children to behave indiscreetly or disrespectfully on social media are all potential threats to the wellbeing and good name of both the nuclear and the extended family. Mansa, a young baker living in Tema, was discussing the threat posed by social media on the obedience and reputation of children. She told me that her niece, who lives in her house,

124 *In a relationship with God*

uses a unique application that blocks access to her mobile phone, including individual applications. For example, entering her WhatsApp account requires a unique password. This application prevents family members from prying through her phone if it is left unwatched.[3] One day Mansa's niece left her phone unlocked, and Mansa finally managed to look through her chat logs. She found intimate conversations with other boys and girls, including sexual interactions.

Mansa's niece attends boarding school, and most of the interactions on her social media were with female peers. Sending children to boarding schools has been highly prevalent in Ghana since the British colonial period. These schools are often remembered for their strict disciplinary rules and their role as a 'melting pot' for teenagers of various backgrounds. However, 'as an opposing sphere to home, boarding-schools represent a space beyond the control of the family and setting for homo-erotic playground sexualities' (Dankwa, 2009: 196). In that sense, just like an evening in a dark pub or a day in the local internet café, boarding schools are seen as an opportunity for privacy. This privacy, of course, is only relational to the family but far from being absolute.

According to Dankwa (2009), it is the combination of 'homo-social spaces' (united in gender, age, or social position) and 'indirect language' that allows such hidden sexual practices to exist. However, if in the past boarding schools carried an aura of discipline and surveillance, the introduction of new technologies enhanced the rumours and stereotypes about what happens behind these walls. As Gwen, a social media user, commented online:

> It's crazy ooo. My landlord's 15 yrs old girl took my laptop to browse when she was home two weeks ago, she forgot to log out, and I got curious to read some of her chats, jeeeeeez nudes? What that gal is doing at age 15, I haven't done in my 33 yrs lifetime.
>
> Instagram (2017)

Many Ghanaian parents delay their children's access to technology as much as possible by preventing them from owning their own devices. As in the case of women in India, minors are given access to technology only under direct supervision (Venkatraman, 2017). However, unlike India, where the ban on mobile phone ownership and social media usage specifically targets women (Venkatraman, 2017: 38), the sanctions in Ghana are much more age-oriented than they are gendered. Nevertheless, the right to own a technological device is associated with power, age, class, sexual maturity, and life achievements.

For instance, Yaw, an entrepreneur and construction manager living in Tema, conditions his daughter's future ownership of a mobile phone with her school achievements and good behaviour. Yaw has a 15-year-old daughter named Grace and although she dreams of having her own phone, he is scared of the sexual scenarios his daughter may be exposed to if she were to

In a relationship with God   125

own a mobile phone before attending boarding school. 'We do not educate our children like you in the West,' he told me. 'We are becoming too Western, and I do not allow my girl to have a phone until she finishes school because now, she should study and help us in the house.'

In her article about Cuban girls and visual media, Pertierra (2015: 194) discusses the Quinceañera ritual, when 15-year-old girls shift from full family control to 'having sexual agency.' At this age, Cuban girls engage with a variety of digital and visual content 'both as consumers of global media and as producers of their own images for local and transnational circulation' (Pertierra 2015: 194). The mobile phone camera and the social media platforms that accommodate it become 'technologies of sexiness,' in which teenagers explore their online visibility by negotiating between global consumer culture, post-socialist economy, and traditional familial expectations.

Like the Cuban girls in Pertierra's (2015) article, who negotiate between capitalist consumer culture and post-socialist collective norms, Ghanaian teens (both boys and girls) live in an exceptionally complex time: their parents are shifting from traditional structures of extended families and communal culture towards the Christian Pentecostal ideal of nuclear families, public morality, and consumerist prosperity. These inter-generational ruptures are a daily point of reference, as the Pentecostal movement sweeps young urban middle-class households to break ties with parents, siblings, and extended kin to achieve spiritual and material prosperity (Marshall-Fratani, 1998; Maxwell, 1998; Meyer, 1999).

Mansa explained that her niece's move to boarding school meant that social media was often utilised for unwanted interactions and even to facilitate 'lesbian and homosexual influence.' This relates to what Peter, a 28-year-old social media manager, told me regarding gays 'coming out after darkness' (Chapter 4). Boarding schools, night-time, and social media, therefore, are seen as sites of invisibility and therefore as dangerous sites. Once these platforms gain their reputation as spaces of liberation and escape, they also become associated with taboos, secrets, infidelity, pre-marital sex, nude pictures, and same-sex interactions. In both cases, social media privacy is entangled with environmental and material conditions, echoing the recent discussions about 'bedroom culture' in media studies about Western households (Livingstone, 2007; Horst, 2009).

Yaw, Mansa, and Peter connect their suspicions about digitisation to the increasing loss of control over children by elders, in an age of rapid urbanisation, modernisation, and transnational migration. In recent years, young Africans around the world (many of whom are the children of migrants) have developed a shared online conversation about this unique experience of parental surveillance, especially using the hashtag #Africanparentsbelike. This conversation mostly takes place on Twitter and Instagram – two applications that are not frequently used by the older generation and therefore have a more liberated tone. For instance, a satiric Instagram sketch by Nigerian comedian and social media figure Dami Olatunde (also known as

126 *In a relationship with God*

'AfricanApe06') depicts a mother gathering her 'fellow African parents' to a special meeting. In the sketch she states:

> This month we have just three major tasks we must accomplish. Number one, we must make sure that every morning we send our children daily broadcast messages. These messages must be very long so when they look at it, it will terrify them... but we will now call them and make sure they read it... The second part, we should call them and make sure they talk to people they don't even know; for example, the auntie who took care of them when they were two-months-old, or the doctor that circumcised them, you get the point. In the third part, we should call them and complain about every picture they post on the Internet – any questions?

As previously discussed concerning memes, the sketch indirectly confronts a general familial experience. The fictional mother suggests three types of surveillance, which are in fact three common practices. A Ghanaian Instagram user gave an example of the third one (calling and complaining) by telling her followers that she changed her WhatsApp profile picture to a picture of 'Groot,' a fictional non-human creature featured in the 2014 American superhero film *Guardians of the Galaxy* (Figure 6.2). When her mother saw the photo, she called the family pastor worried about its 'demonic' style and demanded that she take down the picture. This could be a fictional story (or joke), but it aims to reference real familial surveillance. Pentecostalism sets a negative discourse on indigenous mythical creatures such as gnomes, trolls, witches, and demons as signs of danger and evil, so such a parental reaction is not unreasonable (Meyer, 2010).

Figure 6.2 Monitoring profile pictures, Instagram post.

In a relationship with God 127

Ghanaian parents, therefore, use a variety of methods to monitor both the 'consumption and self-representation that digital technologies and economic reforms have afforded their generation' (Pertierra, 2015: 203). Moreover, parents try to establish their authority by repressing their child's sense of privacy. For instance, an Instagram post from July 28, 2017, shared a parental conversation about privacy: the daughter confesses about confronting her mother who invaded her privacy online and the mother, in response, says 'You came out of my privacy' (Figure 6.3). The mother's message is clear: I gave you life, and therefore I am entitled to know your personal matters.

While it demands the act of sharing information, an irreversible action of exposing parts of yourself and your family to the world, social media also allows you to hide in unprecedented ways.[4] In the same way that curtains and walls cover a house's interior, and iron gates monitor the movement in and out of it, young social media users find creative ways to hide and monitor access to their information. Direct and instant messages (known as 'DM'), closed virtual groups, automatically disappearing content, and control over specific contacts' exposure are all part of this mechanism. Many Ghanaians even turn off their mobile data transmission so that messages they receive won't appear as 'seen' on the sender's device.

Marwick and boyd (2014) stress that the technical affordances of social media can divide and collide different social contexts, which brings new challenges and threats to many teenagers. The public persona of teenagers is expressed in their online profile and in the information they share. Thus, Marwick and boyd (2014:13) argue that 'recognising that privacy is networked suggests that privacy might best be maintained through

Figure 6.3 Motherhood and privacy, Instagram post.

128 *In a relationship with God*

shared social norms over information-sharing.' This claim that privacy is 'networked' is highly relevant in the Ghanaian context, and so is the idea that social coherency is maintained by enforcing social norms about what is appropriate or inappropriate to share online.

However, a significant difference in the Ghanaian case is that the overlapping of multiple groups in public space ('hetero-social spaces' to paraphrase Dankwa 2009) and the strict identity management it requires are all pre-existing and ongoing experiences. While the American teenager faces a new reality whereby he or she is 'performing' to a diverse audience in a unified stage, Ghanaian teenagers grow up with a firm understanding that their identities should be carefully exhibited and cautiously performed. For instance, while Marwick and boyd (2014) talk about 'coding' private information on public platforms, Lange (2007) describes 'publicly private' content, and Spyer (2018) analyses encrypted information; Ghanaians see indirect communication as an essential component of culture, language, and social norms.

To sum, there is a chain of socio-technical transformations to familial surveillance and domestic privacy: bedrooms, boarding schools, dark pubs, and internet cafés are 'homo-social spaces' (Dankwa, 2009) that offer an escape from certain types of surveillance. At the same time, these spaces are conjoined with mobile phones, pre-purchased internet data, and social media platforms that offer individual enclaves of privacy. Consequently, young Ghanaians discover new ways to visualise, represent, and express themselves online. This leads to a firm response by their parents and supervisors, who wish to establish their control in a rapidly changing environment.

6.2 Polymedia: Facebook is the street; WhatsApp is the house

The increasing attempts of Ghanaians to supervise each other's online behaviour is noticeable between couples, parents and children, pastors and worshipers, and employers and employees. However, the proliferation of alternative platforms to Facebook, such as Instagram and WhatsApp, allowed some people (especially the young and technologically savvy) to 'migrate' from Facebook and cleverly negotiate between content, platform, and audience (Miller, 2016). This idea of choosing between multiple communication platforms is theorised by Madianou and Miller (2012), following their ethnographic work about Filipino mothers working abroad. The relationship between migrant mothers and their children (who were left behind) was mediated by an abundance of communication tools such as video calls, phone calls, and letters.

Inspired by classic questions in structuralism, Madianou and Miller (2012) asked what the meaning was behind each medium and how this medium is defined in relation to its opponents. For instance, they state that 'Email is not simply Email; it is defined relationally as also not a letter, not

In a relationship with God 129

a text message and not a conversation via webcam; which, in turn, is not a phone call' (Madianou and Miller, 2012: 174). 'Polymedia' is a concept that theorises and describes these daily choices and media ecologies while focusing on their emotional and cultural meaning. According to Madianou and Miller (2012: 171), this meaning is heightened whenever 'the responsibility of choice shifts from technical and economic, to moral, social and emotional concerns.' An increasing number of young urban adults around the world can now choose between a wide selection of mediums, regardless of cost, access, or literacy (Madianou and Miller, 2012: 170).

Enyonam, a 28-year-old architect living in Tema, is active daily on both WhatsApp and Facebook. She is a member of several groups on WhatsApp such as her high-school peers' group, her architecture colleagues' group, a church group, and a group of young tech-savvy professionals living in Tema. However, on Facebook, she feels as if she's the only one sharing 'authentic' content as she reveals personal aspects of herself. She compares her experiences writing on Facebook to that of Twitter, another social media app that she often uses:

> Facebook is like a room full of spirits. You know everyone so what you say is restricted. On Twitter, my audience is undefined and so is my mind. The smart and creative people are on Twitter. Facebook posts are unoriginal, and people show a fake and vain face. When people dare to show themselves on Facebook, it ends in fights and judging.

Enyonam's point demonstrates how the Facebook audience is perceived as oppressive regarding creativity and individual liberties – it is a place where everyone is expected to follow norms and keep their position as ideal modern Christian urbanites. A flood of Christian messages and imagery that bring the 'watching eye' of God, the church, and the community into the digital realm reinforces such norms. Facebook is where the monitoring, guiding, and even policing of spirituality and faith takes place, where technology overlaps with Christianity.

A popular Ghanaian Facebook page depicting this point is titled 'Word on the street Ghana'; this page is dedicated to religious activists who brave the streets of Tema, Kumasi, and Accra, carrying signs with Pentecostal spiritual messages, mostly about being born again, forgetting the past, overcoming spiritual enemies, and connecting to the global kingdom of God. Photos of these activists holding signs in various urban spots are posted to the page, encouraging discussion and sharing.

This merger of urban streets, digital media, and religious order is a classic example of how Ghana's public landscape is reflected on Facebook by occupying it with Pentecostal values. Moreover, it reveals attempts to bridge between private media and public surveillance by monitoring intimacy (as described in Figure 1.1). As one post from this page poetically stated: 'Christianity is when no one is looking' (Figure 6.4). This post, by a young

130   *In a relationship with God*

pastor in Tema, also emphasises the issue of solitude and who looks at us when we're alone:

> I pray for you today that the eye that sees when no one is mindful of your presence will keep watch over you. The one who knows what you can't tell the closest person around you will meet your heart desires.
> (Facebook, 2017)

The public expectation to be a 'good Christian' is expressed continuously through the type of content people share on Facebook. Much of this content comes from the users themselves in status updates such as 'anything that will not take you to heaven is not worth it!!!' or 'What have you done today for Jesus?' Pictures and videos from Sunday church services, funerals, and weddings are an essential part of the Facebook news feed, visually portraying this public sphere. The concept of visibility, morality, and spiritual gaze, therefore, is a repeating theme in many posts. As Sinanan (2017: 1) explains in her ethnography of social media in Trinidad:

> Social media heightens the fields of visibility between the individual self and wider society. As a consequence, there is a general anxiety of what appearance, and being judged on appearance, imply about what it means to be human.

Figure 6.4 Facebook and Christianity. Courtesy of the managers of 'Word on the streets Global' Facebook page.

In a relationship with God   131

Sinanan's (2017: 204) work demonstrates that in an age of social media, 'visibility is a central manifestation of normativity.' Each culture, place, and group has a dynamic idea of normativity, correctness, and appropriateness that people strive to materialise through their public visibility online. The community gaze on Facebook is also expressed in the responses to those who try to challenge this normativity through individualism or 'non-normative' behaviour. Unlike the concept of 'zombie' (*jiangshi*) contacts in China, referring to Facebook contacts who never interact with each other (Wang, 2016: 100), Enyonam's description of Facebook as a 'room full of spirits' means that users are present and interactive but do not express their true selves. Instead, they follow conventions, re-post existing content, and simply observe others without sharing anything personal. Enyonam knows well that if she ever broke her silence, people would not hesitate to remind her about the 'proper' way to use Facebook.

Last year, Enyonam struggled with depression following an upsetting experience at her university. Her teacher and dissertation supervisor, who is also a pastor, sexually harassed her, which deeply damaged her confidence and livelihood during her studies. The fear of being exposed as a woman who complains about sexual harassment or mental depression is incredibly intense for a young and aspiring person like Enyonam. As she phrased it: 'everybody is connected.' Her actions could affect peers, friends, family, other lecturers, and many more. However, after overcoming this dark time in her life, she wanted to help other men and women who may be suffering in similar ways. She wanted to share her experience publicly on Facebook, demonstrating the power of prayer, hope, and family support to overcome the pain of depression.

Enyonam decided to share a controversial blog article by Freda Obeng-Ampofo (2015), titled 'A Real Face of Depression.' The article revealed the writer's story about depression to increase public awareness, which included some intimate confessions such as the following:

> I must confess, prior to my depression, I was heavily involved in church, but during the years I was depressed, church was usually a one-off thing. Deep inside I knew God was the only being who could sustain me but just didn't have the desire or bandwidth to draw closer to God. Frankly, I prayed but I always felt the more I prayed, the worse things got, and nothing was getting better. And I was extremely upset at God when my relationship ended because, at the time, that was all I was holding on to. It's safe to say I was bitter towards God.
>
> (Freda Obeng-Ampofo 2015, blog post)

Publishing an article about depression, instead of declaring it on a personal basis, was a typical way of using indirection on social media. Referring to Spyer's (2018: 59) division between 'lights on' and 'lights off' domains online, indirectness protects people's public persona by discussing personal matters in a public sphere.

132 *In a relationship with God*

However, after Enyonam posted the link, certain relatives, friends, and co-workers confronted her on Facebook. Many claim that depression is a sign of being a non-believer and Enyonam got into an argument with a Facebook friend, who responded: depressed people are selfish, focusing on themselves instead of the community. Enyonam tried to convince him that such a condition is sensitive, and that no one chooses to suffer from it. So he sent her a private message, where he confesses about the abuse he went through as well: 'Look at me! I am not crying I just moved on,' he wrote.

Enyonam's Facebook friend moved from the public post on Facebook to the private messaging function (Facebook messenger) when he wanted to discuss a profoundly personal issue. This choice of one medium over another according to content and context is a case of polymedia. Moreover, this 'switch' reflects the emotional management of each medium, determined mainly by its level of privacy. For instance, Madianou and Miller (2012) discuss the choice between voice and text messages as significant for the emotional management of migrant mothers and left-behind children. Also, in her research about breakups in the digital age, Gershon (2011) shows how choosing between Facebook, SMS messages, phone calls, and face-to-face interactions may carry a moral and emotional burden when disconnecting romantic relationships.

Enyonam's attempt to be non-normative on Facebook (even if indirect) demonstrates how discourse about depression can threaten social order and essential Christian values such as spiritual uplift, care for others, and prosperity as fulfilment. The social order is maintained by obeying the divisions of private and public, proper and improper, visible and invisible. Users are free to explore new forms of communications using alternative mediums and platforms. The possibility to choose between different mediums carries a moral responsibility: 'an individual has no external excuse as to the choice they've made, so they are held personally responsible for the decision' (Madianou and Miller, 2013: 180). Where should Enyonam have turned?

While conducting this ethnographic study, and especially during its digital ethnography component, I received only a handful of Facebook friend requests but dozens of new WhatsApp contacts. According to Elikem, a blogger and computer engineer living in Accra, in Ghana, Facebook is not as common as people would think. 'A quick attempt to run a paid advert to all Ghanaian users on Facebook, generates about 900,000 users.' WhatsApp, as opposed to Facebook, is considered a much more discrete platform. This is due to its physical ability to create multiple channels of interaction with varying levels of privacy – what Miller had called 'scalable sociality.' According to Miller (2016: 3), social media currently offers a range of interactions varying from 'most public' to 'most private' and from small to large groups. This spectrum allows different people and cultures to move along it according to particular values, beliefs, habits, and power structures.

Why is this possibility so crucial to urban Ghana? There are many reasons and advantages for using WhatsApp over Facebook, but the heart of the

In a relationship with God   133

matter is that Facebook is experienced as too exhibitionist. As illustrated above, Facebook provides access to dangerous terrain, full of biographic and visual details. Much like a town's central circle, church, or marketplace, Facebook is used for more public exchanges of information. Many urbanites promote their small or informal businesses on Facebook, offering privately sold food, clothes, and goods.[5] Other contents on Facebook may include birthday wishes, wedding photos, anniversary blessings, and of course Christian spiritual messages.

WhatsApp, alternatively, allows careful navigation between what you show and exactly whom you show it to, which better suits this often reserved and suspicious urban climate. WhatsApp is perceived as a more private application because it syncs only with mobile phone numbers, maintaining a sense of control over who sees what. Also, WhatsApp provides an easy and straightforward private messaging platform specially designed for both smartphones and simpler mobile phones. Unlike the family computer, landlines, or internet cafés, mobile phones in Ghana are used as personal and individual objects, offering unprecedented privacy.

Urban Ghanaians use WhatsApp in a dynamic, lively, and productive manner: whenever WhatsApp introduces new technical features Ghanaians tend to adopt them quickly and smoothly. For instance, broadcast messages, time-limited multimedia 'stories,' direct replies to specific messages, and the long-awaited 'un-send' function. The latter was celebrated on Instagram as a Godly blessing that can prevent unfortunate situations such as accidentally sending a gossip message to the wrong person. Profile pictures are replaced on a daily or weekly basis, serving as visual updates, alongside the regular updates of status/bio lines, which usually includes religious phrases and slogans.

WhatsApp offers an additional platform for familial and intimate relationships. Updating a profile picture on WhatsApp to that of a parent or a cousin, for instance, is an 'effective' way to express familial love and honour to the 'outside' world. Samuel, a young IT consultant, often posts portraits of his mother as his profile picture and once added a caption saying: 'I am blessed to have this great woman of God. "God bless you, mummy."' By doing so, WhatsApp 'adds a further layer to the visibility of those relationships – both for other family members and for wider community networks' (Sinanan, 2017: 108). While many Ghanaians are members in nuclear and extended WhatsApp family groups, these tend to be less active, perhaps due to the strict surveillance they entail.

Apart from adding a layer of visibility, WhatsApp's most important role is of adding a layer of invisibility (like houses and dark pubs). WhatsApp groups that contain friends, colleagues, and church members, or people with similar interests such as motherhood or technology, are much more popular than family groups in urban Ghana. The importance of the enclosed digital group is that content can be directly targeted to a particular audience: jokes, news updates, prayers, rumours, and political commentary are distributed

134 *In a relationship with God*

between groups while private chats are reserved for everything else. These chats may include discrete content such as family feuds, economic hardships, neighbourhood gossip, secret affairs, and nude pictures.

'I'm sure the inspiration to increase the WhatsApp group limit from 50 to 250 members was from Ghana!' declares Ayisi, a blogger and entrepreneur living in Accra. 'There are many WhatsApp groups for what we call "fun" – you can meet boys and girls there.' People are added to the groups Ayisi mentioned only if they know at least two or three other members so that the others can feel secure and trusted. The group is used like a networking space from which people can move to private chats, almost like moving from a house's courtyard to one of the rooms (see Chapter 5). Other groups are restricted to women or men only so that each can recommend or share a potential hook-up with his or her friends. Ayisi explains that 'fun' groups are often platonic but carry a playful sexual atmosphere:

> I used to party a lot, so we created a group called Party Crew... The group had guys and girls that party together; trust each other, do sexually suggestive dancing with each other. Spouses can't be there so if someone posts pictures and videos in the group and less than five minutes later her boyfriend calls her, she knows there's a traitor in the group.

Apart from reaffirming Pertierra's (2015: 194) discussion about 'technologies of sexiness,' and their new forms of self-representation, Ayisi's description of secret, hidden, and playful WhatsApp groups provides virtual access to otherwise enclosed spaces. It provided me with clues about spaces that I could not penetrate but knew existed. In that sense, it resembled private houses that I visited but only saw from the outside. Following these symbolic parallels, I suggest an internal division of Ghana's WhatsApp, similar to that of the private house: individual chats are entirely private, groups are semi-private, and the profile is semi-public, containing minimal information and visible only to phone contacts. Application-blocking apps and unique passwords resemble iron gates, as they monitor the movement in and out of this digital space (see Section 5.2).

WhatsApp, like the house, plays a dual role: it is a space where one escapes the public gaze of the street (in this case Facebook) but enters a more particular type of domestic surveillance. The WhatsApp account is divided into groups that act as rooms within a house, but this virtual house is individually planned, and its architecture is unique to each mobile phone owner. The ownership of two devices, as commonly seen in Ghana, offers an even more sophisticated version of polymedia, not only through the multiplicity of platforms but also through the multiplicity of mobile phone numbers (Sinanan, 2017: 110). This media ecology offers a dynamic and flexible spectrum of privacy and regulation.

Miller (2016: 5) argues that 'scalable sociality' replaced the traditional dichotomy between 'the private dyad and the public broadcast.' I suggest that this dichotomy was not completely replaced but simply challenged by the introduction of WhatsApp. Going back to Gal's (2002) semiotics of public and private spheres as 'fractal recursions,' WhatsApp sets a private sphere as opposed to Facebook but has its own private/public divisions as well (for instance, family groups versus 'fun' groups). While Facebook in Ghana is seen as entirely public, faithfully recreating the city's 'hetero-social spaces,' WhatsApp offers a rare commodity – individual and group privacy. The digital migration from Facebook to WhatsApp, as a choice afforded by polymedia, reframed WhatsApp and Instagram as individual spaces, leaving Facebook as an entirely 'group-oriented platform' (Sinanan, 2017: 202).

6.3 Digital witchcraft & dangerous visibility

Odame is a Hip-life musician living in Tema, who sings in Twi and English about politics, religion, and society. Just before one of my return visits, he suddenly sent me a peculiar GIF image on WhatsApp.[6] It showed dozens of snakes crawling out of a basket and going back in repeatedly (as GIFs do), without any caption or explanation. I immediately felt uncomfortable with the image, as if the snakes were released out of the image into my phone and energetically into my life. Based on the repeated warnings I had heard in Ghana, I suspected this to be digital witchcraft. 'Why did you send this to me?' I asked him. 'To scare you,' he replied.

Although I was a bit shaken by the experience, I didn't take it too seriously. Instead, I decided to take it up as a conversation topic about witchcraft and its digital dangers. Auntie Madi, who sells palm oil in Tema's market, was alarmed by the story. She refused to watch the message (like a few others) and told me to delete it quickly and block the sender. Such a firm handling of the situation is considered a harsh response for it defies the lingual rules of indirection and might put shame on Odame and his family. Why was her advice so assertive?

The answer lies in the spiritual framing of online visual culture in Ghana. Auntie Madi explained that many Ghanaians are digitally illiterate or impatient about typing; so, instead, they choose videos and images that convey their message to the other person. She showed me her WhatsApp account, which was full of graphic images with various blessings, wishes, and tips (see Figure 6.5). These memes often have a temporal component, matching the content to segments of the day (e.g., 'good morning'), the week (e.g., 'happy Sunday'), or the annual events approaching (e.g., 'happy Christmas'). They are usually Christian, with a range of decorated fonts, colours, shapes, backdrops, and music, spread mostly in church and family WhatsApp groups, as well as Facebook pages and profiles. As Venkatraman (2017: 93) argued about such memes in their Indian context, spreading them is often seen as 'God-given opportunities to build good Karma,' encouraging a generous sharing culture and attributing these images 'a social life of their own.'

136 *In a relationship with God*

'You see?' Auntie Madi asks while showing me her most recent WhatsApp interactions. 'I don't need to write anything – it is all in the message so I can just send it to my friends and family and wish them well.' Auntie Madi was trying to demonstrate that Ghanaians use visual messages to communicate online and to express meaning. This practice was termed as 'phatic photo sharing' by Lobinger (2016: 481) and as 'visual chitchat' by Villi (2012: 42), whereby the content and information are only secondary to 'the pleasure of communication and connectivity' and to 'the ritual view of communication.' Moreover, it relates to the old tradition of visualising ancestral wisdom in West Africa, as seen in Ghana's Adinkra signs and the use of Sankofa birds during Nkrumah's regime (see chapter 3, page 38).

Visualising proverbs on clothes, architectural features, or digital memes is a common semiotic strategy of indirection. The temporal and visual significance of memes in urban Ghana explains why Odame's messages were so dangerous from Auntie Madi's perspective. However, there was a broader context to this fear of digital sorcery. Odame's clever use of temporality, visualisation, movement, and spiritual conventions led Auntie Madi to conclude that he must be connected to the movement of *Sakawa*. Often referred to as cult or local religion, *Sakawa* is a widely discussed form of spiritual ritual aimed at enhancing and ensuring the financial success and protected identity of digital scammers and cyber-criminals (Warner, 2011: 744).

Sakawa tales circulate in urban streets and social media in the form of rumours and gossip (Armstrong, 2011; Burrell, 2012). These rumours typically describe teenage men who meet secretly after dark and perform rituals that combine digital scamming with black magic practices such as drinking

Figure 6.5 Visual communications, WhatsApp meme. Author recreation.

In a relationship with God   137

blood, ritual killings, sleeping in coffins, and public nudity. It is frequently discussed in the public sphere (churches, radios, magazines, news blogs, and street preachers), and especially in Ghanaian and Nigerian films dealing with 'juju-money' or 'blood-money' (Wendl, 2007). With rapid modernisation and an emerging neoliberal market economy as the backdrop, *Sakawa* rituals relate to what Comaroff and Comaroff (2008) have termed 'occult economy,' whereby magical techniques are deployed for material gain, sometimes violently. According to Weiss (1998), rumours about blood-stealing by greedy sorcerers among the Haya people express a postcolonial notion of bodies as commodities, the suspicion towards biomedical institutions, and the analogies between blood, gasoline, and electricity as quantified substances that become avenues for wealth and power. *Sakawa* internet scammers share this intersection of rumours, modernity, technology, and suspicious wealth.[7]

Sakawa boys are usually identified by their luxurious lifestyle, new cars, and imported clothes, which are attributed to the fortune they've made through scams. This makes them essential actors in local perceptions of middle-classness as a social category that depends on visibility and invisibility. In other words, they represent the risk, jealousy, and moral speculation that any expression of wealth and success may bring with it in urban Ghana, requiring a careful manipulation of privacy online and offline. The formal and informal debate about *Sakawa* therefore influences privacy practices and fears online among all urbanites. These fears are especially true concerning one's social visibility and photographic portrayals.

According to Meyer, Pentecostal media uses radio, television, and cinema to 'mediate between frustrations and anxieties, and the wish for a better, more prosperous life' (2006: 298). This media, digital and electronic, is a space for emotional and spiritual engagement with forces of good and evil (Meyer, 2006). The advantage of visual representations over observed reality in Pentecostalism (by making the invisible visible) situates photographs and videos 'as an important medium of divine intervention in the life of the (biblically informed) viewer' (Gordon and Hancock, 2005: 389).

However, unlike cinema or television, which is mostly public and at times censored or age restricted, social media adds a personal, private, and unsupervised layer to this phenomenon. It reaches anyone, anywhere, even in the vulnerable state of being alone or at home. According to Meyer, Pentecostal Christianity attributes so much power to photographs that even seemingly pure and sacred Jesus posters may contain hidden wicked spirits, looking at innocent worshipers through the wandering gaze of the picture's subject (Meyer, 2010).

In that sense, Auntie Madi's speculation that the GIF image I received was enchanted by *Sakawa* boys, and that the snakes would penetrate my mobile phone, and through it, into my life, requires a detailed investigation into digital witchcraft, social media, and photography. Anthropologists and historians have studied the attribution of supernatural powers to photography

138   *In a relationship with God*

by looking at the role of photos in traditional societies (Michaels, 1991; Behrend, 2003; Wright, 2004). In his classic book on comparative religion, *The Golden Bough*, Frazer (1890) describes several incidences of native peoples being terrified of or hostile towards cameras. Behrend (2003: 133) explains that early missionaries and European explorers in Africa used the camera to obtain spiritual power over natives, as 'the unfamiliar media evoked fear, terror, panic, and submission.'

According to Pinney (2011: 70), 'the anthropological literature abounds with accounts of suspicion and hostility towards the presence of the camera.' For instance, Wolbert (2000) brings a detailed description of Evans-Pritchard's camerawork in his book *The Nuer*, claiming that the distanced and blurry photos capture the natives from behind, or without them even knowing. 'The pictures were taken in secret,' she states, 'he avoided lifting his camera to focus and shoot the picture' (2000: 334).

During my fieldwork, I was systematically refused permission to take pictures of people, the interiors of their houses, and many other mundane or 'natural' situations. In some cases, where I'd snapped a photo without permission, I was immediately scolded. One time, when Violet and I drove around town, I took a photo of a food stall because I was amused by its sign: 'don't tell your wife food joint.' Sitting nearby were three men on a bench, who'd assumed I took their photo without permission and they demanded I delete it, or they'd 'beat' me. It was only after Violet firmly explained to them in Twi that I'd just snapped a picture of the sign that they gave up. Although I encountered a lot of resistance when snapping photos of traders, shopkeepers, pedestrians, or home-dwellers, when I'd visit a Sunday church service, wedding, funeral, or other festivities my camera was embraced and at times encouraged, or just casually ignored. I was even invited to take pictures at several weddings, as the locals took notice of my impressive Canon camera and my love of photography.

As Violet explained, the introduction of social media has made the issue of tourist photography somewhat sensitive because the locals now worry about the public distribution of their image. Many of them resisted the role of representing 'Africa' or 'Ghana,' especially if they were wearing their unglamorous work clothes or sat in the sun by their market stall. As mentioned, social media heightens the collective importance of visibility, which becomes a central way of materialising relationships and the self. This often raises anxieties, self-awareness, and a desire to align with 'normative' visual cultures (Sinanan, 2017).

Avoiding the mundane and preferring stylish and ideal representations online also relates to the social mobility of Ghanaian urbanites and how they maintain their public persona through photography and social media. As members of a modern and upwardly mobile community, many Ghanaians choose to keep their unglamorous, 'natural,' or spontaneous selves private, making room for a carefully performed visual identity. As Wendl (1998: 154) showed through the case of studio photography, the mundane,

In a relationship with God   139

economical, and rational reality is not crucial in Ghanaian photographs 'insofar as they are more interested in the exploration of the mysteries of exterior appearance.'

Therefore, unlike the writings on 'natives' resisting photography as a whole, it was the nature, timing, and context of the photo that determined if people embraced or resisted it.[8] The discomfort around intimate or 'naturalistic' photographs is strongly associated with a fear of witchcraft. It seems that people feel more exposed and vulnerable to sorcery and evil spirits when their photos are not composed and lack aesthetic. Saul, a 32-year-old marketing agent, discussed this issue very frankly. I asked him about the reluctance of middle-class Ghanaians to share and post intimate photos online:

SAUL: Ghanaians are a bit worried when it comes to having their picture taken for a few reasons. First, they don't know where this picture will go and what will be done with it, second, they want to look very good when the photo is taken.

ME: When you say they don't know what will be done with the picture what do you mean?

SAUL: hmm for example Juju. It is something to worry about because once you have the person's photograph, it is stronger than having their name even, you can use it to do bad things.

ME: So, knowing someone's name is also risky?

SAUL: Yes. You can use the local name or hometown for witchcraft.

Saul referred to a photo as a powerful tool for witchcraft and mentioned that any personal detail about someone can be used for putting evil spells on him/her. Names, faces, and hometowns are all coordinates on an energetic map that lead the way to a potential victim of witchcraft. Displaying these details on Facebook, therefore, is considered dangerous. Made-up residential details and fictional or generic names become boundaries between the self and his/her more extensive networks of belonging both online and offline.[9] A photo, however, is considered superior to all personal details for it provides direct access to someone's identity, and therefore his soul.

It is perceived across different cultures that the photograph captures shades, souls, or spirits of its subject, and therefore can be used to harm or even kill them. As Frazer quotes: 'When a copy of the face of a person is made and taken away from him, a portion of his life goes with the picture' (1890: 461). Alfred Gell (1998: 99) developed this point by distinguishing between 'contagious magic' and 'sympathetic magic': while the former requires physical features of the victim, such as hair or nail clippings, the later relies merely on shared visual properties – drawings, sculptures, dolls, or photographs. 'Sympathetic magic' is the main risk when posting photos online.

In February 2017, the African-American pop singer Beyonce shared an artistic photo on Instagram, announcing: 'we have been blessed two times

140   *In a relationship with God*

over. We are incredibly grateful that our family will be growing by two.' This post raised a debate on West African social networks about pregnancy photos, which was further illustrated in another humoristic video by Nigerian comedian Dami Olatunde ('AfricanApe06'). The sketch portrays a 'typical' African mother's reaction to Beyonce's post. It begins as the child informs his mother that Beyonce is pregnant. At first, she is excited and happy, but when she asks her daughter how she discovered this news, she realises it was through a social media photo and changes her tone. The soundtrack turns tense and horrific as the mother says:

> She posted a pregnant picture on Ingramgram? [the mispronunciation is on purpose] ... Does she know that everybody can see it? She is not scared of witches doing something to her? My daughter, unfollow her! When you find a husband, and you get pregnant if I hear that you want to post your pregnant picture on Ingramgram I will personally deliver you to god myself – unfollow her!

Notice that this viral Instagram meme brings together two elements of Ghana's social media – family surveillance and a fear of witchcraft. As a video meme, the sketch uses humour as indirection but relies on 'an understanding of shared circumstances and a sense of inclusion in order to "get" their meaning' (Sinanan, 2017: 206). The mother's negative reaction to Beyonce's publication comes from the perception that people should keep certain things to themselves. Beyonce's post seems careless in the mother's eyes for it might bring danger on her and (even worse) on her child. Eventually, she requests that her daughter unfollow Beyonce due to the negative influence she might have on her. Although this sketch is satiric, it taps on the tension between pre-existing privacy etiquettes, taboos, and new modes of sharing online. These findings relate to the 'pregnant' state of unfinished houses in Ghana, which are also kept hidden from social media (see Chapter 5). Such norms are profoundly different from the emergent genre of ultrasound, pregnancy, and infant photos among social media users in England (Miller and Sinanan, 2017: 60–66).

A closer example of this tensed alliance between visualisation, familial intimacy, and the dangers of witchcraft occurred when Ama posted photos of her cousin's baby girl online. Growing up in London, Ama had no idea that sharing baby photos might pose a cultural or spiritual problem. However, her cousin Louisa lives in Ghana and as a devoted born-again Christian, she has strict rules against exposing her children online. After seeing her child's face posted online, she immediately called Ama and asked for the photos to be removed. When I later asked Louisa about the incident, she explained:

LOUISA: Well... In Africa, we prefer not to expose our children on social media for the whole world to see. When they are old enough, they can decide for themselves but as for now its Dangos.

In a relationship with God   141

ME: What is that?

LOUISA: Danger. If you see just the back, it is fine, but if you see the face, someone can take it to a special traditional doctor and ask for something bad to happen to the person. It happens oo! There are bad people around. Once you have the picture, you don't even need the name. But it's not even just that – why would you like your picture shown to everyone?

ME: I see your point. Louisa: Our pastor tells us that we should get ahead with times and use more technology, but we shouldn't publish our photos anywhere for everyone to see- if I want you to see my picture, I will send it to you, so it's better to use emails and WhatsApp. I never post my son's photos online. You don't know whom might want evil for you. So, just keep it to yourself.

Such fear over witchcraft and jealousy on Facebook resembles that associated with the taboo of new-born baby pictures in India, where women avoid the 'evil eye' on Facebook by circulating photos to close family members via WhatsApp (Venkatraman, 2017: 112). In both cases, Facebook is associated with an envious and destructive gaze that one may not even be aware of. However, Louisa also used the term witchcraft to describe something much less mystical than it may seem: the fear of being exposed to a community in a non-controlled, de-contextualised, and almost chaotic manner. Following the contextual approach to photographs in Ghana, family pictures are encouraged and welcomed by Louisa and her pastor, but they prefer to distribute them via WhatsApp. This way they have a stronger sense of control over the exposure, distribution, copyright, and social visibility.

The overlapping meaning of witchcraft as an actual fear and as local terminology for privacy, safety, and caution is therefore crucial (especially if one wishes to avoid overly exotic interpretations of Ghanaians). Peter, a 28-year-old social media manager, told me that 'African beliefs' (his term) comprise practical/rational and religious/supernatural elements. 'Once they say it can bring spells upon you,' he explains, 'you'll be really careful.' Therefore, the spiritual side taps on one's nerves, their emotions, and becomes more efficient in leading people's lives and governing their morality. Noah, a 35-year-old tailor and fashion designer living in Tema, says, the culture of fear around witchcraft is first and foremost a safety precaution:

As children, we were told not to sing in the shower because it summons ghosts, but it's actually so we wouldn't accidentally swallow the water. If someone always shows himself off as big and rich people may rob him or ask him for money, so they warn him of witches who wish him harm. It's like that.

Going back to Sakawa boys, and per Weiss (1998), the idea of 'blood-stealing' as a reaction to postcolonial economies suggests witchcraft doesn't exist

142   *In a relationship with God*

'outside' modernity, consumerism, or digitisation, but within its context. By processing 'translocal discourses into local vocabularies of cause and effect,' witchcraft becomes a form of response to urban modernity (Comaroff and Comaroff, 2008: 286). This has an impact on class mobility as it translates the global economy into local terms of moral and immoral accumulation of wealth and power (Geschiere, 1997; Weiss, 2004; Ferguson, 2006; Comaroff and Comaroff, 2008).

As discussed earlier, social media heightens social visibility and issues of self-representation (Pertierra, 2015; Sinanan, 2017). In Ghana, these anxieties are often reframed to concern witchcraft, reputation, safety, and privacy. Digital photographs are especially powerful vehicles for these concepts, due to their dual magical properties: first, as iconic representations (or 'sympathetic magic') and, second, as objects with indexical virtues (the required physical presence of its subject).[10] In various cultures around the world, people believe that by destroying an image they can destroy the person captured in it, based on this visual/indexical connection (Frazer, 1890: 461), it is intriguing to wonder whether deleting a digital photo would have a similar effect.

6.4 Snapchat: a liberating application

During my fieldwork, I logged into Facebook, Instagram, Snapchat, and WhatsApp every day and documented the relevant data in my field notes. Whether I was in Ghana, immersed in the 'actual' field, or in my native home of Israel sitting in a café, these platforms gave me direct access to the daily lives of Ghanaian urbanites. Whenever I opened Snapchat, the first screen I'd see was the front camera, encouraging me to take a selfie[11] or explore the latest filters and animations. I wouldn't usually take pictures of myself but swipe straight to the Stories section, where I'd watch the exciting aspects of urban Ghana come to life.

Snapchat Stories are a collection of images, texts, and videos that appear in the chronological order that the user took them, like a slideshow. By clicking on any one of the 'Stories,' I was able to see people document their daily lives; some Stories are available for an hour and others for up to 12 hours. When watching these stories, I could see anything from a man boiling yams for lunch to a woman driving whilst listening to her favourite Afro-beat song, people adding photo effects and animations such as bunny ears, enlarged eyes or shrunken heads, nature trails, holiday poolside snaps, clubs, bars, and plenty of other self-generated videos of daily scenarios. This content generated more data about direct lived experiences than any other social media I examined.

Launched in September 2011 as an image and multimedia-messaging app, Snapchat was developed by three students from Stanford University.[12] The app has over 166 million daily active users, making it the fastest growing social media platform to date (Smith, 2017). What makes the app unique is

In a relationship with God 143

its ability to limit the audience's exposure to users' content by using time frames – the content simply disappears after anything from 10 seconds to 12 hours. This platform offers the most original service for social media privacy, significantly changing the way we think about sharing information online. 'Ghanaians like Snapchat and I'm always amazed at how free they are on there,' says Elikem, blogger and computer engineer:

ELIKEM: There are many things they'll post there, but they will never post on WhatsApp, they see it as very different worlds.
ME: What sort of things?
ELIKEM: A woman can snap a picture of her boobs and send it on Snapchat, but she'll be scared to do that on WhatsApp because there is a file, he [the man] can pass it on, but on Snapchat she decides it's only available for 10 seconds and then poof it disappears!

In 2017, Facebook Messenger, Instagram, and WhatsApp all followed in Snapchat's footsteps adding the Story feature to their social media platforms. People I'd observe online were cautious and hesitant to use WhatsApp and Facebook stories, due to the audience clash these applications suffered from. However, Instagram and Snapchat stories became an instant success due to their more liberated, individualised, and playful nature. Why is Snapchat experienced as 'clean,' free of judgemental adults and community surveillance?

According to Marwick and boyd (2014), 'searchability' – when a person becomes searchable online – is one of the defining features of social media. People find other people using parameters of location (e.g., Grindr, Tinder), first name and surname (Facebook, Instagram), or mutual friends (Facebook, Myspace). In similar ways, Ghanaians place high significance on private names, residential addresses, and hometowns as parameters that give away valuable personal information. Alternatively, Snapchat makes it intentionally difficult to find someone without his/her unique username. It even offers individually generated visual QR codes, also known as 'handles' or 'display names.' These display names make users less traceable and identifiable or simply 'privately public' (Lange, 2007).

Furthermore, as discussed before, visual materials and photographs are believed to have the power to harm a person through witchcraft or ill intention. Snapchat enters this context by producing photos with 'situational relevance' that are neither preserved nor documented (Lobinger, 2016: 482). Therefore, Snapchat does not only liberate users from social norms and community surveillance but it also liberates them from the spiritual dangers intertwined with it. The photo can be shared momentarily, without duplicating itself to the recipients. The recipient cannot blackmail the person who sent him 'nudes' (naked pictures) nor can he print the photo or republish it in distorted contexts.[13]

144 *In a relationship with God*

Another important boundary offered by Snapchat's developers is its relatively complicated design interface, making it a non-welcoming platform for supervising adults and authoritative figures. As Elikem explains:

> I actually find it hard to operate. I can't really understand it. It's not by chance. I saw an interview with the developers of Snapchat, and they said that they designed the interface differently on purpose, so it's not familiar. It made it harder for adults to work out and understand the app, giving an advantage to teenagers. The idea was to keep adults away.

Elikem refers to an interview with the developers where they admit making the user experience complicated and confusing to avoid the migration of supervising adults to the app. This strategy aims to maintain a sense of exclusiveness and expertise around the app. There is an extensive debate online about Snapchat's user experience design, often blaming it as an example of 'bad design.' As stated in an article about Snapchat's adult users: 'Snapchat makes almost everyone over the age of 25 feel old – even people who had never felt particularly old before. And that might be its greatest appeal' (Oremus and Oremus, 2015). According to the influential book *The Design of Everyday Things* (Norman, 2002), 'Good design is actually a lot harder to notice than poor design, in part because good designs fit our needs so well that the design is invisible.'

This perception that design should be 'intuitive,' self-explanatory, and 'simple' is a strong convention in the world of digital design, influenced by sub-disciplines such as HCI (Human-Computer Interaction), cognitive design, ethnographic design, and more (Forty, 2005; Smith-Atakan, 2006; Gunn, Otto and Smith, 2013). Snapchat, however, has challenged this convention and encouraged debate around 'Sharable Design' (Elman, 2016). According to Elman, 'shareable design understands this deeply social nature of how humans learn.' By abandoning the 'intuitive' ideal, Snapchat designed a space that requires peer-to-peer learning and gradual mastering.[14] Such design creates intimacy and exclusiveness by limiting access. How do all these boundaries influence the content shared on Snapchat?

In their research about Snapchat selfies among Australian teenagers, Charteris et al. (2014: 389) explain that Snapchat is a kind of 'underground technology that inherently evades detection.' The new and appealing genre of ephemeral messaging returns to a more private form of communication whereby one's words and expressions are not documented or archived, and thus cannot be used against him or her in the future. Charteris et al. (2014) claim this offers new possibilities for identity formation and self-surveillance in the circulation of teen culture. This opportunity for ephemeral messages and being un-searchable is so popular among young urban adults in Ghana that some telecommunication companies offer additional internet data bundles just for Snapchat.

In a relationship with God 145

The possibility of taking automatically deleted selfies is especially valuable in Snapchat, loosening 'the burden of social visibility' (Nicolescu, 2016: 60). The recent literature about selfies deals with their ability to promote self-representation and generate public attention around individual identity (Marwick, 2015; Abidin, 2016). Anthropologists who examined selfies in their fieldwork challenged their common conception as signs of self-centred teen culture, narcissism, and individualism by emphasising their collective, normative, and social role (Haynes, 2016; Miller et al., 2016; Nicolescu, 2016; Miller and Sinanan, 2017; Sinanan, 2017). Whether these photographic self-representations display symbols of upward mobility through fashionable clothes and trendy accessories (Spyer, 2018: 74), or nonchalant spontaneous scenarios by 'making faces' (Haynes, 2016: 64), their interdependence with social media clearly demonstrates that these 'are in fact a product of society itself' (Sinanan, 2017). For instance, in less individualistic societies (such as Ghana), selfies often become 'a means of showing one's association to family or church' (Miller et al., 2016: 186).

What the case of Snapchat in Ghana adds to the above debate on selfies is the ability to take self-portraits without the self-consciousness and anxiety that is usually experienced with public distribution, audience clash, digital witchcraft, and community surveillance. Snapchat selfies form a unique genre of social visibility whereby the past and future cease to worry the picture's subject, marking the present as this extraordinarily liberating moment in time. This temporal difference situates Snapchat selfies as opposites to the orthodox church, wedding, or family selfie that embodies collective aesthetics of normativity.

Snapchat forges the possibility for more daring, mundane, sexual, and personal visibility than is usually accepted in Ghana's public sphere. As discussed in previous chapters, age, gender, and class may govern relatively private spaces such as dark pubs and bedrooms. Snapchat, however, expands the possibilities of these spaces by offering undocumented and unregulated sociability for any user with a mobile phone. When constantly interacting with these informal urban spaces, users can share the more casual, natural, and playful parts of their lives, daring to push social boundaries.[15]

Elikem connects this need for enhanced privacy to the previously discussed aspects of judgement, conservatism, jealousy, and community surveillance. The 'forbidden' aspects of daily life remain hidden but still linger with the desire to be shared, discussed, and witnessed. Snapchat became an outlet which finally provided the ability to share the 'hidden self.' This 'hidden self' is not a fictional or virtual second identity purely created online, as described in Boellstorff's (2008) ethnography of the game Second Life or in Coleman's (2014) account of Anonymous. Instead, it is an identity strongly embedded in alternative urban spaces such as dark pubs and clubs, bedrooms, and other hidden corners that just can't be visualised in a public social media sphere.

One of the results of this sharp division between private and public visualisation is a growing gap between the self-image people maintain versus

146 *In a relationship with God*

how they are in secret. An entire genre of humorous memes is dedicated to peoples' secret lives and the gap between their image online and actions offline. Many of these memes relate to adultery, fake personas, nightlife, and vanity. For instance, a Nigerian viral meme distributed among Ghanaians comically portrays this polymedia state by comparing a man's Snapchat Story to his WhatsApp Story: the Snapchat Story shows him drinking alcohol with friends at a club while the WhatsApp Story shows him studying for an exam. Knowing his family aren't present on Snapchat, the young man chooses to post his 'illegal' activities here and his desired 'correct' activities on WhatsApp.

These two (or more) sides of the same person are not always perceived as contradictory, mutually exclusive, or deceiving, but certainly distinct. 'I have some friends and colleagues that I added on Snapchat, and I was so surprised,' Akosua comments. 'I was like Wooow I thought you were a quiet person now I see you are wild!' Humour about offline/online dichotomies also refers to physical 'rituals of becoming,' whereby people transform their appearance before exhibiting themselves online (see Chapter 5). For instance, the comment 'Some girls don't pick up video calls after 10 PM because their faces are back to factory setting' relates to gaps in physical appearance.

Apart from gaps in physical appearance and the importance of 'lavish' online personas, hidden relationships are facilitated by these private platforms, causing a rift in love lives, marriages, and friendships. For instance, an Instagram user called upon her fellow female followers to 'stop hiding their men from social media.' According to her post, 'three women could be dating the same guy and not even know.' A viral meme depicts a man caught in a mousetrap with the caption: 'When your girl creates a fake account and you DM [direct message] that account' (Figure 24, Two secret life collide, Instagram post. (6.6)). The meme portrays a scenario where the secret lives of both spouses collide and are revealed. Women often discuss male infidelity on Instagram and Snapchat, including the need to check a partner's phone when he's away, getting access to his passwords, and to keep secret boyfriends who'll shower them with gifts. Polymedia, in that sense, facilitates a form of polyamory.

To sum, Snapchat joins a rich media ecology whereby Facebook and Snapchat are perceived as semiotic opposites between public and semi-private spheres. Burrell argued that internet cafés are spaces where technology is not appropriated or localised but, on the contrary, transcends and de-localises users (Burrell, 2009, 2012). Similarly, Boellstorff argues that virtual/online identities can be contextualised without their offline counterparts, as contexts for themselves (Boellstorff, 2008). However, the online/offline gap made possible by shifting between Facebook, WhatsApp, and Snapchat in Ghana is not a gap between physical urban life and a virtual de-localised online identity. On the contrary, these applications facilitate, make possible, and re-categorise existing physical interactions deeply embedded in city

In a relationship with God 147

Figure 6.6 Two secret lives collide, Instagram post.

life. In similar ways to the deliberately complicated and clumsy house gates and locks, the technological barriers posed by Snapchat's 'sharable design' and WhatsApp's demand for a phone number follow Latour's claim about the materiality of technology. Technologies 'do not "express", "symbolise", "reflect", "reify", "objectify", "incarnate" disciplinary relations' but 'form them' (Latour, 2000: 19). As a result, the interior space of Snapchat becomes discrete and seclusive like dark nightspots hidden from daylight publicity (Chapter 4) or a hidden bedroom versus a public street (Chapter 5; Figure 6.6).

6.5 Loud infrastructure, silent believers, and 'noisy polymedia'

A nuanced and detailed examination of privacy practices online and offline shows how the Pentecostal/Charismatic movement forges its own private and public realms, reflected in a creative division between media platforms. Facebook, as shown in this chapter, is one urban space that was primarily occupied by Pentecostal values and norms. Apart from church groups, Christian fan pages, and biblically inspired status updates, Pentecostal prophets and pastors often publish posts about praying to destroy bad relationships and protect against people who secretly work to fail others. Reinforcing this discourse about dangerous strangers, jealous relatives,

148 *In a relationship with God*

and sinful non-believers is a common feature of how Ghanaians occupy Facebook. Moreover, family feuds, economic failures, and other misfortunes are all judged from a suspicious spiritual perspective. As Annan, a history teacher living in Tema, explained: 'When a European man dies, they ask **what** killed him, but when an African man dies, we ask **who** killed him.'

A popular Facebook account under the name 'Prophet Kofi' offers various ways to overcome this spiritual climate. For instance, the proclaimed prophet posted a photo of a sleeping man whose spirit encounters an evil sorcerer, with a call for action: 'TYPE CATCH FIRE AND SHARE THIS POST TO PROTECT YOUR LIFE AND YOUR FAMILY' (Figure 6.7, capitals in source).[16] The comment section, where people are instructed to type 'catch fire,' became a space for replying to the prayer and reciprocating the prophet's calls. In addition to commenting, the sharing function of Facebook becomes a weapon for publicly spreading the gospel and distributing the presence of God online. Facebook becomes a highly public platform with a strong moral and spiritual voice. This interaction can be framed as a digital version of 'call and response' prayers commonly practised in Pentecostal churches when, for instance, the pastor hails 'Praise the Lord' and the audience replies 'Hallelujah.' This 'migration' of church interaction patterns into Facebook's universal functions is an essential way of how Ghanaians 'find themselves in this environment and at the same time try to mould it in their own image' (Miller and Slater, 2001: 1).

Apart from shifting between public and private communication platforms, Ghanaians overcome this battle with an abundance of posts about the importance of silence and discreteness. For instance, a digital flyer was distributed online, compiling proverbs and biblical quotes about 'When to keep your mouth shut.' At the bottom of the flyer was a biblical quote from the Book of Proverbs (13:3): 'Whoso keepeth his mouth and his tongue Keepeth his soul from troubles.'[17] Other posts include moral memes with warnings such as 'sometimes you have to keep your good news to yourself, everybody is not genuinely happy for you' (Figure 6.8). Inspired by such quotes, 'Mr Godisthereason,' a Ghanaian Instagram user living in Dubai, who mostly posts photos from his travels to luxury hotels and restaurants around the world, wrote:

> Samson's parents had known the secret of Samson's strength, since his birth. Yet they told no one. The day Delilah heard of it she told Samson's enemies and brought him down to ordinary... Nothing can be more dangerous and painful than to share your secrets with your enemy thinking they are your friends.
>
> (Instagram, 2017)

This post borrows the biblical story of Samson[18] as a lesson on discreetness and privacy, conveying that in an age of heightened visibility and information sharing, disclosing secrets can be dangerous. Delilah turned Samson

ANY BAD MAN THAT WILL USE YOUR SPIRIT
TO OPERATE TO DESTROY YOUR DESTINY
AND FUTURE TYPE CATCH FIRE AND SHARE
THIS POST TO PROTECT YOUR LIFE AND YOUR
FAMILY GOD IS WORKING

Figure 6.7 Importing 'call and response' prayers to Facebook's Pentecostal realm.

from 'incredible' to 'ordinary' simply by knowing his secret. From the Ghanaian perspective, if this biblical affair happened today, Delilah would probably post a Facebook status about her lover's secret weakness or even Snapchat herself while cutting his hair.

The emphasis on silence as a boundary for privacy stands in opposition to two other components of Pentecostal digitisation in Ghana: first, the strong link between Pentecostalism and noise, loud preaching, and high-volume audio-visual dominance in public spaces (van Dijk and Studiecentrum, 2001), including its assertive occupation of urban night-time as a symbolic agent of light (see Chapter 4). Second, the constant presence of unstable and irregular infrastructure, such as electricity, water, and wireless internet, which denies its otherwise silent and invisible character (Star, 1999; Gupta, 2015). Describing the historical and cultural connection between infrastructure and media in Nigeria, Larkin (2008: 10) marked noise as both 'the technical interference and breakdown that clouds and even prevents that signal's transmission' and 'the interference produced by religious and cultural values.' What can this semiotic opposition, between remaining silent and discrete, on the one hand, and battling technological and religious 'noises,' on the other, teach us about polymedia and privacy?

According to Postill and Pink (2012: 129), in an age of polymedia, 'digital ethnographers must practise media switching and media-mixing to create and maintain social relationships with research participants across space and time.' By following the same informants across multiple social media platforms, I was able to identify the different moral choices

150 *In a relationship with God*

and emotional framings of each one. Furthermore, by taking a contextual digital anthropology approach, I matched these findings with people's practices offline, in houses, streets, pubs, and churches. This holistic approach suggested a dialectic process whereby infrastructures and financial routines shape technological use, digital technology bypasses previous material restrictions, and social, spiritual values set a moral, ethical point of reference in daily navigations between public and private spheres.

In that sense, the 'noise' of material infrastructure and Pentecostal reformation was crucial for the navigation between various communication platforms. Infrastructures and their limitations (or 'noises') mean people often switch between their trendy smartphones and dated 'yam phones,' go to an internet café because there is a power cut and they ran out of battery, or choose text messages over voice calls because of bad reception. The scarcity of Wi-Fi infrastructure and the dependence on pre-paid quantified mobile data mean Ghanaians often switch sim cards for better rates, transfer media to each other via Bluetooth technology to bypass the internet, choose voice calls over video calls to save data, and generally avoid media streaming. This 'semiotics of interference' (Tsivian, 1994, quoted in Larkin, 2008: 238) means that technological marginality, sustainability, and deficiency are an integral part of the media itself.

Madianou and Miller (2013) stress that issues of access, economy, infrastructure, and literacy to multiple communication tools must be eliminated before the choice between them becomes moral and emotional. Hence, they define a rather idyllic media ecology as a condition of polymedia. However, the conditions described above means it is impossible to isolate 'moral choice' between mediums from economy, infrastructure, and access in Ghana. Polymedia cannot be fully understood in this context without considering these limitations and how they influence peoples' daily choices between various platforms of communication. Instead of declaring that 'polymedia remains an aspiration and not the current state for much of the world' (Madianou and Miller, 2013: 175), the case of Ghana suggests a different version of polymedia – a version I call *Noisy Polymedia* (Ben Elul, 2020). The noise I refer to is not only infrastructural and cultural but also theoretical. For instance, when an academic theory is used to interpret unique field sites it often encounters 'noise' – data that does not fit the theory neatly. In this case, the theory of polymedia requires an ideal media user who is frequently found in wealthy Western cities while the data from urban Ghana (and other cities in the Global South) suggests a messier and unstable media experience.

In Chapter 5 the findings on domestic architecture and privacy in Ghana challenged the theory of domestication in media studies and household technology. Similarly, this chapter uses a contextual analysis of digital privacy in Ghana and breaks any previous assumptions about coherent, flowing, and wholesome media ecologies. Narratives about *Sakawa* scams, taboos about pregnancy and children's photos online, the omitting of full names from Facebook profiles, and the practice of sharing religious posts to combat evil

In a relationship with God 151

spirits are all part of how this ecology forges new realms of privacy and publicity. The public ones (such as Facebook and WhatsApp family groups) demand silence, surveillance, and normativity, while the private ones (such as Snapchat and direct messaging) offer new ways to interact without 'the burden of social visibility' (Nicolescu, 2016: 60). These new practices reflect the ongoing battle between technology, visual culture, morality, religion, and social class (Figure 6.9).

Figure 6.8 Overcoming jealousy and evil intentions. Author recreation.

Figure 6.9 Keep your good news, Facebook post, 2016. @WestAfrikanman.

152 *In a relationship with God*

References

Abidin, C. (2016) '"Aren't These Just Young, Rich Women Doing Vain Things Online?": Influencer Selfies as Subversive Frivolity', *Social Media + Society*, 2(2), p. 2056305116641342. doi: 10.1177/2056305116641342.

Armstrong, A. (2011) *'Sakawa' Rumours: Occult Internet Fraud and Ghanaian Identity*. UCL working paper 08/2011. London: University College London. Available at: https://www.ucl.ac.uk/anthropology/research/working-papers/082011.pdf (Accessed: 3 August 2017).

Behrend, H. (2003) 'Photo Magic: Photographs in Practices of Healing and Harming in East Africa', *Journal of Religion in Africa*, 33(2), pp. 129–145. doi: 10.1163/15700660360703114.

Ben Elul, E. (2012) 'Memory Sticks: Domestic archiving among Ghanaian families abroad in a cross-cultural perspective'. University College London.

Ben Elul, E. (2020). 'Noisy Polymedia in Urban Ghana: Strategies for Choosing and Switching between Media under Unstable Infrastructures', *New Media & Society*. doi: 10.1177/1461444820925047.

Boellstorff, T. (2008) *Coming of Age in Second Life: An Anthropologist Explores the Virtually Human*. Princeton, NJ: Princeton University Press.

Bourdieu, P. and Whiteside, S. (1996) *Photography: A Middle-Brow Art*. Redwood City: Stanford University Press.

Burrell, J. (2009) 'Could Connectivity Replace Mobility? An Analysis of Internet Cafe Use Patterns in Accra, Ghana', in Bruijn, M. de, Nyamnjoh, F., and Brinkman, I. (eds) *Mobile Phones: The New Talking Drums of Everyday Africa*. Bamenda, Cameroon: Langaa RPCIG, pp. 151–169.

Burrell, J. (2011) 'User Agency in the Middle Range: Rumors and the Reinvention of the Internet in Accra, Ghana', *Science, Technology & Human Values*, 36(2), pp. 139–159. doi: 10.1177/0162243910366148.

Burrell, J. (2012) *Invisible Users: Youth in the Internet Cafés of Urban Ghana*. Cambridge, MA: MIT Press.

Charteris, J., Gregory, S. and Masters, Y. (2014) 'Snapchat "Selfies": The Case of Disappearing data', in Hegarty, B. and Loke, S. (eds) *Rhetoric and Reality: Critical Perspectives on Educational Technology*. Dunedin: Proceedings Ascilite, pp. 389–393. Available at: https://www.researchgate.net/profile/Jennifer_Charteris/publication/277186349_Snapchat_'selfies'_The_case_of_disappearing_data/links/5564487808ae86c06b6987c3.pdf (Accessed: 15 August 2017).

Coe, C. (2008) 'The Structuring of Feeling in Ghanaian Transnational Families', *City & Society*, 20(2), pp. 222–250. doi: 10.1111/j.1548-744X.2008.00018.x.

Coleman, G. (2014) *Hacker, Hoaxer, Whistleblower, Spy: The Many Faces of Anonymous*. New York: Verso.

Comaroff, J. and Comaroff, J. L. (2008) 'Occult Economies and the Violence of Abstraction: Notes from the South African Postcolony', *American Ethnologist*, 26(2), pp. 279–303. doi: 10.1525/ae.1999.26.2.279.

Dankwa, S. O. (2009) '"It's a Silent Trade": Female Same-Sex Intimacies in Post-Colonial Ghana', *NORA - Nordic Journal of Feminist and Gender Research*, 17(3), pp. 192–205. doi: 10.1080/08038740903117208.

van Dijk, R. A. and Studiecentrum, A. (2001) 'Contesting Silence: the Ban on Drumming and the Musical Politics of Pentecostalism in Ghana', *Ghana Studies*, 4, pp. 31–64.

In a relationship with God 153

Elman, J. (2016) *Intuitive Design vs. Shareable Design, Greylock Perspectives.* Available at: https://news.greylock.com/intuitive-design-vs-shareable-design-88ff6bb184bb.

Ferguson, J. (2006) *Global Shadows: Africa in the Neoliberal World Order.* Durham, NC: Duke University Press.

Forty, A. (2005) *Objects of Desire: Design and Society since 1750.* London: Thames and Hudson.

Frazer, S. J. G. (1890) *The Golden Bough.* Abridged edition. Mineola, NY: Dover Publications.

Freda, O.-A. (2015) 'A Real Face of Depression', *Circumspecte*, 4 September. Available at: https://circumspecte.com/2015/09/guest-post-by-freda-obeng-ampofo-a-real-face-of-depression/ (Accessed: 25 July 2017).

Gal, S. (2002) 'A Semiotics of the Public/Private Distinction', *Differences: A Journal of Feminist Cultural Studies*, 13(1), pp. 77–95.

Gell, A. (1998) *Art and Agency: An Anthropological Theory.* Oxford: Clarendon Press.

Gershon, I. (2011) *The Breakup 2.0: Disconnecting over New Media.* New York: Cornell University Press.

Geschiere, P. (1997) *The Modernity of Witchcraft: Politics and the Occult in Postcolonial Africa.* Charlottesville: University of Virginia Press.

Gordon, T. and Hancock, M. (2005) '"The Crusade Is the Vision": Branding Charisma in a Global Pentecostal Ministry', *Material Religion*, 1(3), pp. 386–404. doi: 10.2752/174322005778054023.

Gunn, W., Otto, T. and Smith, R. C. (2013) 'Design Anthropology: A Distinct Style of Knowing', in *Design Anthropology: Theory and Practice.* London: A&C Black, pp. 1–29.

Gupta, A. (2015) 'An Anthropology of Electricity from the Global South', *Cultural Anthropology*, 30(4), pp. 555–568. doi: 10.14506/ca30.4.04.

Haynes, N. (2016) *Social Media in Northern Chile.* London: UCL Press.

Horst, H. (2009) 'Aesthetics of the Self: Digital Mediations', in Miller, D. (ed.) *Anthropology of the Individual: A Material Culture Perspective.* New York: Berg Publishers, pp. 99–113.

Ingold, T. (2000) 'Making Culture and Weaving the World', in Paul Graves-Brown (ed.) *Matter, Materiality and Modern Culture.* London: Routledge, pp. 50–71.

Lange, P. G. (2007) 'Publicly Private and Privately Public: Social Networking on YouTube', *Journal of Computer-Mediated Communication*, 13(1), pp. 361–380. doi: 10.1111/j.1083-6101.2007.00400.x.

Larkin, B. (2008) *Signal and Noise: Media, Infrastructure, and Urban Culture in Nigeria.* Durham, NC: Duke University Press Books.

Latour, B. (2000) 'The Berlin Key or How to Do Words with Things', in Graves-Brown, P. (ed.) *Matter, Materiality, and Modern Culture.* London: Routledge, pp. 10–21.

Livingstone, S. (2007) 'From Family Television to Bedroom Culture: Young People's Media at Home', in Devereux, E. (ed.) *Media Studies: Key issues and Debates.* London: Sage Publications, pp. 302–321.

Lobinger, K. (2016) 'Photographs as Things – Photographs of Things. A Texto-Material Perspective on Photo-Sharing Practices', *Information, Communication & Society*, 19(4), pp. 475–488. doi: 10.1080/1369118X.2015.1077262.

Madianou, M. and Miller, D. (2012) *Migration and New Media: Transnational Families and Polymedia.* Abingdon, Oxon; New York: Routledge

154 In a relationship with God

Madianou, M. and Miller, D. (2013) 'Polymedia: Towards a New Theory of Digital Media in Interpersonal Communication', *International Journal of Cultural Studies*, 16(2), pp. 169–187. doi: 10.1177/1367877912452486.

Marshall-Fratani, R. (1998) 'Mediating the Global and Local in Nigerian Pentecostalism', *Journal of Religion in Africa*, 28(3), pp. 278–315. doi: 10.2307/1581572.

Marwick, A. E. and boyd, D. (2014) 'Networked Privacy: How Teenagers Negotiate Context in Social Media', *New Media & Society*, 16(7), pp. 1051–1067. doi: 10.1177/1461444814543995.

Marwick, A. E. (2015) 'Instafame: Luxury selfies in the attention economy', *Public Culture*, 27(1 (75)), pp. 137–160. doi: 10.1215/08992363-2798379.

Maxwell, D. (1998) '"Delivered from the Spirit of Poverty?": Pentecostalism, Prosperity and Modernity in Zimbabwe', *Journal of Religion in Africa*, 28(3), pp. 350–373. doi: 10.2307/1581574.

Meyer, B. (1999) *Translating the Devil: Religion and Modernity among the Ewe in Ghana*. Trenton, NJ: Africa World Pr.

Meyer, B. (2006) 'Impossible Representations. Pentecostalism, Vision, and Video Technology in Ghana', in Meyer, Birgit and Moors, A. (eds) *Religion, Media, and the Public Sphere*. Bloomington: Indiana University Press, pp. 290–312. Available at: http://dare.uva.nl/record/1/261248 (Accessed: 19 July 2016).

Meyer, B. (2010) '"There Is a Spirit in that Image": Mass-Produced Jesus Pictures and Protestant-Pentecostal Animation in Ghana', *Comparative Studies in Society and History*, 52(1), pp. 100–130. doi: 10.1017/S001041750999034X.

Michaels, E. (1991) 'A Primer of Restrictions on Picture-Taking in Traditional Areas of Aboriginal Australia', *Visual Anthropology*, 4(3–4), pp. 259–275. doi: 10.1080/08949468.1991.9966564.

Miller, D. and Sinanan, J. (2017) *Visualising Facebook: A Comparative Perspective*. London: UCL Press.

Miller, D. and Slater, D. (2001) *The Internet: An Ethnographic Approach*. First Edition. Oxford; New York: Bloomsbury Academic.

Miller, D. (2016) *Social Media in an English Village*. London: UCL Press. doi: 10.14324/111.9781910634431.

Miller, D. et al. (2016) *How the World Changed Social Media*. London: UCL Press.

Nicolescu, R. (2016) *Social Media in Southeast Italy*. London: UCL Press.

Norman, D. A. (2002) *The Design of Everyday Things*. New York: Basic Books.

Oremus, W. and Oremus, W. (2015) 'Is Snapchat Really Confusing, or Am I Just Old?', *Slate*, 29 January. Available at: http://www.slate.com/articles/technology/technology/2015/01/snapchat_why_teens_favorite_app_makes_the_facebook_generation_feel_old.html (Accessed: 14 August 2017).

Pertierra, A. C. (2015) 'Cuban girls and Visual Media: Bodies and Practices of (still-) Socialist Consumerism', *Continuum*, 29(2), pp. 1–11. doi: 10.1080/10304312.2015.1022950.

Pinney, C. (2002) 'Photographic portraiture in Central India in the 1980s and 1990s', in Buchli, V. (ed.) *The Material Culture Reader*. London: Berg, pp. 87–104.

Pinney, C. (2011) *Photography and Anthropology*. London: Reaktion Books.

Postill, J. and Pink, S. (2012) 'Social Media Ethnography: The Digital Researcher in a Messy Web', *Media International Australia*, 145(1), pp. 123–134. doi: 10.1177/1329878X1214500114.

Sarvas, R. and Frohlich, D. M. (2011) *From Snapshots to Social Media - The Changing Picture of Domestic Photography*. New York: Springer.

Shifman, L. (2013). 'Memes in a Digital World: Reconciling with a Conceptual Troublemaker', *Journal of Computer-Mediated Communication*, 18(3), 362–377.

Sinanan, J. (2017) *Social Media in Trinidad*. London: UCL Press.

Slater, D. and Kwami, J. (2005) 'Embeddedness and Escape: Internet and Mobile Use as Poverty Reduction Strategies in Ghana', *Information Society Research Group (ISRG) Report*. Available at: http://www.researchgate.net/profile/Janet_Kwami/publication/228635823_Embeddedness_and_escape_Internet_and_mobile_use_as_poverty_reduction_strategies_in_Ghana/links/00b7d530253d3b70b1000000.pdf (Accessed: 6 July 2015).

Smith, C. (2017) *135 Amazing Snapchat Statistics and Facts (June 2017)*. DMR. Available at: http://expandedramblings.com/index.php/snapchat-statistics/ (Accessed: 14 August 2017).

Smith-Atakan, S. (2006) *Human-Computer Interaction*. Boston: Cengage Learning EMEA.

Spyer, J. (2018) *Social Media in Emergent Brazil*. London: UCL Press.

Star, S. L. (1999) 'The Ethnography of Infrastructure', *American Behavioral Scientist*, 43(3), pp. 377–391.

Strassler, K. (2010). *Refracted Visions: Popular Photography and National Modernity in Java*. Durham, NC: Duke University Press.

Venkatraman, S. (2017) *Social Media in South India*. London: UCL Press.

Villi, M. (2012) 'Visual Chitchat: The Use of Camera Phones in Visual Interpersonal Communication', *Interactions: Studies in Communication & Culture*, 3(1), pp. 39–54. doi: 10.1386/iscc.3.1.39_1.

Wang, X. (2016) *Social Media in Industrial China*. London: UCL Press.

Warner, J. (2011) 'Understanding Cyber-Crime in Ghana: A View from Below', *International Journal of Cyber Criminology*, 5(1), pp. 736–749.

Weiss, B. (1998) 'Electric Vampires: Haya Rumours of the Commodified Body', in Lambek, M. and Strathern, A. (eds) *Bodies and Persons: Comparative Perspectives from Africa and Melanesia*. Cambridge: Cambridge University Press, pp. 172–194.

Weiss, B. (2004) *Producing African Futures: Ritual and Reproduction in a Neoliberal Age*. Leiden: Brill.

Wendl, T. (1998) 'Portraits and Scenery in Ghana', in Léon, S., Martin, P., and N'gone, F. (eds) *Anthology of African and Indian Ocean Photography*. Illustrated edition. Editions Revue Noir. New York: Distributed Art Pub Incorporated, pp. 143–155.

Wendl, T. (2001). 'Entangled Traditions: Photography and the History of Media in Southern Ghana'. *RES: Anthropology and Aesthetics*, 39(1), 78–101.

Wendl, T. M. (2007) 'Wicked Villagers and the Mysteries of Reproduction: An Exploration of Horror Videos from Ghana and Nigeria', *Postcolonial Text*, 3(2). Available at: http://postcolonial.org/index.php/pct/article/view/529 (Accessed: 26 July 2018).

Wolbert, B. (2000) 'The Anthropologist as Photographer: The Visual Construction of Ethnographic Authority', *Visual Anthropology*, 13(4), pp. 321–343. doi: 10.1080/08949468.2000.9966807.

Wright, C. (2004) 'Material and Memory Photography in the Western Solomon Islands', *Journal of Material Culture*, 9(1), pp. 73–85. doi: 10.1177/1359183504041090.

Yankah, K. (1989) 'Proverbs: The Aesthetics of Traditional Communication', *Research in African Literatures*, 20(3), pp. 325–346.

156 *In a relationship with God*

Notes

1 In August 2008 Vodaphone took over Ghana Telecom, the national telecommunication company in Ghana, by purchasing 70% of its assets. Vodaphone's nationwide reach is expressed in a proud cultural and localised marketing approach (*Acquisition of a 70% Stake in Ghana Telecom*, 2008).

2 There is an ongoing debate about the methodological meanings of terms such as digital ethnography, virtual ethnography, and digital anthropology. Overall, this project took a digital anthropology contextual approach. This means I observed the same informants in their online and offline worlds. However, I use the term digital ethnography in this chapter because it focuses on data and findings from social media platforms. See more about these distinctions and definitions in Pink et al. (2015) and Chapter 1 in this book as well.

3 I had never encountered these apps before my visit to Ghana but saw them regularly while I was there. I was also exposed to an extensive usage of phone tracing applications in case of theft, passwords, app blocking apps, and battery saving apps used due to unstable electricity.

4 Recently WhatsApp and Instagram introduced an 'unsend' button which allows retrieving messages. When one of my informants shared this news, he received dozens of relieved and humorous comments thanking God for hearing their prayers and introducing this 'life-saving' function.

5 This economic aspect of Facebook is especially relevant to the middle class that often relies on multiple incomes by opening small businesses and utilising social media and community ties to promote it. See Chapter 3 for more information about informal economies in the middle class.

6 GIF is an acronym for Graphics Interchange Format, which is a type of animated image displaying a sequence of frames in a repeating manner.

7 *Sakawa* boys, and other internet fraudsters, also represent an escape from community surveillance, strongly associated with 'generational deregulation that leads to crime, teenage pregnancies, HIV/AIDS, family breakdown, disrespect' (Slater and Kwami, 2005: 9). While mostly operating in internet cafés via emails and dating sites, they also use mobile phones and social media sites such as Facebook. As Burrell (2012: 190) points out, the rumours about spiritual rituals involved in internet scamming reflect the mystification of these new technologies and require the re-localisation of victimhood: no longer the foreign stranger behind the screen, who gave out his credit card details but, now, the scammer's closest relatives. Thus, rumours about their immoral practice 'extended the moral scripting of the technology' they use (Burrell, 2012: 190).

8 In my ethnography about Ghanaian family photography in London, I argued that the division between contexts or modes of photography relates to the solemnised perception of photos in Ghana, as objects of formality, ritual, and memory (Ben Elul, 2012). The significance of visual representation in such solemnised events is usually attributed to historiography (e.g., Bourdieu and Whiteside, 1996, about rural France) while the literature about contemporary domestic photos emphasises the shift to playfulness, spontaneity, and informality (Sarvas and Frohlich, 2011).

9 In fact, although I knew the full names of my research informants, I could not trace them on Facebook by myself – they had to give me the specific name they use there.

10 This indexical relation between the image and its subject, often compared to a person's fingerprint, was elaborately discussed in Linguistic Anthropology and visual culture (Bourdieu and Whiteside, 1996; Wendl, 2001; Pinney, 2002; Strassler, 2010).

In a relationship with God 157

11 Selfie is a common global term in the digital age, describing the widespread habit of people taking their own photo by stretching the arm forward while holding a camera, or by standing in front of a mirror with the camera. There are many sub-genres of this self-visualisation technique, including 'groupies' (selfies of more than one person), 'couplies' (selfies of a couple), and even 'footies' (selfies of one's own feet). Selfies are highly associated with social media, teen culture, and pop culture.

12 The founders of Snapchat are Evan Spiegel, Bobby Murphy, and Reggie Brown.

13 The risk of someone taking a screenshot of an image before it disappears still lingers but recently Snapchat even added a feature that informs its users if someone screenshots their message. This feature alone shows how attentive the designers are to the fears and worries of digital users, whether they are Australian teenagers or Ghanaian professionals.

14 Anthropologists have written rich ethnographies about the socio-cultural value of learning, imitating, and mastering a technique. See Ingold's article about weaving baskets as a mother-daughter transmission of knowledge as an example (Ingold, 2000).

15 Snapchat is so incredibly popular in Ghana that in the latest elections (2016) a major news story was about John Dumelo, an actor who shared a photo of his ballot on Snapchat, showing his vote for President John Mahama (who later lost the elections). Vodaphone, Ghana's major telecommunication company, often offers free data for Snapchat users, indicating the popularity of the application nationwide.

16 This horrific scenario happens in a bedroom, which paradoxically serves as a private haven from chaotic city life (see Chapter 5) but also as the most dangerous space for demonic spirits and witchcraft attacks, for people are most vulnerable when they are asleep, and especially at night. Meyer (2010) analyses these demonic attacks on bedrooms through Pentecostal Nigerian and Ghanaian cinema.

17 Such de-contextualisation of biblical texts and their use as a neutral authority in new contexts is highly common online and offline.

18 Book of Judges, chapters 13–16.

7 Conclusions
Towards an ethnography of privacy

7.1 Urbanisation, digitisation, and thinking beyond 'rights'

Public, journalistic, and academic debates in the US often present the entire digital realm as a dualistic battle between the 'public,' which is described as governmental, corporate, or commercial, and the 'private,' often described as individual, personal, and interiorised (Nissenbaum, 2004; Solove, 2004; boyd, 2008; Wicker, 2013; Trottier, 2016). In these debates, privacy is predominantly measured and discussed concerning abstracted and (at times) vague entities such as the state and its public records (Landau, 2016; Srinivasan et al., 2018) or commercial companies and its consumer data (Trottier, 2016; Rider, 2018). Other technological 'threats' to privacy are biometric and satellite monitoring, credit card tracking, face recognition, and video surveillance. As a result, digitisation is perceived as a threat to privacy and perceived as a risky exposure to an 'Orwellian horror of relentless scrutiny' (Wacks, 2015: 4). Privacy, accordingly, is 're-conceptualised in the popular imagination as a commodity of ever-declining value' (Campbell and Carlson, 2002: 592).

In Ghana, comparatively, people tend to worry less about the abstracted 'big brother' gaze or the declining value of privacy. Instead, they cope with generational, financial, and interpersonal relations, both online and offline. Living in a much less economically privileged part of the world, Ghana's middle-class members, whether they like it or not, rely on community ties, religious affiliations, and extended kin, for financial wellbeing. Meanwhile, state authorities and NGOs are often dismissed as corrupt, dysfunctional, and irrelevant, due to their corrupt mismanagement and inadequate infrastructure.[1] For instance, the disturbance of water, electricity, and internet supply in the home requires the extension of domestic space into urban and digital spaces, raising new concerns about privacy, visibility, and sociality.

In the context of direct face-to-face interactions and tight connections, as people talk about each other and observe each other every day, the digital realm poses new, yet not exclusive, opportunities for a 'secret life.' Alongside the dark spots of the city (especially during *Dumsor*) and the hidden yards or bedrooms of middle-class houses, social media platforms become a refuge

DOI: 10.4324/9781003187424-7

Conclusions 159

from informal urban and familial surveillance. In addition to the enclosed and protected spaces of small groups (e.g., nuclear families, prayer circles, or nightclubbers), mobile phones and tablets offer complete individual privacy. While having to share 'illegitimate' or stigmatised spaces (e.g., nightclubs) with others means that they become co-owners of private information (Petronio, 2002), hand-held smartphones allow the enticing possibility to be completely discrete. What are the reasons for this gap between the ethnographic findings and the dominant literature about privacy and digitisation?

The political theories of Arendt (1958/2013) and Habermas (1989), critical thinkers in the sociology of private and public spheres, were based on sharp dichotomies between 'the polis and the household' or between state administration and market economy (Weintraub, 1997). Due to this dualism, which inspired countless scholars and thinkers, these theories are difficult to apply outside Euro-America, carrying an excess 'baggage of Western imperial hegemony' (Thompson, 2003). The historical construction of the individual (or 'interiorised self') in Western Europe, for instance, is seen as an important pre-condition for the claim over privacy (Chakrabarty, 2009). As Marwick and boyd (2018: 1158) point out, the right to be 'left alone' is a privilege, often denied from marginalised groups such as minors, activists, and poor people.

Feminist scholarship (e.g., Pateman, 1983; Landes, 2003; Meehan, 2013) seemed to offer a useful critique and alternative framework to these rigorous divisions of political theory, and to the internet-related literature that they inspired. However, at least in a Ghanaian context, the feminist opposition between the domestic sphere and the market economy, or male as public and female as private, are also inapplicable. These gendered divisions later inspired the feminist readings of digitisation as public male domains (Turkle, 1988; Laurence Habib and Tony Cornford, 2002; Srinivasan Ramani, 2008). While making a universal claim, these readings often ignored alternative experiences around technology, especially in other parts of the world (Freeman, 2000; Guta and Karolak, 2015; Tacchi and Chandola, 2015). For instance, in his ethnography of social media in southeast Turkey, Costa (2016: 26) found that digital technologies 'produced a new idea of "public", characterised by a more visible presence of women.'

According to Gal (2002: 84), much of the feminist literature about private and public divisions reproduced the classic theories they strove to resist by mostly presenting alternative distinctions, 'without explicating their logic.' In other words, although the feminist critique challenged pre-existing divisions between private and public, this was done by suggesting alternative ones and not by deconstructing the very notion of privacy and culture. Gal's (2002) semiotic division between public and private spheres as fractally recursive and culturally constructed categories was an especially useful concept in this study, providing a nuanced, contextual, and dynamic observation of privacy. To quote Gal (2002: 80), 'Public and private are co-constitutive cultural categories, as many have pointed out. But they are also, and equally importantly,

160 *Conclusions*

indexical signs that are always relative: dependent for part of their referential meaning on the interactional context in which they are used'.

Together with Bourdieu's reading of the Kabyle house (see Chapter 5), fractal recursions were particularly important for the understanding of middle-class Ghanaian houses and their complex divisions between outdoors and indoors. These divisions are infinitely reproduced between the street and the yard, the living room and the bedroom, the house tenants and their mobile phones. For example, a humorous Instagram meme illustrates the feeling when receiving a direct message (DM) from a stranger online – the experience is visually compared to a locked door with a small viewing window, or wicket, with the caption: 'Me every time I get a DM from a random' (Figure 7.1). The private mechanisms of the house, therefore, are re-imagined through the materiality of social media and vice versa.

The rapid adaptation of new communication tools allows many people to experience a whole new social world of seeing and being seen (Marwick and boyd, 2014; Costa, 2016; Sinanan, 2017). The discourse about privacy and how one protects his or her reputation, consequently, takes on new shapes and forms in its digital and non-Western context. Lange's (2007) notion of being 'privately public' and 'publicly private' online provided another valuable frame to describe these nuanced and tensed avenues for privacy. Changing one's Facebook name to control anonymity, attending a church service dedicated to keeping one's 'good name' online, or posting prayer memes for prosperity and success are all creative ways of enacting privacy through sociality, or despite it.

Even though American developers designed these digital functions, settings, and layouts in their Silicon Valley offices while imagining a completely

Figure 7.1 The physical is a metaphor for the virtual, Instagram post.

Conclusions 161

different audience (Hahn and Kibora, 2008), Ghanaians do not only consume, domesticate, and 'urbanise' those new tools in masses but they also establish their own culture – their own set of rules – while using them (Miller and Slater, 2001). Deconstructing this culture with ethnographic methods shows that Africa's middle class is not simply a peripheral version of America's middle class but a frontier of digital innovation. For instance, Ghana's version of polymedia – the conscious choice between various communication tools – is not as 'sterile' as it is for other middle-class urbanites (Madianou and Miller, 2013). Instead, it can be described as 'noisy' polymedia whereby infrastructure, local traditions, and religion shift and shape individual choice.

The central discourse on digitisation and the meaning it carries among urban middle-class Ghanaians, therefore, is not perceived as a threat to privacy but as an opportunity for privacy. It is also not a set of trade-offs whereby privacy is 'sacrificed' for the sake of goods and services (Landau, 2016; Srinivasan et al., 2018) but a strategic use of devices, spaces, and audiences. As a result, church leaders worry about their followers engaging in sinful activities online, parents worry their children are bypassing house rules via social media, and couples worry about their spouses having secret love affairs enabled by password-locked messaging apps. Such exciting opportunities for privacy significantly minimises any concerns about an 'invisible' commercial or governmental gaze often discussed in relative literature (Nissenbaum, 2004; Vitak, 2012; Wicker, 2013).

However, I do not wish to give the impression that Ghana poses a binary opposite to this Western-oriented literature. Tema, unlike Cairo, Bengal, Casablanca, or even Accra, the nearby capital, was founded on the grounds of European distinctions between private and public spheres, and between the individual (or the nuclear family) and the community. The city was 'exported' almost like a fixed entity, under the 1945 British New Towns act (d'Auria and De Meulder, 2010). This 'urban experiment' yielded unexpected results, as the exact parallels between forms and content – between the Euro-American architectural appearance and the actual socio-cultural practice in the city – began to fall apart. The cultural and infrastructural 'noise' in Tema is expressed through irregular electricity, busy nightlife, unstable urban roads, restricted banking access, religious reformations, and (of course) new technology.

Postcolonial readings of non-European cities showed how the assumption that private and public spheres can be neatly divided and reflected in the material layout of the city is naïve at best and misleading at worst (Mitchell, 1991; Chakrabarty, 2009). According to Ferguson (1999: 210), the inability to trace coherent, stable, and culturally homogenous divisions in African cities challenges the very idea of anthropology, forcing the ethnographer to 'maintain decent respect for the social significance of the unintelligible.' In his ethnography of modernity, myths, and meaning in urban Zambia, Ferguson (1999: 210) argues that anthropologists rely excessively on the assumption that culture is a system of communication when it is actually, also, a system of miscommunication. Hidden, private, and ruptured communication,

162   *Conclusions*

an essential component of modern life in urban Africa, should not escape anthropological analysis.

Studying what is not there rather than what is there, what is miscommunicated rather than what is communicated, is what the ethnography of privacy tries to do. By this, I do not mean that such ethnography seeks to intrude and expose private information. It does, however, try to take into account what is concealed alongside what is revealed and most importantly the relationship between the two. Ethnography relies heavily on what people 'show,' by doing actions or exhibiting materials, and 'tell,' by speaking to the researcher or between each other in his/her presence. Privacy, on the other hand, is about what people hide or avoid, which can pose a lot of tension and contradiction in the field.

Throughout my research, I had to stop and ask myself: what am I not seeing? what is being communicated and miscommunicated? what is exhibited and what is hidden? I then navigated these binaries through conversations, negotiations, and alternative paths. For instance, humorous discourse about secrets and surveillance on social media revealed many hidden or unspoken practices indirectly (see Chapter 6). Other ways I achieved knowledge about privacy was by reflecting on what personal information and aspects of my own identity I chose to either share or hide in different fieldwork situations (Chapter 2). I mainly had to map the points where publicity ends and discreteness begins (Nippert-Eng, 2010) and whether it was present in language patterns, informal economies, nightlife practices, domestic architecture, or social media technologies (see Chapters 4–6).

As for members of Ghana's middle class, although local, ancestral, rural, and collective frameworks have a firm grip on them, they also have 'a special relation to that which is not (in localist terms) expected proper, or normal' (Ferguson, 1999: 211). The hidden and the ruptured, accordingly, are strongly intertwined, channelling their desire to resist local frameworks of meaning and ideally 'make a complete break with the past' (Meyer, 1998). They strive to engage in modern cosmopolitan systems of thought by negating local and traditional ones. The rapid consumption of mobile phones and the faithful engagement with international institutions such as the Pentecostal church are all experienced as cosmopolitan practices against a peripheral 'background.'

Cosmopolitanism is a significant component of 'grounding' the internet in the city. It's an essential part of the multi-layered process of digitisation – domestic, urban, local, universal, private, and public. Social media brings together Africans from across the nation, the continent, and the world; family members from across the country and the diaspora reunite in family WhatsApp groups; young Ghanaians discuss cultural differences and national boundaries with neighbouring African nationalities on Instagram; and American Pentecostal pastors engage daily with their Ghanaian followers on Facebook. Cosmopolitanism is also encouraged by the Pentecostal movement that often aims to virtualise, universalise, and de-localise urban identities (Marshall-Fratani, 1998: 299).

Conclusions   163

Exploring digitisation in its urban context, accordingly, shows that the physical and the virtual, the public and the private, are in constant negotiation. The city comes to life in a new digital environment with all its infrastructural and cultural 'noises' (Ferguson, 1999; Larkin, 2008). The ability of digital technologies to become a vessel for urban culture in such a way may explain how people around the world become familiar with such technologies so quickly. Incorporating digital anthropology and 'internet-related ethnography' (Postill and Pink, 2012) into urban anthropology will enrich and expand the understanding of city life and the divisions of space within it.

The city of Tema and its middle-class inhabitants invite us to suspend liberal notions of public and private spheres as binary categories of political order by immersing into a complex network of veiling and unveiling, performance and withdrawal, invitation and denial. In this uncertain, rapidly changing, and paradoxical urban landscape, urbanites achieve a sense of order and coherency through the quest for privacy. I use the word quest and not 'demand' or 'right' because these are also out of context. For instance, electrical power cuts (*Dumsor*) are seen as an opportunity for privacy, but no one will explicitly demand artificial darkness as his or her 'right' to conceal certain social activities. What is the significance of this distinction between rights and strategies?

Much was written about the birth of human rights and the philosophical discourse around them as a direct result of Western democratic citizenship and Christian morality (Cobbah, 1987; Taylor, 1999; Montgomery, 2001; Asad, 2003; Chakrabarty, 2009). The civil rights movements of the 1960s and 1970s placed great importance on individual autonomy and freedom of expression. Claiming, demanding, and fighting for one's 'right to privacy,' as we've increasingly witnessed in the US, is a highly privileged position with strong roots in the Western nation-state (Warren and Brandeis, 1890; Marwick and boyd, 2018). Moreover, the US has an abundance of laws about privacy rights, personal harm, and informed consent that can be waived by civilians both legally and morally (Solove, 2004).

As Taylor explains, the opposite of 'right' is 'wrong,' and certain communities place more weight on the moral duties of their members, instead of their moral entitlements (Taylor, 1999). According to Asad, such different perceptions of rights and obligations mean 'the essence of the human is quite different in both cases – sovereignty on the one and dependence on a network of obligations on the other' (2003: 130). In his classic book, *Good Natured*, primatologist and ethnologist Frans de Waal critiques the concept of rights and autonomous space, arguing that

> A morality exclusively concerned with individual rights tends to ignore the ties, needs and interdependencies that have marked our existence from the very beginning. It is a cold morality that puts space between people, assigning each person to his or her little corner of the universe.
>
> (Waal and Waal, 1996: 167)

164 *Conclusions*

Privacy in Ghana, therefore, is not perceived as an individual 'right' that is granted to all civilians by a governing power (whether it is families, states, or corporations), but as the 'decent' and 'correct' behaviour expected from members of an interdependent community. At the same time, privacy is the escape from these restricting frameworks of 'correct' behaviour. As mentioned, middle-class Pentecostals seek out cosmopolitanism – 'that which is not (in localist terms) expected proper, or normal' (Ferguson, 1999: 211). As a result, privacy is mostly understood as a strategy, a tool, and a weapon for individual fulfilment and meaning, within an existing social order. Staying discrete is an essential part of navigating and retaining power between social classes, religious cosmologies, technological advancements, and familial transformations.

7.2 Coda: religion, internet, discontinuity, and continuity

A lady recently reported on an FM radio station that her husband and father in law were 'fighting' over where or how her new-born baby should be 'outdoored' – either by Christian rituals in the church or by African traditional rites at home! She explains that whilst her zealous penteco-charismatic Christian husband insists that the baby boy (who was to be named after the husband's father) should be 'outdoored' or christened in the church for more Godly blessings, her husband's father, a die-hard traditionalist, would rather the ceremony be done at the house and in the traditional way. She was worried over the controversy this may pose, and thus wanted some counselling. Yes, you could easily pity her plight!

(Daily Guide, 2015)

The column articulates how the ideological crossroads of urban Ghanaians are a constant issue for debate and negotiation, between family members, pastors, and social media users. Later in the text, the rupture that so many urban Ghanaians face with their conversion to Pentecostalism is demonstrated in the writer's condemnation of pouring libation for the ancestors on the ground while performing a naming ceremony for the new-born. To back up her objection, the writer quotes one of the English versions of Deuteronomy 18:11–12: 'There shall not be found among you anyone... who consults the dead, anyone who does this is an abomination to the Lord... and the Lord, your God will drive out such people from you.'

Therefore, by accepting the gospel and the scriptures (as their pastors understand them), many Ghanaians ultimately decide to break away from their culture, tradition, and kin members. Their online persona is yet another platform to either express or escape this endeavour. Facebook and WhatsApp, in other words, can liberate an individual from their family as much as they can show its collective unity. As more and more cultural trades become associated with sin and pagan worship, many remain with feelings

Conclusions 165

of uncertainty: how can they be 'good' Christians (a somewhat universal category) but still live within their local life-worlds? This question alone teaches me a lot about the importance of privacy in Ghana.

Ghana's postcolonial urban vision is based on modernity, nationhood, and Westernisation that adopted carefully chosen indigenous elements as national symbols of heritage and culture. For instance, Kwame Nkrumah adopted the Akan Sankofa symbol depicting a bird looking backwards to emphasise the value of borrowing from the past to sustain the present. Feld describes this process as 'a matter of hybridising the hybrid through re-articulation of roots' (2012: 56). The Charismatic church, unlike this carefully articulated national project, takes a more global and uncompromising approach to local ontologies, promoting modern cosmopolitan subjects who take a radical break from their local roots and traditions (Marshall-Fratani, 1998; Meyer, 1998).

It's no coincidence that these churches began to flourish after the structural reforms, democratisation, and privatisation of state entities that Ghana (and many other African states) led in the 1980s and 1990s. According to Weiss (2004: 9–14), this process constructed a 'neoliberal personhood,' which demands 'greater openness' alongside 'rigorous closure,' a 'reorganisation of temporality to envision alternative futures,' and the reinvention of tradition and sanctity. Additionally, the weakening of the state as a result of such neoliberal privatisation has brought Africa into a particular state of modernity that differs from Asia and Euro-America, whereby social and material infrastructures are dysfunctional, futures are uncertain, and informal 'shadow' economies are more prevalent than formal sectors (Ferguson, 2006: 13–15). Privatisation and privacy, in that sense, are strongly connected; one allows the other, forges new spaces for it, and increases the need for it.

Pentecostal Christianity operates in similar ways to digitisation, offering an alternative framework that explains and copes with the uncertainties, tensions, and contradictions experienced with modernity. Both 'technologies' offer a universal language, form, and epistemology that have a unique capacity to contain and interact with pre-existing scripts and ontologies. Thus, digitisation and Pentecostal reformation act as a skeleton with a pre-determined form and shape that allow different cultural expressions to grow around it. As Burrell (2012: 167) pointed out in her study of internet cafés in Accra, both technologies offer escape, transcendence, and meaningful engagement with the world. Pentecostals have a complicated relationship with visual and material expressions of faith, due to their association with the Protestant church and its long-term promotion of immaterial, abstracted, and subjective divine experiences (Meyer and Moors, 2005). However, when it comes to digital media, the church seems to utilise it for its preaching and community, even more than their Catholic peers. To quote Miller and Horst (2012: 14): 'Protestants have seen media, unlike images, as a conduit to a more direct, unmediated relationship with the divine.'

166 *Conclusions*

In his ethnography of deathbed practices in Fiji, Tomlinson argues that expressing a 'good' or 'happy' death in Fiji, and under Christian ideals, requires the deceased to reject any prayers, rituals, and beliefs that originate from his/her traditional cosmology. He describes that under the supervision of missionary priests, these prior traditions didn't vanish entirely but were pushed out of the public realm and into the private one, in death and in life. This process of re-categorisation, he argues, means ancestral spirits are labelled as demons or devils, which create a new 'ambiguous, shadowy' private realm of spirituality, expressed through gossip, taboos, hidden narratives, secret myths, and sometimes moral torment (Tomlinson, 2008). Similar processes were described by Meyer in her work on Christian conversion among the Ewes of Ghana (1999) and by Robbins in his ethnography on the Urapmin in Papa New Guinea (2004b).

The importance of these studies on transitions from tradition is in the way re-socialisation entails re-categorisation of boundaries, taboos, and norms. Akin to neoliberal privatisation (and perhaps as a result of it), religion has an immense impact on the issue of privacy; the process of spiritual and cultural rupture, very much like the migration of the urban community in Tema to the internet, 'entails the local creation of new realms of privacy configured against the dominant new Christian public' (Tomlinson, 2008: 713). As Robbins (2013: 450) states, Charismatic Christianity 'insists on its relevance to all domains of life, both public and private.' Thus, due to its potential to be present in one's consciousness even when no one else is around – mainly through spiritual agency – Pentecostalism forms privacy as an essential commodity. In other words, due to its attempt to eliminate private lives, Pentecostalism increases the need for privacy on a personal, spiritual, and financial level.

Going back to the columnist quoted above, and the dilemma of naming ceremonies outside of the church, she eventually proposes a kind of fusion for the event: 'I am thus envisaging a name-giving ceremony in the Christian home where the church pastor will be invited to exclusively officiate, with Christian prayers (instead of libation pouring).' The writer, like many other urbanites, uses this digital medium as a space for re-articulating who she is and how her society continues to shape around her. Therefore, this study suggests that spiritual aspects of privacy are negotiated in a broader context where class mobility, urbanisation, and digitisation also shape new categories. As users adopt social media tools such as Facebook, WhatsApp, and Snapchat, they assign (consciously or unconsciously) new roles, norms, and boundaries around them and navigate fluidly between them.

Modernity is often described as the movement 'forward' from one end – religion, irrationality, conservatism, ignorance, locality, and 'tribalism' – to another end – secularism, rationality, enlightenment, universality, liberalism, and individualism.[2] The case of middle-class Ghanaians illustrates a different route where religion serves as a vehicle for globalisation, modernisation, and progress. In similar ways, the assumed route from

Conclusions 167

non-digital private life to a privacy-threatened digital life is challenged, as the migration of Ghanaians to digital spaces opens up new possibilities of privacy. It is of great importance to identify these alternative routes from an emic or subjective perspective, instead of imposing 'objective,' ideological, and 'universal' sociological structures that pre-determine them. The construction of African modernity, thus, demands a unique and dynamic juxtaposition and opposition of such abstract categories into a common social purview (Weiss, 2004: 5–6).

Imposing pre-existing structures based on Western or secular temporalities of modernity may put ethnographers (and their informants) at the risk of mistaking the movement of people forward as backward and vice versa. For instance, Mahmood (2011) argued that feminist scholars often misinterpret the participation of women in Islamic movements as a retreat back to patriarchal patterns of subordination, while the Muslim women themselves experience their religious engagement as pacing forward towards piety and meaning. The movement of post-Soviet societies from a communist past to a capitalist future (Haukanes, 2013), the Cambodian practices of 'forgetting' memories of Genocide towards a happier future (Kidron, 2012), and the revival of witchcraft as a response to modern economy in Cameroon (Geschiere, 1997) are just a few examples to stress that different societies shift back and forth on different routes, between different dyadic poles.

What those experiences have in common are the central roles of privacy as a strategy and tool, which help conceal and reveal elements of the self or the group, while constructing a new vision for society. Further research on privacy as a semiotic and contextual tool, rather than a 'right' or an endangered legal status, can highly benefit ethnographers, as it seeks to discuss what is concealed and what is exhibited, while understanding the ethical and social structures of individuals during times of uncertainty, transition, and change. I believe that the case of middle-class urban Ghanaians demonstrates this vividly.

References

Arendt, H. (2013) *The Human Condition: Second Edition*. Chicago, IL: University of Chicago Press.

Asad, T. (2003) *Formations of the Secular: Christianity, Islam, Modernity*. Redwood City: Stanford University Press.

boyd, danah (2008) 'Facebook's Privacy Trainwreck', *Convergence*, 14(1), pp. 13–20. doi: 10.1177/1354856507084416.

Burrell, J. (2012) *Invisible Users: Youth in the Internet Cafés of Urban Ghana*. Cambridge, MA: MIT Press.

Campbell, J. E. and Carlson, M. (2002) 'Panopticon.com: Online Surveillance and the Commodification of Privacy', *Journal of Broadcasting & Electronic Media*, 46(4), pp. 586–606. doi: 10.1207/s15506878jobem4604_6.

Chakrabarty, D. (2009) *Provincializing Europe: Postcolonial Thought and Historical Difference*. Princeton, NJ: Princeton University Press.

168 Conclusions

Cobbah, J. A. M. (1987) 'African Values and the Human Rights Debate: An African Perspective', *Human Rights Quarterly*, 9(3), pp. 309–331. doi: 10.2307/761878.

Costa, E. (2016) *Social Media in Southeast Turkey*. London: UCL Press.

Feld, S. (2012) *Jazz Cosmopolitanism in Accra: Five Musical Years in Ghana*. Durham, NC: Duke University Press Books.

Ferguson, J. (1999) *Expectations of Modernity: Myths and Meanings of Urban Life on the Zambian Copperbelt*. Berkeley: University of California Press.

Ferguson, J. (2006) *Global Shadows: Africa in the Neoliberal World Order*. Durham, NC: Duke University Press.

Freeman, C. (2000) *High Tech and High Heels in the Global Economy: Women, Work, and Pink-Collar Identities in the Caribbean*. Durham, NC: Duke University Press.

Gal, S. (2002) 'A Semiotics of the Public/Private Distinction', *Differences: A Journal of Feminist Cultural Studies*, 13(1), pp. 77–95.

Geschiere, P. (1997) *The Modernity of Witchcraft: Politics and the Occult in Postcolonial Africa*. Charlottesville: University of Virginia Press.

Guta, H. and Karolak, M. (2015) 'Veiling and Blogging: Social Media as Sites of Identity Negotiation and Expression among Saudi Women', *Journal of International Women's Studies*, 16(2), pp. 115–127.

Habermas, J. (1989) *The Structural Transformation of the Public Sphere*, trans. Thomas Burger, Cambridge, MA: MIT Press, 85, pp. 85–92.

Hahn, H. P. and Kibora, L. (2008) 'The Domestication of the Mobile Phone: Oral Society and New ICT in Burkina Faso', *The Journal of Modern African Studies*, 46(01), pp. 87–109. doi: 10.1017/S0022278X07003084.

Haukanes, H. (2013) 'Belonging, Mobility and the Future: Representations of Space in the Life Narratives of Young Rural Czechs', *YOUNG*, 21(2), pp. 193–210. doi: 10.1177/1103308813477467.

Heath, C. W. (1997) 'Children's Television in Ghana: A Discourse about Modernity', *African Affairs*, 96(383), pp. 261–275.

Kidron, C. A. (2012) 'Alterity and the Particular Limits of Universalism: Comparing Jewish-Israeli Holocaust and Canadian-Cambodian Genocide Legacies', *Current Anthropology*, 53(6), pp. 723–754. doi: 10.1086/668449.

Landau, S. (2016) 'Choices: Privacy & Surveillance in a Once & Future Internet', *Daedalus*, 145(1), pp. 54–64. doi: 10.1162/DAED_a_00365.

Landes, J. B. (2003) 'Further Thoughts on the Public/Private Distinction', *Journal of Women's History*, 15(2), pp. 28–39. doi: 10.1353/jowh.2003.0051.

Larkin, B. (2008) *Signal and Noise: Media, Infrastructure, and Urban Culture in Nigeria*. Durham, NC: Duke University Press Books.

Laurence Habib and Tony Cornford (2002) 'Computers in the Home: Domestication and Gender', *Information Technology & People*, 15(2), pp. 159–174. doi: 10.1108/09593840210430589.

Madianou, M. and Miller, D. (2013) 'Polymedia: Towards a New Theory of Digital Media in Interpersonal Communication', *International Journal of Cultural Studies*, 16(2), pp. 169–187. doi: 10.1177/1367877912452486.

Mahmood, S. (2011) *Politics of Piety: The Islamic Revival and the Feminist Subject*. Princeton, NJ: Princeton University Press.

Marshall-Fratani, R. (1998) 'Mediating the Global and Local in Nigerian Pentecostalism', *Journal of Religion in Africa*, 28(3), pp. 278–315. doi: 10.2307/1581572.

Conclusions 169

Marwick, A. E. and boyd, D. (2018) 'Privacy at the Margins| Understanding Privacy at the Margins—Introduction', *International Journal of Communication*, 12, pp. 1157–1165.

Meehan, J. (2013) *Feminists Read Habermas (RLE Feminist Theory): Gendering the Subject of Discourse*. New York: Routledge.

Meyer, B. (1998) '"Make a Complete Break with the past." Memory and Post-Colonial Modernity in Ghanaian Pentecostalist Discourse', *Journal of Religion in Africa*, 28(3), pp. 316–349. doi: 10.2307/1581573.

Meyer, B. (1999) *Translating the Devil: Religion and Modernity Among the Ewe in Ghana*. Trenton, NJ: Africa World Pr.

Meyer, B. (2004a) 'Christianity in Africa: From African Independent to Pentecostal-Charismatic Churches', *Annual Review of Anthropology*, 33(1), pp. 447–474. doi: 10.1146/annurev.anthro.33.070203.143835.

Meyer, B. and Moors, A. (2005) *Religion, Media, and the Public Sphere*. Bloomington: Indiana University Press.

Miller, D. and Horst, H. (eds) (2012) *Digital Anthropology*. First Edition. London: Berg Publishers.

Miller, D. and Slater, D. (2001) *The Internet: An Ethnographic Approach*. First Edition. Oxford; New York: Bloomsbury Academic.

Mitchell, T. (1991) *Colonising Egypt: With a New Preface*. London: University of California Press.

Montgomery, H. (2001) 'Imposing Rights? A Case Study of Child Prostitution in Thailand', in Cowan, J. K., Dembour, M.-B., and Wilson, R. A. (eds) *Culture and Rights: Anthropological Perspectives*. Cambridge: Cambridge University Press, pp. 80–101.

Nippert-Eng, C. (2010) *Islands of Privacy*. Chicago, IL: University of Chicago Press.

Nissenbaum, H. (2004) 'Privacy as Contextual Integrity Symposium - Technology, Values, and the Justice System', *Washington Law Review*, 79, pp. 119–158.

Pateman, C. (1983) 'Feminist Critique of Public/Private Dichotomy', in Gaus, G. F. and Benn, S. I. (eds) *Public and private in social life*. London : Croom Helm ; New York : St. Martin's Press. Available at: https://trove.nla.gov.au/version/46390557 (Accessed: 9 April 2018).

Petronio, S. (2002) *Boundaries of Privacy: Dialectics of Disclosure*. Albany: State University of New York Press.

Postill, J. and Pink, S. (2012) 'Social Media Ethnography: The Digital Researcher in a Messy Web', *Media International Australia*, 145(1), pp. 123–134. doi: 10.1177/1329878X1214500114.

Rider, K. (2018) 'The Privacy Paradox: How Market Privacy Facilitates Government Surveillance', *Information, Communication & Society*, 21(10), pp. 1369–1385. doi: 10.1080/1369118X.2017.1314531.

Robbins, J. (2004a) *Becoming Sinners: Christianity and Moral Torment in a Papua New Guinea Society*. Oakland: University of California Press.

Robbins, J. (2013) 'Beyond the Suffering Subject: Toward an Anthropology of the Good', *Journal of the Royal Anthropological Institute*, 19(3), pp. 447–462. doi: 10.1111/1467–9655.12044.

Sinanan, J. (2017) *Social Media in Trinidad*. London: UCL Press.

Solove, D. J. (2004) *The Digital Person: Technology and Privacy in the Information Age*. New York: NYU Press.

170 *Conclusions*

Srinivasan, J. *et al.* (2018) 'Privacy at the Margins| The Poverty of Privacy: Understanding Privacy Trade-Offs From Identity Infrastructure Users in India', *International Journal of Communication*, 12(0), p. 20.

Tacchi, J. and Chandola, T. (2015) 'Complicating Connectivity: Women's Negotiations with Smartphones in an Indian Slum', in Hjorth, L. and Khoom, O. (eds) *Routledge Handbook of New Media in Asia*, New York: Routledge, pp. 191–200.

Taylor, C. (1999) 'Conditions of an unforced Consensus on Human Rights', in Bauer, J. R. and Bell, D. A. (eds) *The East Asian Challenge for Human Rights.* Cambridge: Cambridge University Press, pp. 124–144.

Thompson, E. (2003) 'Public and Private in Middle Eastern Women's History', *Journal of Women's History*, 15(1), pp. 52–69. doi: 10.1353/jowh.2003.0037.

Tomlinson, M. (2008) 'Publicity, Privacy, and "Happy Deaths" in Fiji', *American Ethnologist*, 34(4), pp. 706–720. doi: 10.1525/ae.2007.34.4.706.

Trottier, D. (2016) *Social Media as Surveillance: Rethinking Visibility in a Converging World.* London: Routledge. doi: 10.4324/9781315609508.

Turkle, S. (1988) 'Computational Reticence: Why Women Fear the Intimate Machine', in: Kramarae C., (ed). *Technology and Women's Voices: Keeping in Touch*, New York: London: Routledge & Kegan Paul, pp. 41–61.

Vitak, J. (2012) 'The Impact of Context Collapse and Privacy on Social Network Site Disclosures', *Journal of Broadcasting & Electronic Media*, 56(4), pp. 451–470. doi: 10.1080/08838151.2012.732140.

Waal, F. de and Waal, F. B. M. de (1996) *Good Natured.* Cambridge, MA: Harvard University Press.

Wacks, R. (2015) *Privacy: A Very Short Introduction.* Second Edition. Oxford, New York: Oxford University Press (Very Short Introductions).

Warren, S. D. and Brandeis, L. D. (1890) 'The Right to Privacy', *Harvard Law Review*, 4(5), pp. 193–220. doi: 10.2307/1321160.

Weintraub, J. (1997) 'The Theory and Politics of the Public/Private Distinction', in Kumar, K. (ed.) *Public and Private in Thought and Practice: Perspectives on a Grand Dichotomy.* Chicago: University of Chicago Press, pp. 1–39.

Weiss, B. (2004) *Producing African Futures: Ritual and Reproduction in a Neoliberal Age.* Leiden: Brill.

Wicker, S. B. (2013) *Cellular Convergence and the Death of Privacy.* First Edition. New York: Oxford University Press.

Notes

1 As Meyer explains in her review of Christianity in Africa, current African politics seems to express the decline of nation-states as a central economic power in the continent. In her words: 'the state seems to reach its limits in the face of both small-scale autochthonous incentives and transnational movements such as political Islam or PCCs' (Meyer, 2004a: 466).

2 The words 'tribe' and 'tribalism' are associated with a long tradition of colonial rule and its often-derogatory perception of what are in fact complex and diverse social structures (Keim, 2013: 113). According to Lowe (1997), these terms are inaccurate and ambiguous, nowadays rejected by most African scholars. However, I have borrowed this term here to express the dichotomies that middle-class urbanites and Pentecostal worshipers often face in their spiritual, financial, and social discourse.

Index

Note: *Italic* page numbers refer to figures; page numbers followed by "n" denote endnotes.

Africa 4, 13, 76, 99, 165
Altman, I. 5, 7, 22n2, 29, 33, 96
architecture/architectural 40–41, 42, 86, 89–90, 91, 94, 96, 98–99, 102, 112, digital 134
art 107–108

bedroom 7, 104, 107–110, 125, 145
Bourdieu, Pierre 87, 108, 160
boyd, Dana 5–6, 8, 110, 127, 128, 143, 159

camera *see* photography
Christianity 13–17, 75–76, 129, 165–166
community surveillance *see* surveillance
compound houses *see* houses
cosmopolitan/ism 14, 43, 44, 78, 91, 162, 164–165

darkness 59, 60, 65–66, 163; and privacy 62–63, 72–78; symbolic 72–74, 80–81, 89; urban 68–70
digital anthropology 4, 9–11, 150, 156n2, 163
digital ethnography 24, 122–123
digital photographs *see* photography
digitisation 2, 9, 11–13, 92, 158–166
domestication 43, 70, 96, 105, 161; theory of 86, 110–113, 150
Dumsor 64–66, 76, 78, 81, 105, 163

electricity 39, 63–64, 66, 67, 78, 89, 95, 105, 111, 161

Facebook 6, 24, 27, 128–135, 141, 143, 146, 148, 164, 166

family/familial 5, 6, 9, 10, 48, 66, 91, 101, 103, 106, 162, 164; digital 133; home 90, 110; honour 14, 24, 25, 28, 30, 32, 69, 71, 123–124, 126, 146; nuclear/extended 40, 42, 43, 46, 77–78, 98, 104; photos 103, 108, 141, 143
feminism 5, 159, 167
film/cinema 43, 67, 71, 72, 85n5, 120n18, 120n20, 126, 137

van der Geest, S. 9, 25, 72–73
gender 26, 28–29, 68, 72, 74, 87, 104, 107–108, 124, 159
Ghana 15, 25, 27, 38, 48, 50, 61, 68, 94, 108, 150, 161
God 1–2, 14–16, 65, 76, 77, 79, 91, 96, 129, 131, 133, 148, 164
Goffman, Erving 6–7, 49, 101, 110

houses 24, 39, 86, 88, 90–91, 96, 99, 104, 111, 138, 160
human rights *see* rights

indirect speech 48–50, 71, 72, 122, 123, 124, 131, 135, 136
infrastructure 11, 23, 42, 89, 111–113, 147, 150, 165

Jewish 26, 31–32, 75

Latour, Bruno 97, 112, 147
LGBT 27–30, 77, 125
living room 87, 102–106, 110

material culture 11–12, 62, 93–98, 102, 112

172 *Index*

materiality *see* material culture
media studies 109–110
memes 121–123, 135, 136, 146, 160
Meyer, Brigit 2, 14–15, 38, 76–77, 96, 108, 137, 166
middle-class 24, 44–47, 79–80, 94, 106, 112, 158, 164, 166–167
Miller, Daniel 4, 9, 12, 61, 87, 89, 121, 128–129, 132, 134, 145, 165
mobile phones *see* smartphones
modern/modernity 2, 13–14, 16, 23–24, 40, 42, 77, 79, 86, 93, 99, 102–104, 110, 137–138, 142, 161, 165–167

neoliberalism 4, 39, 137
Nigeria/Nigerian 38, 41, 46, 64, *74*, 77, 79, 94, 105, 125, 140, 146, 149
night 60–62, 63, 67–68, 76–77, 79, 97, 101
nightlife *see* night
Nippert-Eng, Christine 6–7, 26, 162
Nkrumah, Kwame 14, 38, 41, 67, 165
noisy polymedia 147, 150

Pentecostal church *see* Pentecostalism
Pentecostal media 2, 137, 79–80, 106, 149
Pentecostalism 13–17, 31, 43, 75–76, 80–81, 88–91, 125, 126, 129, 137, 147, 162, 164–166
photography 92, 108, 137–139, 141–143
poloymedia 128–129, 132–134, 146, 147–149, 150, 161
privacy 2, 68, 92, 123–124; literature on 5–9, 10–11; as methodology 25–26; online 127–128; right for 158–164, 166; urban 43, 49–50
power cuts *see* electricity
public media 10, 30, 38, 121, 122, 131, 134, 148, 151
public sphere 3, 5, 7, 9, 11, 12, 13, 15, 16, 25, 26, 33, 44, 50, 60, 62, 63, 68, 71, 74, 80–81, 87, 99, 101, 102, 105, 108, 112, 128, 129, 130, 135, 145, 147, 158, 161, 163, 166
publicly private/privately public/public secret 7, 46, 50, 87, 122, 128, 143, 160

rights 8, 27, 66, 110, 124, 158–159, 163–164, 167

scalable sociality 10, 132, 134
shaming 27
smartphones 47–48, 80, 97, 105–106, 112, 133, 150
Snapchat 24, 142–147, 151
social media 8, 10–11, 24, 30, 50, 92, 110, 121, 123–125, 127, 130, 137–138, 142–143, 158, 161–162, 166
surveillance 8, 14, 59–61, 94–95, 97, 110, 121, 123–128, 133, 143, 145, 158–159

television 10, 15, 63, 66, 67, 71, 103–104, 106, 109, 110, 137
Tema 23, 39–41, 65, 78, 99, 102, 163
tradition/traditional 2, 4, 15, 16, 24, 38–40, 43, 75, 76, 89, 92, 98–99, 101–102, 106, 125, 134, 136, 141, 164–166

urban 39–41, 42–43, 86–87, 99, 106, 133, 145, 163–164; churches 13–14, 79; middle class 123, 161; security 61–62, 93
urbanisation 39, 63, 158
urbanites 2, 13, 24, 25, 39, 41–44, 47, 60, 64, 67, 76, 81, 95, 108, 111–112, 133, 137, 161, 163

village 39–40, 42–43, 67, 72, 77–78, 98–99
visibility 4, 77, 80, 92, 108, 130, 131, 135, 138, 148, 158; /invisibility 30, 47, 67, 110, 125, 133; social 49, 137, 141, 142, 145, 151
visual culture *see* photography

West Africa *see* Africa
WhatsApp 47–48, 57n13, 126, 128–135, 141, 143, 147, 162, 164
witchcraft 15, 77, 135, 139, 140–141
Why We Post (project) 10–11; studies from the 50, 121–122, 130, 131, 132, 134, 140, 145, 159, 151